The Library of Sexual Behaviour
General Editor: Professor Hans Giese

Editor of the English Language Edition:
Professor Fernando Henriques

Incest

Incest

Herbert Maisch

Translated by Colin Bearne

 **ANDRE DEUTSCH**

First published 1973 by
André Deutsch Limited
105 Great Russell Street London WC1

English translation copyright © 1973
by André Deutsch Limited

First published in German under the title
INZEST
© Rowohlt Taschenbuch Verlag GmbH
Reinbek bei Hamburg, 1968
All Rights Reserved

'Incest in English Law' copyright
© J. W. Hall Williams, 1972

Printed in Great Britain by
Butler & Tanner Limited, Frome and London

ISBN 0 233 96165 8

Contents

Foreword *7*

Introduction *9*

1 Incest from the point of view of cultural history *11*
2 Incest taboo *41*
3 The law and criminal statistics on incest *65*
4 Family sociology, psychology and psychopathology of incest *93*
5 Personalities and interpersonal relationships of the married couples *124*
6 The personality of female incest victims *146*
7 Conditions giving rise to incestuous relationships, and the course of these relationships *169*
8 Incest and abnormal sexual behaviour *196*
9 The effects of incest *207*
10 Conclusion *216*

Incest in English law *219*

Glossary of terms *229*

Bibliography *233*

Index *245*

Foreword

Anyone who comes across cases of incest in the course of his forensic work as a youth pyschiatrist, or as a psychological specialist, has as a rule the task of examining the youthful victims of and participants in the act of incest with a view to resolving the legal question of their suitability to give evidence and of whether they are actually telling the truth about what happened. These questions are less easily solved by an analysis of the relations between the victim and the offender, and thereby of the personality of the offender himself, than by an analysis of the family situation in which such a set of circumstances was able to arise. Except in cases of attempted murder in couples living in intimacy, there is hardly any other set of legal circumstances which bind offender and victim so closely together in such a tight, often tragic, network of affection and distance, fear and fascination, care and lack of consideration; in short all the ambivalence which is an integral part of the closest human relationship. The question of the personality and trustworthiness of the child or adolescent victim can therefore never be separated from the question of the development of the incest affair, the factors which favoured or accompanied it, and finally those which put an end to the occurrence and led to its discovery. On the other hand, both the courts and specialists are equally concerned with the results of the affair. It is natural to abhor the destructive effects of incestuous abuse, often lasting for years, if the victim's personal development proves to have been adversely affected. Yet how far is this abhorrence justified, especially as it can play a role in the degree of legal punishment meted out? Might it not be the same factors which had a decisive influence on the development of the affair, which also damaged the character of the victim?

Lack of skilful analyses linked with an exact statistical evaluation of the empirical data acquired, means that, in the field of moral offences, both the theory and practice of law and, not least, the youth psychiatrist and psychological expert, must fall back on general human, or personal-scientific experience. This circumstance has an unfortunate effect on the practice of legal theory and forensics; a fact which prominent jurists are not backward in bewailing. The following monograph contains extensive material, well examined and subjected to analysis from a multitude of angles. To my knowledge this material has never before been published in such a complete form. It is an attempt, with the help of exact data, to throw light on all aspects of the problem of incest and to make it possible to judge such sexually deviationary behaviour objectively; a form of behaviour which otherwise seems most prone to be examined from a prejudiced and emotionally coloured point of view.

The examination of the social, anthropological, sociological, psychoanalytical and comparative forensic aspects of the problem of incest, which the author has also undertaken, gives an impressive insight into mankind's ambivalent attitude towards incest, with its combination of fascination and taboo. It covers the whole of history up to the present time. Against this background could be illumined those motives, only apparently rational, but in fact irrational, which determine our approaches and attitudes even today, in this as in many other fields of our social life. The conclusions, arrived at by the author on the basis of his critical analyses, may possibly surprise or even shock. At the same time they are to a great degree capable of preparing the way for an objective and rational critical approach, which should alone be decisive both for the legal evaluation of incest and for the forensic judgment of offenders and victims.

Hamburg, August 1968   PROF. DR HEDWIG WALLIS

Introduction

> What a strange state of affairs. A pretty girl must not lead me into temptation – because I have brought her into the world!
> MARQUIS DE SADE

Looking at the background of the manifold mythological literary and scientific representations of incest in cultural history, one gains the impression of dealing with a phenomenon which man has always approached with a peculiar kind of ambivalent fascination. Attraction and repulsion, approval and stigmatising, 'fire and ice' (Sartre, 1965) typify the polarity of human attitudes and values which betrays the ambivalence of the feelings behind it. Even conceptual abstractions and scientific systems of observation can at times hardly conceal the emotional participation which especially affects the moral and ethical interpretation of the problem of incest and the motivation behind the laws. It is one of the tasks in exploring forensic sexological questions to separate the object of their study from the emotional and moralising climate of official and unofficial attitudes and approaches, and to point to an unprejudiced picture of reality.

This book is concerned with the manifold problems of incest in the past and present. Without any claim to be comprehensive there is, first, an attempt to sketch a cultural, historical outline of the theme, to depict the considerations which gave rise to the incest taboo, and to cast a critical light on the legal aspects. The second part of the book, based on the experiences of specialist observers in German courts, presents new findings and those of previous psychiatric and psychological research on incest.

1. Incest from the point of view of cultural history

Etymological interpretation

The study of the linguistic origins of the words 'incest' and *'Blutschande'* (blood dishonour) reveals that their original meaning and application were quite fluid and in no way exclusively limited to sexual relations between people related by blood.

According to Többen (1925) the word *'Blutschande'* is a direct translation of *'sanguis contumelia'* in *lex 38 1 Dig. ad legem Juliam de Adulteris*. Curiously enough, the concept was also originally used for 'any neglect of the honour' which one owes one's parents (Grimm, 1860). H. Rohleder (1912) draws a distinction between 'incest' and 'inbreeding'. According to this, 'incest' can be taken to mean quite generally that sexual intercourse between close blood-relations which is forbidden by law, and 'inbreeding' will mean sexual intercourse or bearing of children by that wider blood-relationship, such as is allowable under the law. At an appropriate point we shall explore further the present-day legal definition in this country and abroad.

The word 'incest' is probably derived from the Latin *'castus'* (pure, chaste), and from *'incestus'* (impure, immodest, lewd) (Heyse, 1879; Walden, 1938). *'Incestare'* means to stain, defile, ravage (*Sexual Scientific Lexicon*, 1928), and in medieval Latin–German glossaries we find under *'incestus'*, 'immodesty with blood-relations or maidens'. It was, however, also understood to mean 'adultery' (Diefenbach quoted by Többen, 1925).

Another, more symbolically orientated, etymological interpretation seeks the original meaning in the Latin *'cestus'* – girdle (of Venus), which 'should arouse love' and in marriage counts as a sign of feminine loyalty (Georges, 1869).

In fact the loosing of the girdle is in Greek tradition a symbol of sexual activity (Rank, 1912). In Homer the god of marriage, Hymen, bears the attribute 'the girdle loosener', and the seat of the erotic magic charms of Aphrodite, the goddess of love, is placed in the girdle (Homer II, xiv). In the Norse Thidrek saga a magic girdle gives Brunhilde the power on her wedding-night to defend her virginity against Günther, and it is only Siegfried who overpowers her, wearing his cap of invisibility and tearing off her girdle. Here the stealing of the girdle appears directly as a symbol of rape. Thus against the background of this symbolism the following interpretation of the word 'incest' sounds quite plausible: with the exception of the husband the loosing of the girdle was for any other male member of the family an offence against the (girdle-) taboo or an 'incest', that is an offence against a family sexual taboo, and at the same time an injury to feminine loyalty (Caprio and Brenner, 1964).

In ancient Rome '*incestus*' or '*incestum*' was taken to mean both immodesty of the Vestal Virgins (Roman priestesses) and defiling of the holy places and – in connection with marriage inhibitions – sexual contacts between blood-relations to the sixth or seventh degree (Lubker, 1914). T. Mommsen (1899) is of the opinion that the concept of incest referred originally to offences against modesty which ran counter to religious ordinances. Only later was the concept more narrowly defined by the monk Gratianus (*Decretum Gratiani*, 1139–42) in order to separate the so-called offence against the 'blood' from all other possible meanings (Herzog, 1897).

Epic and dramatic writing

Man invents his gods, saints and heroes. And he endows them with those very qualities and forms of behaviour which are his own or which correspond with his more or less conscious wishes, tendencies or ideals. Mankind's cultural history shows that the incest motif possesses a tradition in the imagination over two thousand years old. The continuity with which this theme – involving both heaven and earth, both God and Man – has been treated over the course of thousands of years in various literary variations, emphasises the fact that it is a matter which men find fascinating.

'If the young wild beast were left to itself, and if the untutored mind of the child in the cradle were combined with the violence of passion of a man of thirty, then he would break his father's neck and ravish his mother.' This was the phrase of the French poet and philosopher, Diderot, in his satire *Le Neveu de Rameau*, and it was used by Sigmund Freud over a hundred years later in his *Interpretation of Dreams* (1900) first as the basis of the oedipus theory, and something that had taken place in the ancient Greek myth-building thousands of years before: the oedipal situation, incest.

In Greek mythology there arose from out of the primeval cosmic chaos Gaa, Mother Earth, who in incestuous love-embrace with the son of her own body, Uranos, gave birth to six male and six female Titans. Kronos, one of these Titan-sons of Uranos, knew of his father's evil deeds and that he was also his brother. Moreover he had an especially close relationship with his mother and hated his father as an oedipal rival. One day Kronos surprised his brother-father, Uranos, as he was having marital coitus with Gaa, and he castrated him:

'And mighty Uranos came and brought the night with him; filled with love he embraces Gaa . . . but then from hiding the son reaches out with his left hand, with the right he grips the huge hip, and long and sharp of tooth, he mows off quickly his own father's shame and, fleeing, throws it behind him again. . . .'

Kronos seizes power and marries his sister Rhea, who bears him three sons and three daughters. But his happiness is short-lived; his father's fate is repeated. Kronos is unmanned by his son Zeus, who mounts the throne of the gods and marries his sister Hera. And in the incestuous brother–sister pair Minos and Britomartis, the children of Zeus, the Olympian incest-tradition is maintained. Incestuous love amongst the gods is, in fact, as a rule, love between brother and sister. In comparison – according to the German pamphleteer Rudolf Walter Leonhardt (1969) – only a few father–daughter pairs could exist, and those mostly of lower rank. Thyestes and his daughter Pelopeia are the most prominent: their son Aegisthus was a victim of the curse of the Atrides. Also not to be forgotten is the child-jewel of the father–daughter union of Cinyras–Myrrha: he was called Adonis and was the most beautiful of the demi-gods – a proof that the Greeks had still not recognised any degeneration theory.

From a psychoanalytical point of view the myth of the incest of the gods reveals some of the central facets of the oedipus complex: in the scene in which Kronos surprises his father during marital coitus and castrates him there is the complete infantile root of the hatred for the father, which arises out of the sexual rivalry for the mother. Yet the incestuous wish impulses of Kronos are not realised in mother-incest, but are transferred to the sister: Kronos marries Rhea. Thousands of years later a writer was able to give meaning to this development. J.-P. Sartre, who in his childhood had slept in a double bed with his mother, recognised in 1963, in the first part of his autobiography, incestuous fantasies and wishes which he transferred from his mother to an imagined sister:

'Lovers kiss and promise to sleep in the same bed. (A peculiar custom: why not in a double bed, like my mother and I?) I knew no more than that, but was vaguely aware of the existence of a hairy mass beneath the shining surface of the idea. At all events as a brother I would have committed incest. I dreamt of it. An aberration? The concealing of repressed sensitivities? Quite possibly. I had an older sister, my mother, and I wished for a younger sister. I have committed the grave mistake of seeking such a non-existent sister amongst other women: my complaint was rejected, I had to bear the costs of my misdeeds.' (1965, pp. 41–2)

In these confessions Sartre reveals not only his oedipal-incestuous attachment to his mother in early childhood, but also a piece of the basic dynamic drive of the oedipal conflict, which is expressed in the resistance to, and the transference of, the incest fantasies originally orientated on the mother, and thus – under the guise of the sister-image – it remains fixed for a lifetime: 'Even today – in the year 1963 – this is the only bond of relationship which makes any impression on me' (Sartre 1965, p. 41). Sartre himself points to the link between individual experience and his literary production, even if only in a footnote:

'When I was ten years old I was delighted with Abel Hermant's novel *The Transatlantics*. In it there is a young American and his sister. I put myself in the boy's place and through him loved the little girl Biddy. For a long time I have dreamt of writing a story about two lost and discreetly incestuous children. Traces of this dreaming can be found in my works: Orestes and Electra in *Les Mouches*, Boris and Ivich in *La Liberté*, Franz and Leni in *Les Sequestrés d'Altona*. These last are the only ones to actually commit physical incest. What engages me about this family bond is less the erotic temptation than the forbidden love: fire and ice, a mixture of rapture and renunciation; I liked incest, so long as it stayed platonic.' (1965, p. 42)

Almost all the most important writers in world literature have dealt with the incest theme 'with a frankness . . . which is only prevented from being indecent by a series of typical and all too transparent disguises, as well as by the transformation of something childishly enjoyable into something tragically guilt-bearing' (Rank, 1912, pp. 13-14). For many writers the incest theme is quite obviously an object of dramatic or, perhaps, according to Shelley, even 'a very poetic' impact. The long tradition of 'literary incest' represents a piece of cultural history in which human passions and temptations are revealed. If one analyses the life and works of great writers from a psychoanalytical point of view, as for example Rank (1912) tries to do, then one discovers increasingly manifold connections between individual experience, life history and the literary working over of the incest motif.

Stendhal, a writer who became famous in his lifetime with the appearance of *La Chartreuse de Parme* (1839) and *Le Rouge et le Noir* (1830), wrote quite openly: 'I was always in love with my mother. I was always kissing my mother and wishing that we had no clothes on. . . . I kissed her with such ardour that she felt to a certain degree in duty bound to withdraw. *I detested my father* when he came and interrupted our embraces. I wanted to kiss her breasts always' (quoted in Rank, 1912, p. 32.)

Is it mere chance or caprice that the same writer, Henri Beyle (to give him his real name), depicted in his novella *Cenci* an historical father–daughter incest and patricide?

Marcel Proust, whose life and works were undoubtedly influenced by a strong attachment to his mother and by oedipal rivalry, wrote as a boy in the 'question and answer' diary of Antoinette Felix-Faure in answer to the question 'what are you afraid of most?' the sentence 'Being parted from Mama' (Maurois, 1964, p. 20). The hysteria-like love and exceptional inner life of the young Proust are well known, and Maurois has shown that one scene which occurs in *Swann's Way* did actually take place in the writer's childhood. One evening Proust's mother had invited some friends round and could not come to give him his goodnight kiss. Marcel became almost unconscious from fear and when his mother finally did come after all he could no longer resist the desire to kiss her, and even prevailed upon her to spend the night with him.

Is it the ubiquity of man's infantile incest-wishes, as postulated by psychoanalysis, which explains the long tradition of this poetic material? Maybe. At all events it is worth noting that in recent years the incest motif has gained increasingly in importance in the drama and in the novel, and that it may possibly become even more important in future.

The prototype of literary incest is Oedipus (Sophocles, fifth century B.C.) who unwittingly kills his father and marries his mother. If the depiction of this motif in Greek mythology and in Aeschylus, Sophocles and Euripides has undergone psychologically interesting modifications through the progressive disguising of the family relationship, according to Rank part of the process of repressions, then one will not be surprised at the richness of the variations in the Oedipus tragedies by Seneca, Julius Caesar, Corneille, Voltaire, Dryden, Lee and Hofmannsthal, up to Cocteau.

Whilst the incest theme was relatively seldom dealt with in medieval and Renaissance literature – with the exception of the medieval fables and Christian legends, e.g. Marguerite de Navarre's *History of an Incest* – and also appears only in isolated instances in the adventure novel of the seventeenth and eighteenth centuries, it takes on new life amongst the English Romantics (e.g. Shelley, Byron) and more especially the American novelists and short-story writers of the nineteenth century (e.g. Melville) and twentieth century (e.g. Metalious). The European writers of the twentieth century also devote attention to the incest theme. The best-known literary figures for the English reader are perhaps Giovanni and Annabella in John Ford's *Tis Pity She's a Whore*; for Americans possibly Pierre Glendenning and his half-sister Isabel in Melville's novel *Pierre, or the*

Ambiguities; for Scandinavians Oswald and Regine in Ibsen's *Ghosts*; and for Germans most likely Ulrich and Agathe in Musil's *Der Mann ohne Eigenschaften*. There are admittedly other authors; writers of such different literary rank as L. Frank (*Brother and Sister*), Thomas Mann (*Wälsungenblut*), W. S. Maugham (*The Book-Bag*), I. Murdoch (*A Severed Head*), H. Frisch (*Homo Faber*) and A. Moravia (*Incest*). And we should not omit mention of the eighteenth-century tales, *The 120 Days of Sodom* and *Crimes of Love* by the Marquis de Sade.

According to our understanding there are three characteristic forms of representation of the motif of incest: the unconscious and conscious perpetration of incest, as well as the subconscious incest wish in all its more or less concealed variations. Both the first two forms (mainly the first) are to be found in Greek mythology, and both to an equal degree in myths and fairy tales. Unconscious incest has its model in Aeschylus' and Sophocles' *Oedipus*, but the occurrence in dramatic and epic literature of the subconscious incest wish is purely a discovery of psychonalysis. It is a discovery in two respects: whilst many authors in this century try to give form to the results of psychoanalytical discoveries of the subconscious (Tennessee Williams, for instance), psychoanalysis is trying to discover in the writers' creations the subconscious motivation of human behaviour. According to the psychoanalytical interpretation there is an inner link between the three presentation forms of 'literary' incest.

Oedipus, ejected by his parents in early childhood, kills his father and marries Jocasta, his mother. Every step in the chain of events is forecast by the Delphic oracle, and incest is committed by Oedipus in ignorance of his blood-relationships. According to Sophocles, men steer unerringly towards their predestined fate. Even Oedipus' attempt to avoid the oracle's evil prophecy by fleeing from his supposed parents, Polybos and Peribola (in reality his fosterparents), is a failure. The discovery and knowledge of the patricide and incest with his mother come too late – the guilt is tragic destiny. Psychoanalysis interprets these events as 'an unsuccessful attempt at repressing' Oedipus's oedipal-incestuous tendencies, and sees the tragic destiny which is laid upon the hero by fate – from the belief in an intact cosmos – as the concealed realisation of original, still unconscious, infantile, incestuous impulses. A contrived psychoanalytical interpretation? A look at the other end of the long series of writings on the Oedipus theme makes more evident the progressive process of repression and concealment, as for example in Hofmannsthal's *Oedipus and the Sphinx*, a dramatisation of the events prior to Sophocles' material. Here Oedipus learns of the incest and the patricide not from the oracle, but in a dream. But the faces of the parents are veiled, Oedipus does not recognise them – an expression of a psychological defence against unacceptable impulses, unconscious, yet painful to the consciousness:

'There lay a cloth upon his face, and groaning at the memory of the murdered man which suddenly came forth, my heart was seized with pain, and I awoke.'

With the knowledge of Freud's teaching, new variants of unconsciously committed incest were developed in the twentieth century. We encounter one of the literarily and psychologically interesting variants in M. Frisch's *Homo Faber*, in which the taboo on the father–daughter relationship loses, *a priori*, something of its sharpness owing to the illegitimacy of the daughter. In Frisch the perception, the similarity association (Sabeth–Hanna/daughter–mother) set up by external phenomena, takes over the function of the oracle. But the notion of a connection between Sabeth (daughter) and Hanna (Faber's ex-mistress and Sabeth's mother) is the more repressed, the closer the relations between Faber and Sabeth become. The fateful nature of the (apparently chance) meeting between father and daughter is as it were transformed to the human plane by Frisch with the help of psychology, the inevitability of the Delphic oracle is operative in the sphere of the dynamics of psychological motivation. The recognition scene, in which Faber gains 'conclusive proof' of the identity of his daughter, becomes a situation of conflict, but remains without consequences. In resisting his feelings of guilt Faber twists reality until 'the sum really comes out right, the sum as such'. And later, after vain attempts at repression and rationalisation, when the certainty of the incest can no longer be shut out from his consciousness, Faber's thoughts of suicide increase; although, 'I don't think much of suicide, it won't change anything about the fact that one has lived – and what I wished at this moment was never to have been!'

Frisch adds weight to the motif of guilt and sin by the repetition of fragments of classical material, when he makes Faber, after he has returned to Hanna, reflect in the bath: 'I had not locked the bathroom door, and Hanna (so I thought) could come straight in and murder me from behind with an axe.'

The Atrides tragedy of Aegisthus does not take place, Hanna is no Clytaemnestra – at most a personified conscience – and Faber's end is more profane; he dies of cancer. Perhaps the engineer Walter Faber is 'the only likeable "outrager of his daughter" known to world literature'? (Leonhardt, 1969, p. 206).

At all events he is more likeable than de Sade's Count, who deliberately prepares his daugher for incest, in full knowledge of the blood-relationship. This case, so extremely rare in modern literature, of consciously committed and premeditated incest, represents the most extreme consequence of the ubiquitous incest-wish. In Sade's *Eugénie de Franval* incest is not only consciously committed but, with allusions to the morality of the French Enlightenment and the Bible, given philosophical justification and ethical acceptance. Here sex is not only practised against a taboo, but the taboo is by-passed, the child is brought up to incest. Franval to his daughter Eugénie: 'Is not the world full of such weaknesses. Is not this how man had to begin populating the earth? Should what was then not evil now become so? How strange! A beautiful girl must not tempt me simply because I brought her into the world! Should that which binds me most nearly to her now be a matter to set us apart? Because she looks like me, because she stems from my blood, because she carries within her a reason for the greatest love, should I observe her coldly? Oh, what sophistry! How absurd! Let us crush these disgusting prejudices which are hostile to happiness; even if they have sometimes been able to delude the reason, then it has always happened at the expense of the most beautiful enjoyments' (p. 158). These 'introductory manœuvres' of Franval's come, in a psychological sense, quite near the criminological reality of incest; nearer than Stendhal's or Shelley's historically staged abnormal case of a violent and sadistic father in *Cenci*, or than Sade's own sadomasochistic daughter–father seduction in *Juliette*.

Since the Freudian revolution there has been a growth of works of literature which seek to give expression to the exploration of the unconscious, and earlier works now appear in a new light when seen through the mirror of psychoanalysis. The more or less unconscious motifs of the affective reactions of love, hate and jealousy between members of one family arise from the sphere of psychosexual experience; they have become part of the internal action of the system of psychological co-ordinates in works by Tennessee Williams (*Cat on a Hot Tin Roof*), O'Neill (*Mourning becomes Electra*), Lawrence (*Sons and Lovers*) and even those of Sartre (*Les Mouches*). Admittedly in these cases the unconscious incest-wish, the oedipal rivalry, are no more a completely central theme than in Shakespeare's *Hamlet*, or Schiller's *Don Carlos*, but they colour the heroes' interpersonal relationships, evoke tension and complications: oedipal components achieve dramaturgical functions, quite divorced from the inescapable doom-laden Delphic oracle in *Oedipus*.

If one looks for common external characteristics of the three extremely divergent representational forms or types of literary incest, then there are – with the exception of Greek mythology – again and again the motifs of guilt and sin, of internal and psychosocial conflicts in the characters depicted. In this process incest can be a tragic and fateful damnation, as in Sophocles' *Oedipus*, or an individual statement visible in the conflict-laden defence-processes and revitalised with the help of psychology, as in Frisch's *Homo Faber*. The moral and ethical evaluation of the characters performing may vary according to author, epoch and culture: 'being guilty' can be inescapable as in classical tragedy or in Ford's drama, *Tis Pity She's a Whore*, or the punishment can be directly meted out in the condemnation by society, as in Sade's *Franval*, or inflicted by self-blinding, as in the Sophoclean *Oedipus*; but the situation of conflict and guilt almost always characterises as a *leitmotif* the literary portrayal of the incest theme. Interestingly enough there are some cases of brother–sister incest which do not follow this *leitmotif* rule: 'For in all world literature intercourse between brother and sister – in contrast to father – daughter relationships – is portrayed as something perhaps socially undesirable, but basically moving and lovable' (Leonhardt, 1969, p. 219).

These few proofs will have to suffice to make clear to the reader what a considerable gallery of fictional forebears is involved in the literary and poetic treatment of the incest theme.

History

Our knowledge of the spread of incest in pre-Christian times is indeed sketchy, but that it occurred amongst various peoples and cultures is hardly to be doubted. The Greek, Roman, Egyptian and Persian myths which have come down to us, and the Old Testament narratives of the Hebrews, with their numerous examples of incest (from Zeus – Rhea/Hera – Isis to Lot and his daughters) reflect primeval human tendencies, which were ascribed to the gods, and Lucian (second century A.D.) is probably correct in his assumption that in early times incest amongst the gods merely sanctioned man's corresponding earthly behaviour. In fact historical evidence has come down to us that in a whole series of cultures, some very highly developed, sexual relations between members of the same family, which took as their model godly behaviour, were not only entered into willingly but were sometimes even required.

What is remarkable is the number of marriages in ancient times between brother and sister, cousins, etc. While Morus (1965) is of the opinion, without mentioning detailed sources, that the earliest marriages of the Pharaohs were sexually quite normal, and that brother and sister marriages amongst the Egyptian rulers only became the practice many centuries later, most experts on antiquity are agreed that such marriages in ancient Egypt were a relatively early phenomenon (Schiller-Tietz, 1892; Erman, 1885; Wilcken, 1891; Kayser and Roloff, 1908 *et al.*

Such unions were apparently most common in the XVII and XVIII dynasties of the Ptolemies, where their existence is recorded for a period of over three hundred years in papyrus and tax records (Kohler and Wenger, 1914). The most famous product of an Egyptian marriage of this kind was Cleopatra, who was at one and the same time her husband's niece and his sister (Schiller-Tietz, 1892). Sekenenre-Taa II married his sister Aahutep, whose great-uncle Ahmose married his sister Nefretete

(Cassin, Bottero and Vercoutter, 1966) and Ptolemy II his older sister Arsinöe, who according to Grimal (1965) had been deified even before her death and revered as the 'Goddess of Happiness'. Yet it was not only for the royal rulers of ancient Egypt that incestuous marriage seemed to be the 'easiest and the most natural thing'. Durant (1954) was in agreement with Erman when he recently established the hypothesis that incestuous marriage was widespread amongst the Egyptian people in both the pre- and post-Christian periods. Thus, for example, under Commodus in the second century A.D., two thirds of the citizens of the town of Arsino lived in incestuous marriage, predominantly between brother and sister. It is interesting that in Egyptian poetry the words 'brother' and 'sister' also have the meaning of 'lover' and 'loved' – which seems a distant echo of a once-permitted custom of incestuous marriage. (Rank 1912)

In the holy writings of the ancient Persians, the *Avesta*, incestuous marriage is directly recommended as a 'pious work' and for a period such unions were legally sanctioned for the ruling and priestly classes (Slotkin, 1947). The best-known case of incest – as told by Herodotus – is that of King Cambyses who married both his elder and his younger sister. Plutarch reports the marriage of the Persian emperor Artaxerxes to his own daughter, and Slotkin, a student of Persian and Greek literary sources, has the following *résumé* at the end of his argument: 'Thus Iranian sources indicate not so much the absence of an incest-taboo but that marriages between close relations were even approved of! One further important conclusion is that all the Iranian writings of all the Zoroasters – and not only of the priests and rulers – seem even at first sight to recommend incestuous marriage' (1963, pp. 230–1, author's translation).

Marriage amongst close relations was most widespread in the civilisations of the Peruvians, who – according to Schiller-Tietz (1892) – married mothers, sisters and daughters without any regard for blood-relationship. Amongst the pre-Colombian Incas, the highest Peruvian nobility who were treated as priests of the sun and the world-spirit, marriage between brother and sister was, according to the chronicles, part of family law for over fourteen generations. H. Többen (1925), who is presumably basing himself on Rohleder (1912), represents the view, however, that incest amongst the Incas can only be historically proved in five generations, and then only in the Huiracocha, Jupanki, Tupac Jupanki, Haayun Capac and Atahualpa tribes.

Incestuous marriage was also allowed in ancient Arabia (Wilutzki quoting Strabo, 1903). Schräder mentions isolated instances of incestuous marriages between parents and children of Indo-European peoples, and amongst the Hebrews in the pre-Mosaic period marriages were allowed between children of the same father, but not the same mother (Morus, 1965; Rank, 1912).

Incest among the Greeks in antiquity is characterised by Többen when he writes: 'In their customs and their legal outlook the Greeks held a middle course between oriental freedom and Roman severity. As a result they preserved ineradicable traces of original incest' (1912, p. 5). If one views the period as a whole from Homeric Greece through the Athens of Solon up until the post-Christian period, both the legal position and public opinion on incestuous relations seem to have moved from a liberal attitude towards a ban on incest, although admittedly this progression was not continuous, either from a legal or a socio-ethical point of view. The attitudes expressed in civil law, in poetry and philosophy varied, not only in a metaphysical sphere, but also geographically. There was no special law involving punishment for incest. Whilst in Athens before the time of Solon marriage to a sister seems to have been allowed, the Themis – a religious and at the same time private law of the Greek goddess of customs and order, which had earthly sanction – forbade marriages between parent and child as well as those between full-born brothers and sisters. Attic law allowed only half-sisters and half-brothers to marry, and Spartan law only such unions between half-sisters or half-brothers on the mother's side. Incestuous marriages, especially those between brother and sister, were not uncommon amongst the families of the social élite (Light, 1953). Nevertheless, public opinion was against unions between parent and child, and also against those between brother and sister.

Socrates, who was a spectator at a performance of Euripides' *Aeolus*, in which incest occurs between brother and sister, reported that there was angry reaction amongst the audience at one stage in the play in which the allusion to incest is: 'For nothing is ignoble or common if it only pleases us!' Quiet was only restored when Antisthenes, sitting in the audience, called out a different version of the lines: 'Ignoble remains ignoble whether it is enjoyed or not!' So says Licht in his sexual history of ancient Greece. Plato reports that the ban on incest was 'an unwritten law' and the breaking of it was a 'godless deed, causing anguish to the gods, the basest ignominy'. Opposed to the ban of Themis were the Sophists, Sceptics and Cynics, and Diogenes praised the Persians for having as few pangs of conscience about incest as, 'fowls, dogs or asses'.

It is obviously uncertain, though, whether the state did in fact uphold Themis' given law, or indeed whether every incestuous union was punished. H. Többen comments on this matter as follows: 'amongst the Greeks the civil law, with the support of public opinion, prevented incestuous union, the religious law excluded the incestuous person from the church community, but the penal law would regard this misuse of individual freedom in private life silently and with indifference' (1925, p. 8). Here are mentioned only some of the better-known cases of incest amongst the Greek civic leaders: the marriage to his sister of Archeptolis, son of the famous Themistocles, and that of Cimon of Athens, son of Militiades. Of the latter Cornelius Nepos observed that: 'for these famous Athenians it was no shame at all to be married to one's sister, for their fellow-citizens had the same custom'. (quoted from Rank, 1912, p. 419)

What amongst the Greeks was hardly tolerated but nevertheless not officially punishable, was forbidden by the ancient Romans. Both the definition of the crime and the kind and amount of punishment varied considerably with the rise and flowering of the Roman Empire. Only slaves were not affected by the ban of the *incestus juris civilis*, but even they came under the ban on incest between 'forebears' and 'descendants', between those related by marriage in both preceding and succeeding generations (*incestus juris gentium*). In his *Annals* Tacitus observes that marriages between cousins of the first degree were unknown in early Rome, and Többen, who is taking his basic information from Tacitus and Livy, reports that the bar to marriage reached as far officially as the sixth degree of relationship, but was liberalised to the fourth degree after the second Punic War (218–201 B.C.).

When Emperor Claudius, who had his bride Messalina poisoned, wished to wed his niece Julia Agrippina, the mother of Nero, he forced the Senate to legalise unions between uncle and niece – a decree which was only reversed three hundred years later (A.D. 274–337) by the Emperor Constantine, who became a Christian.

The punishments for breaking the law on incest were harsh: in the early years of the Republic enforced suicide (Weinberg, 1963), in the first century B.C. death by being thrown from the cliffs at Tarpei. Emperor Constantine's sons also imposed the death penalty, and Emperor Theodosius (A.D. 379–395), who made Christianity the state religion (A.D. 391–392), used death by burning and confiscation of property as a punishment. This was already the time when Augustine (A.D. 354–430) was writing his *De Civitate Dei* (The State of God), and Hieronymus of Stridon (A.D. 345–420) was translating the Bible into Latin. It is quite clear that the Christian Emperors – up until Justinian, who undertook sweeping legal reforms in the sixth century – broadened the ban on marriage between blood-relations and sharpened the penalties for incestuous behaviour.

One of the most famous unpunished cases of incest in Imperial Rome is that of Caligula (A.D. 37–47), who married his sister Agrippina, who, as the wife of Claudius (A.D. 41–54) and Dowager Empress also had sexual relations with her own son by an earlier marriage, the future Emperor Nero (A.D. 54–68) (Többen, 1925; Masters, 1963; Weinberg, 1963).

The Early Middle Ages and the High Middle Ages were the period of the progressive Christianisation of Europe. Gregory I, Bishop of Rome (A.D. 590–604), increased the influence of the Papacy and sent missionaries to England. Pope Gregory II had the Gospel preached in the remaining heathen part of Germany by Boniface, later Archbishop of Mainz (A.D. 748). Pippin, King of the Franks (A.D. 751–768), was anointed by the Bishop and made the Church State secure in Italy, and finally Charlemagne (A.D. 768–814), after he had defeated and converted the Saxons and raised Salzburg and Cologne to Archbishoprics, was crowned 'Imperator Romanorum' in St Peter's by Pope Leo III.

With the spread of the area of power of the Roman Catholic Church, and its influence on the secular rulers, the civil law on marriage becomes increasingly a matter of religious concern. Sexuality is regarded as abhorrent, sinful and promiscuous, and the incest laws are stretched to include an utterly ridiculous degree of relationship. Thus for example in A.D. 800 Leo III told the Bavarian bishops that they should allow no marriages closer than the seventh degree, 'since on the seventh day the Lord rested from all his deeds' (Klein-Mayern, 1784, p. 11). Even godparents were drawn into the ban on incest and marriage, and later the relatives of a priest who had baptised or confirmed a person (Westermarck, 1939). Finally a point was reached where even the two baptismal witnesses of the same child could not marry – 'so deeply rooted was the fear of incest' (Taylor, 1957, p. 59).

Looking at German attitudes to the problem in the Early Middle Ages, Többen remarks: 'The attempts by the Christian Church to spread the ban on marriages between related persons even further than the Roman ban for the newly christianised German tribes only very gradually achieved complete success. Only in the sixth century, when the temporal rulers made the Church's ban part of their own laws, was the ban enforced. In this process the Roman ban was supported on the whole by the older West Gothic, Salian, Ripuarian, Alemannian and Bavarian common law, and the Edict of Rotharis' (1925, p. 11).

In England the Catholic Church's extended ban became part of the King's Law only in the tenth century, while incest in the Early Middle Ages had still been fairly widespread. In A.D. 749 Boniface, the 'Apostle of the Germans', reported to the Archbishop of York on his experiences as a missionary in England of sexual behaviour in that country: 'It is monstrous and simply did not happen in earlier ages that a Christian nation, against the custom and practice of the whole world, against God's commandments, should disregard the law and give itself up to incest, extensive adultery and disgusting whoring with nuns' (Masters, 1963, pp. 28–9). And Taylor, author of a history of sex in England, begins his first chapter with the sentence: 'Rape and incest characterise the sexual life of England during the first century of our era . . .' (1957, p. 23). At all events church norms were only gradually established in the satellites, but achieved more and more the character of the law of the land.

Apparently even the clergy were not untouched by the encroachments of 'accursed' incest. Pope John XII, who was deposed in 963, just after he had crowned Otto the Great Kaiser in 962, was not only accused of incest with his mother and with his sisters, but with having turned the Church of St John in Lateran into a brothel (Lea, 1907). Pope Balthasar Cossa confessed before a Church Council which took place in Constance in 1414 to incest, adultery and other crimes (Taylor, 1957). The Papal legate in France, Cardinal Guala, thought it urgent in the face of the 'unwholesome danger of incest', to publish a decree in 1208, according to which mothers and other relatives should not live in the priest's house, a decree which recurred in various forms until the end of the fourteenth century. According to the legal records of the period more priests even than laymen were accused of incest, although their punishment was only a mild one (Taylor, 1957; Masters, 1963).

Under Innocent III (1198–1216) the Papacy achieved great repute. He not only restored the Church State but liberalised the ban on marriage by making officially possible, at the Fourth Lateran Council in Rome, marriage to cousins beyond the third degree of relationship, a ruling which remained in force until 1918. This council, which took place at about the period of the troubadours Wolfram von Eschenbach and Walther von der Vogelweide, was also responsible for something completely different: the setting-up of the Inquisition, and the start of the persecution of the 'heretics', at first the Christian sects of the Cathars and the Waldenses, but later spreading to cover all who thought differently, or seemed to do so, or all people disliked by the Catholic, and later Reformed, Church.

In the persecution of heretics by the agents of the Inquisition, accusations of homosexual or incestuous behaviour played a not unimportant role.

The Cathars were charged with incest although – according to Taylor – it is highly unlikely that these 'devotees of the horned god' really committed the act, since the rules of their sect advocated sexual abstinence. R. E. L. Masters (1963) mentions the gnostics and the Euchites, of whom it was recorded that they would meet on Good Fridays to commit incest. Of the Cathars and the Luciferans it was said that they had intercourse with their mothers and sisters in the course of their religious observances. The idea of 'incestuous sins' of which the accused was said to be guilty seems to have played a part even in witch-hunting itself. Thus Michelet (1863) believed that according to de Lancre (1613) the main aim of the sabbath was incest, the direct teaching of Satan. Masters (1963, p. 29, author's translation), says of the witches' sabbath: 'Since demons could not commit incest they sometimes called upon witches to join them in incestuous acts. This was considered a normal and even essential part of the sabbath itself.'

In both the witch-hunts and in the persecution of heretics the heresy that was being attacked was more sexual than doctrinal. The most disparate heretical groups were accused, amongst other crimes, of having broken the sexual taboos of Christian dogma. The equation was simple: if a person was a heretic, then he was as a matter of course either a homosexual or a perpetrator of incest.

Here there are – in so far as we are dealing with the process of dynamic drives which are at the base of such phenomena – parallels with our own history: with the Nazi persecution of the Jews who were in no little measure accused of sexual abnormality, and with the 'Red Scare' of McCarthy and his followers. Psychoanalysis gives a quite applicable explanation of this psychological phenomenon. It regards it as the outcome of a certain psychodynamic process, in which the projection mechanism plays an essential role.

'Projection is always a defence against one's own repressed denied excitements and needs, which emanate from the area of the most strongly taboo attitudes, fantasies and tendencies (this holds equally good for the areas of both sex and aggression). It hinders the ability to have an unprejudiced awareness of someone else's or one's own system of values and at the same time gives a pure image of oneself.' A. Mitscherlich (1963, p. 177) remarks in this context: 'Persecuting of heretics is really only the persecution of one's own heresy, one's own mistakes, flight from one's own guilt feelings. . . .'

The exaggerated, and to a great degree false, accusations of the Church point to projections by the inquisitors working in the name of Christ. Like the absurd extension of the ban on marriage to cover the seventh degree of relationship (Pope Gregory III), these projections are also indicators of the sexual tendencies and human behaviour held in the highest taboo by the Christian Church – incest and homosexuality. The motivation was the fear of confronting the realities of human nature.

E. Friedell (1965) has called the Middle Ages the 'period of puberty of Central European humanity, the thousand year long psychosis of sexual maturity in the form of covert sexuality', and has spoken of a kind of 'Renaissance guilt'. The radical change in thinking and attitudes which took place around the turn of the fourteenth century, a change which also affected the behaviour and manners of Central European man, was not only marked by pleasure-seeking, self-aggrandisement and egoism, but also by a newly discovered outlook on the world and equally by the collapse of old-established values. This was also true of norms of sexual behaviour. G. R. Taylor says that the 'sexual guilt feeling was jaded' (1957, p. 129), and Friedell characterises the sexual behaviour of the age with the sentence: 'In relations between the sexes eroticism is replaced by sexuality' (1965, p. 128). Whether these generalisations are admissible or not is something historians must decide. At all events the Renaissance was the period of the joyously sensual and colourful art of Giorgione, Titian, and Raphael, who discovered the beauty of the naked female form, and it was the Rome of Pietro Aretino, the janus-headed littérateur and intriguer who added to Giulio Romano's 'Sixteen Positions' (the 'modi'), his pornographic 'Sonetti Lussuriosi'. Finally, it was the age of the Medicis and the Borgias. The attitude of the Catholic Church towards sex and incest seemed to have become more liberal. Admittedly incest was still a crime, and no rare matter of concern for the Condottiere and the elders of the Church.

From a sexological point of view the most interesting case is that of the House of Borgia. Rodrigo Borgia, since 1492 Pope Alexander VI, involved his daughter in a notorious scandal through her double incest with him and with his son Cesare Borgia. In a Papal Bull he announced himself the father of one of his daughter's children, though in a second Bull he ascribed it to his son, who loved his beautiful sister so passionately that he had throttled her second husband with his own hands (Morus, 1965). The annals of the papal legal clerk Burchard, which contain descriptions of the Pope's orgies with Lucretia, Cesare and prostitutes, remain uncontested by historians.

On the same subject Masters adds: 'The Pope and Lucretia also had other ways of amusing themselves. From a window in the Vatican they would watch enraptured several stallions copulating with mares' (1963, p. 33 ff.). In the same century also Pope John XXII was relieved of his pontificate for incest, and Malatesta, according to Masters (1963, pp. 31 ff.) 'a not completely atypical Condottiere', got his daughter with child. There was also the case of Beatrice Cenci (1594), who was raped by her father and later, after she had murdered him with the help of her stepmother and brother, was beheaded – one of the most famous cases of incest in Italy during the later years of the Renaissance. Both Shelley and Stendhal made use of material from the period, and the latter hinted at the immorality of the Popes during the Renaissance: 'He told the poor girl all kinds of loathsome things, which I hardly dare name. Thus he said to her [Francesco Cenci to his daughter Beatrice] that children who are the product of a father and the daughter of his own body automatically become saints, and that all the great holy figures of the church are the offspring of such parents' (Rank, 1912, p. 402).

Historians and writers of cultural and historical works on sexuality are at least agreed that the Renaissance was one of those great revolutions which opened up a gulf between the law and ecclesiastical norms of behaviour and the realities of human behaviour, a gulf which was perhaps deepest in the Italy of that period. Incest in its extremest, but also in its rarer forms, was only a symptom of the Christian attempt in the Middle Ages to suppress psychological drives. The consequence of this had to be a change either in the law or in manners. The Reformation tried to bring about both, while the Catholic Church's Counter-reformation tried to stabilise the old canon law. Sexual problems played an important role in both movements. Yet they were less concerned with Church law on incest than with the 'sanctity of marriage', its indissolubility, and 'celibacy'. As far as incest was concerned the temporal law of Central Europe in the sixteenth century had, in its end effect, long followed canon stipulations, and the more extreme movements of the Reformation, Puritanism and Calvinism, postulated even heavier punishments for the 'sin' of incestuous behaviour.

In England, where the Reformation occurred almost at the same time as the Renaissance, there was during the whole Elizabethan period a 'deep-seated fear of incest' which 'belonged generally to the suppressed elements of the personality', and could not therefore be spoken of, even in jest. It smouldered in an area of 'tension and anxiety' (Taylor, 1957, p. 138).

There were two reasons for this. One is interesting because it has been preserved into the twentieth century and lies behind our penal code, under the surface, so to speak; the other is linked with certain historical events. Since the excommunication from the Catholic Church of Henry VIII, brought about mainly by the syphilitic king's sexual and marital problems, the Catholic 'law of customs' had indeed been repealed, yet the population continued to be influenced by a mystical and religious way of thinking. The notions of 'making impure', upon which the prescripts of the Catholic Church were based, continued to be at the back of people's minds (Taylor, 1957). The other reason was perhaps the beheading of Ann Boleyn by Henry VIII, who accused her not only of adultery but also of incest with her brother. It is quite likely that Queen Elizabeth, Ann Boleyn's daughter, was influenced by her mother's fate, when in 1583 she empowered the High Court to repeal the death penalty for incest and to introduce fines and imprisonment for the 'crime'. Yet during the Commonwealth, 1642–60, the death penalty for incest came into force again, 'in order to destroy this monstrous sin'.

In Scotland incest was also a contravention of the religious laws and was punishable with death by beheading. Only in 1887 did the Criminal Procedures Act bring some liberalisation so that the offence no longer merited the death penalty, but even the most serious cases were punished simply with life imprisonment (Weinberg, 1963).

The German penal code in the sixteenth and seventeenth centuries also followed the rules of the Church. The penalties were, however, according to the medieval civil laws, different from one state to another. The death penalty for incest with near blood-relations – mostly by decapitation with a sword – seems to have been (according to the evidence of Többen, 1925), more the rule than the exception.

The ban on marriage to relations was moreover extended to

cover step-relations. This weakened the older civil law punishments and distant relatives were less severely punished. This latter point seems above all to have been true of Regensburg, and also of Nuremberg, where incest was said to be 'a very frequently committed offence'. Yet in the imperial city of Speyer, for example, in 1577 a man charged with incest and adultery with his stepmother was 'hanged at the light gallows and the immodest woman brought from life to death by drowning' (Harster, quoted in Többen, 1925, p. 13). It was only towards the end of the eighteenth century that the German penal police laws instituted 'deprivation of freedom for a long period of time'.

In the Swiss Confederation, where Calvinism had its origins, the punishments for incest varied considerably at this time. In serious cases in Zurich the death penalty was employed, whilst in Lucerne the following penalties – obviously religious in origin and based on Reformation models – were the rule: pillory, stocks, dungeon, penance and banishment.

In sixteenth and seventeenth century France the temporal law threatened the wrongdoer with death by the noose (Guyon, 1934). Whilst the beautiful and intelligent Marquise de Brinvilliers was executed for incest with her brothers and murder by poisoning, Cardinal Richelieu was accustomed to maintain with Mme Rousse, his illegitimate daughter, that kind of incestuous relationship which de Sade characterised as the peak of psychic voluptuousness (Bloch, 1904). According to Bloch the French Rococo period was one of those recurring times in cultural history when there is an extraordinary prevalence of incest: The truth of this judgement has yet to be explored. At all events incest was not rare amongst the upper classes and was tolerated by the people.

When Voltaire, in an early play, *Oedipus,* made a veiled reference to the Duke Philippe d'Orleans in his depiction of incest between the King and Jocasta, the duke sat unperturbed in his box. He applauded and kept the young author in reasonable luxury for a year. Philippe d'Orleans, son of the famous Princess Liselotte of the Palatinate, had passionate love relationships with both his daughters: the beautiful and temperamental Duchesse de Berry and Mme de Ségur, one of his illegitimate children (Bloch, 1904). The Duc de Choiseul, Prime

Minister at the time of the Seven Years War, was the subject of a verse about his intimacy with his sister, the Duchesse de Gramont. Bloch says of de Terrai that he enjoyed the favours of a young girl who was the daughter of his former mistress. Of Mirabeau he writes that he not only wrote the Enlightenment work *Essai sur le despotisme*, but also sent secret letters to Mme de Monnier in which he outlined a plan for concluding incestuous marriages for generations to come, between his children and his children's children. Diderot, 'the creator of the *Encyclopédie*', declared incest to be a matter of minor importance, and Nicolardot said one must call it the 'philosophy of sin', since the philosophers of the time justified the rejection of the taboo (Rank, 1912). Indeed the Age of Enlightenment under Voltaire, Hommel, Cella, Soden and Michaelis was one when the punishable nature of the act was seriously doubted.

We cannot here write a complete history of incest, nor do we intend the historical examples scattered here to be a scientifically based apologia for gossip. We have merely attempted to indicate how, in the history of mankind, there have been very different religious and moral attitudes to sexual behaviour and to marriages between people more or less closely related. They vary from age to age and they also show a wide variety of viewpoints ranging from approval through toleration to total disgust and rejection. The reverse side of the religious commandment of the Church (exogamy) is the absurd degree to which the ban on incest is taken. The important role of the Catholic and Reformed Church in the establishment of temporal laws cannot be overlooked. The question of the source and motivation of the ban on incest, and of the legal rulings and punishments, is considered in the following chapter.

Primitive cultures

The life and social structures of 'primitive peoples' which have so far been studied by social anthropology – in the main by Anglo-American social anthropologists – in many respects offer conclusions which run parallel to what has been said above. Most anthropologists and sociologists are continually emphasising the universality of the ban on incest as one, or perhaps the only, institutional characteristic which is common to all human societies (Kroeber, 1948; Murdock, 1949; Weinberg, 1963; König 1964; Schelsky 1965). Murdock, who examined two hundred and fifty societies in a 'cross-cultural study', came to the conclusion that there was no group which allowed incest within the immediate circle of the family, i.e. between mother and son, father and daughter, or between brothers and sisters of the same blood. Yet this rule, which is applicable to most living societies, does have exceptions. Is this sufficient to make us doubt the universality of the ban on incest? The well-known French cultural anthropologist and structuralist Levi-Strauss does not allow any doubt to arise, and maintains that 'one should not count up the well-known exceptions', the small number of which 'traditional sociology has merely tended to emphasise'. And Levi-Strauss continues: 'For every society makes exceptions to the ban on incest if one looks at it from the standpoint of another society with even stronger laws. The thought of the exceptions which a Paviotso Indian could count, for example, is extremely discomfiting. If one takes the three classical exceptions, Egypt, Peru and Hawaii, to which one ought at least to add some others (Asande, Madagascar and Burma), one should not forget that these systems are exceptions when compared with ours, because the ban there has a more limited field of application than here. But even the concept of 'exception' is completely relative, and its meaning would vary considerably for an Australian, a Tongan or an Eskimo. Thus it is not so much a matter of marriages forbidden in one group being allowed in others, but rather of whether there are societies or groups which allow *any* form of marriage. The answer to this is absolutely negative: first because marriages are never allowed between all closely related people, only between certain categories (half-sister with the exception of actual sister; sister but not mother, etc.), and, second, because these incestuous marriages are either only temporary and are ritual in character or are hierarchical and permanent, but in the latter instance the marriage is the privilege of a narrow social caste. Thus, for example, in Madagascar, mothers, sisters, and sometimes cousins are not allowed as brides for the common people, while for the headman and the kings only the mother – but nevertheless the mother – is forbidden' (1966, pp. 86–7). Nevertheless – we could use the following reverse argument – there are equally societies in which some forms of incest, and from a European point of view the most suspicious and heavily penalised, do not fall under the taboo.

Thus Sumner (1960), for example, introduces a whole series of primitive cultures and groups from various societies in which incest is allowed or tolerated, or ones where there is altogether no concept of incest, or where there are unusual ideas of what incest actually is.

Amongst certain hill-tribes in Cambodia marriage between brothers and sisters is allowed, and amongst the Indian Kuki only mother–son incest is forbidden; amongst the Kalangs in Java mother–son marriages are regarded as bringing especial good fortune, while the Baduvis of West Java have perpetuated themselves for centuries by means of incest; the northeast Bantus of Teita in East Africa marry their mothers and sisters, though it must be said that the main reason for this is because they are too poor to buy themselves other women; among the highest castes of the Balinese, brother and sister marriages are allowed between twins of different sexes. The Eskimos of Kodiak, an island south of the Alaska Peninsula, practised all forms of incest during the nineteenth century, without restrictions; the Dyaks of the hinterland of Borneo have no conception at all of incest; the Baigas tolerate incest between grandparents and grandchildren, and on the Solomon Islands father–daughter marriages are allowed. Here one must also mention the brother–sister marriages in Polynesia, Malaya, Burma and amongst the Kamchadals in Siberia quoted by Rank (1912) and Morgan (1891). Many tribes exclude the king or tribal chief from any common ban on incest, as, for example, in Uganda, Siam, Ceylon and on the Sandwich Islands. Amongst the Sakalanis of Madagascar a headman may conclude a marriage with his sister if he cannot find an exogamous bride of equal status, and the Asande of Africa demand of their paramount chiefs sexual partnerships with their own daughters (Ford and Beach, 1968). The Yakuta tribesmen of Siberia and the Ceylonese exercise a marriage ban for members of the chief family, but in the case of the former the sister is deflowered by her brother before she marries, so that she may not take the 'family luck' with her, and in Ceylon this *jus primae noctis* of the brother's which the Senegalese, the Orang-sakai and the eastern Mollucks reserve for the father, is equally legally practised. The American cultural anthropologist Ralph Linton studied the genealogy of a noble family from Samoa: of eight consecutive marriages between brother and sister only one had been concluded with a younger sister. The poor girl thereby drew the anger of the natives and was condemned as immoral. This was because marriage to a brother was the prerogative of the first-born, the elder and not the younger sister. The 'young lady' of Linton's study became an outcast – her incest was not approved of, at least by the Sanwans (Levi-Strauss, 1966).

There is certainly a multitude of such examples, but that does not concern us here. We only wish to point out that the concept of incest is a relative one, that the incest taboo as a social norm is reached through the quality of the relative, and the particular ban on incest can obviously not be in doubt. As far as the exceptions are concerned, it can be said that they are admittedly not absolute; nor, however, are they always the privileges of a socially 'limited caste'. Recent researches into the case of ancient Egypt have strengthened the suspicion that marriages between blood relatives, especially between brothers and sisters, were not only a pre-emptive right of the ruling caste, limited to later dynasties, but seem also to have been a 'custom' practised amongst lesser officials and artisans (Murray, 1934).

Another point is that the mere existence of a ban on incest says nothing at all about its effectiveness. Thus for example, the recent surveys of Edwardes and Masters (1962) in North Africa, and especially in the Jewish quarters of Tangiers, Fez, Marrakesh, Oran, Algiers, etc. have shown that brother–sister incest, although strictly forbidden, is so common as to be regarded as normal. Jacobus points to similar relationships amongst the Hindus in India and East Africa (quoted from Edwardes and Masters, 1962). One thinks involuntarily of the proverb of the Central African Asande: 'The search for a woman begins with the sister.'

Another phenomenon is parent–child masturbation, which can be observed amongst certain primitive tribes and cultures who have an official ban on incest.

Thus masturbatory handling of the children by their parents

belongs to an ancient tradition and is still practised today amongst, for example, the Arabs, Moslems, and the Islamic population of Central Asia, the Turkmens, Uzbeks, Kurds and Kirghizian Kazakhs. The North American Hopi and the South American Siriono frequently masturbate their children (Ford and Beach, 1968). The motives for this behaviour are various and most often connected with superstitious attitudes (*a*) with boys, to encourage the growth of the genitals, (*b*) with girls, to develop and assure vaginal sexuality, (*c*) to keep the child quiet in general. The last-named practice appears to rest on a similar experience to that of a mother's use of feeding in our own cultural circle. R. E. L. Masters (1963) emphasises that in the groups and societies named neither guilt feelings nor psychological harm to the children can be found to exist. It is interesting to note, on the opposite side, that the North American Mojave Indians forbid masturbation of their infants and small children, asserting that this would make them think of incest (Weinberg, 1963). This tribe lives under an exceptionally strict incest taboo, which forbids marriage even to second cousins (Devereux, 1939).

To our knowledge it has not yet been established what specific relationship there may be between the kind of motivation behind the incest taboo, and its effectiveness in the face of sexual behaviour and the incidence of incest.

B. Malinowski (1962), who reports on several cases of brother–sister incest amongst the Trobriands in Northeast New Guinea, is of the opinion that the local prevalent, very strict sexual taboo for brothers and sisters itself creates a favourable climate for incest. He points to the fact that during his investigations he did not find one single case of mother–son incest, although this specialised taboo was not so strictly applied. Incest cases between father and daughter, on the other hand, were not unknown amongst the Trobriands, and not explicitly forbidden by the laws of exogamy, but all the same regarded as reprehensible. But why reprehensible? We do not know. From the Arapesh in New Guinea, who also have a relatively liberal attitude towards their incest taboo, we can discover something of the motivation. For them sexual attraction to one's own mother or sister means something about as reprehensible as the asocial hoarding of provisions. Their attitude towards the incest taboo is very pragmatic: an exogamous marriage is the best means of broadening social and business contacts, and an incestuous marriage would be rejected on these grounds.

The relationships between the strictness of the incest taboo, the nature of its motivation, and its effectiveness, are very much more complicated than will allow them to be brought together into a simple formula. Besides, it is precisely amongst the non-literate primitive cultures that one can establish unpublished exceptions to the taboo, the hidden reasons for which are magical in character. Thus, for example, the warriors of the Australian Dierri tribe are allowed incest on the night before a battle, because it will give them courage for the fight, and provide an emotional catharsis (Niewenhaus, 1929).

Another essential aspect which has a parallel in bourgeois marriage laws and in the sexual penal code of modern civilisation, is the fact that even amongst primitive cultures the rules of exogamy and the incest taboo cover completely different degrees of relationship, and often also differ considerably in direction (Ford and Beach, 1968). Looking at the complicated calculations of degrees of relationship covered by the ban on marriage created by the Catholic Church, one has to agree with Ruth Benedict (1955) when she maintains that no cultural concept has undergone such detailed elaboration as the incest taboo. This is true, as we see from the example of the Kurnai, of many primitive cultures.

Here the endogamy and incest ban involves such a large number of individuals, whose common ancestry can no longer be traced at all, that the choice of a marriage partner is made very difficult. In Australia there is an additional direct fear of marriage with the 'sister', and consequently a unique overdevelopment of the exogamous proscriptions. 'But this sad state of affairs does not make the Kurnai alter their exogamy rules in any way. . . . The only way for a young man to marry is, therefore, to go against the rules: the young couple simply elope' (Benedict, 1955, p. 31).

Thus the exogamy commandments of the Kurnai, once dictated by superstitious fear, are obviated, and the Kurnai use a typical method of extracting themselves from their cultural dilemma – they do what is also done in a modern society, in which lip-service is paid to the traditional moral code of a collapsing social order: they do it covertly. In the absurdity of the Kurnai's rules of exogamy is mirrored a tendency of many human societies, which have to defend their adopted forms of tradition against attack from all quarters.

A word must also be said about the revealing magical superstitions which are linked with incest and its consequences. The results of ethnological surveys by Grimble (1921), Briffault (1927), Krige (1936), Frazer (1940), Devereux (1954), Sumner (1960), to name just a few, have made more likely the conclusion that magical or magical-mystical superstitions are in evidence, connected both with a liberal and a strict attitude to the incest taboo. Most of the superstitions are centred round the act of incest and its consequences.

The inhabitants of the Northern Gilbert Isles believe that the sun will fall from the sky if incest remains unpunished (Grimble, 1921). For the Galdares incest brings on earth-tremors and volcanic explosions, and the Mindanaos believe it to be the cause of flooding (Briffault, 1927). On the Celebes it is partly to blame for failures of the harvest, yet the Kalangs on Java believe that mother–son incest brings fertility and riches (Frazer, 1940). The Mojave Indians connect incest with witchcraft and see it as an evil sign, presaging the ineluctable destruction of the family. Their mystic ideology also links incest very closely with suicide (Devereux, 1954). Certain Central African tribes believe that sexual intercourse with his sister makes a warrior invincible, while the Wayao punish all incest by burning the culprit alive, in order to conjure up magic spirits (Masters, 1963). Jounod reports on an interesting variant superstition amongst the South African tribes on the Nkotami river. 'The inhabitants of certain villages along the Nkotami and other rivers specialise in hunting hippopotami and are well versed in the science, or rather special art, of *butimba*.... The hunter spends his day fishing and watching every move of the hippopotamus. When he thinks the time has come, and is ready to go on a hunting expedition which would last an entire month, he calls his own daughter to his hut and has sexual relations with her. The incestuous act, absolutely taboo in ordinary life, makes him into a murderer; he kills something within himself and thus acquires the courage to accomplish great things in the river. From that moment on and until the end of the campaign, he has no sexual relations with his wives. That same night, immediately after the act [of incest], he leaves with his sons ... he attacks a hippopotamus' (quoted in Gordon, 1949, p. 162).

Amongst the most outlandish and irrational superstitions of these primitive cultures, there are sometimes also those which still belong to the stock prejudices of Western civilisation. They are reminiscent of the dicta of fanatical medieval inquisitors and are centred around the belief that children born of incestuous unions are deformed and wicked monsters, or even witches.

The South African Zulus, for example, believe that children from an incestuous union are at first quite normal and are turned only later by the anger of the 'spirits of the elders' into monsters (Krige, 1936). Amongst other groups the fear of the birth of a child conceived in incest, and of a catastrophe connected with it which might affect all the members of the tribe, is so great that the pregnancy is terminated immediately. Thus the Navajo Indians regard abortion as an absolute need in incestuous pregnancies. G. Devereux (1954), who conducted a survey on this point amongst three hundred and fifty primitive tribes, has a wealth of material on such grotesque superstitions.

These few examples should suffice to show how many-sided can be the irrational and superstitious thinking connected with incest. Where magical-mystical and magical-religious thinking is closely interknit with a rationally unfounded fear of the impact and consequences of incest, the critical eye remains closed to the true nature of events and the real consequences. The rules become over-severe, and judgment and condemnation become intermingled. Thus many tribes which have a strict incest taboo punish those who break it with death. And here one finds parallels with the motivation for, and exercise, of Christian marriage laws. To regard this deduction as controversial would be to overlook a psychologically and socio-culturally determined condition which has been recently brought to our attention by Adorno (1963). The close connection between the incest taboo and cultural-religious and magical beliefs was early recognised by sociologists (Durkheim, 1912), anthropologists (Frazer, 1910), and by Freud (1913). Few proscriptions 'have in our society contained to the same degree the aura of respectful fear which surrounds religious matters. Significantly, incest, in both its real and its metaphorical form of the abuse of juveniles ('old enough to be their father', as the saying goes), in some countries reaches in its effects almost to its opposite pole, i.e., to sexual relations between members of different races, although these represent the most extreme form of exogamy; they are *the most powerful stimulants to disgust and collective vengeance*' (Levi-Strauss, 1966, p. 68). Our modern society and its institutions are full of these.

This digression into history and into cultural anthropological research into incest emphasises the degree to which human sexual behaviour depends on the place, the age and the culture. The emotional side of the problem should not be ignored.

2. Incest taboo

Nineteenth century anthropology consisted predominantly of a discussion about the motives and the historical development of the exogamy rule (a precept under which one must seek a marriage partner outside one's own group or clan) and the incest taboo. This discussion, which went on for over a generation, and in which sociologists, psychologists and ancient history specialists took part, seemed to have been resolved by the discovery of the frequency and number of exogamy rules supported by incest sanctions which occurred in different cultures. The one-sided need for a chain of causality on the part of some experts then led to mutually contradictory hypotheses, and thus by the end of the thirties of this century the discussion of the incest taboo had also come to a stop. The anthropologists had given up, apparently in resignation. L. Lévy-Bruhl (1931, p. 247) writes: 'The famous question of the ban on incest, this much discussed problem, the solution to which ethnologists and sociologists have so long sought after, has no answer.' And Sumner (1960) remarks that the best thing to do would be to leave the whole problem to the philosophers.

Why should we occupy ourselves here with theories which are doubtful or offer at best disputed solutions to the riddle of the taboo? Such a time-consuming activity would indeed have no more than historical interest, were it not for the fact that examination of the origins of the taboo throws a certain amount of light on the moral prohibitions which we ourselves obey. Moreover it can easily be observed that a residue of these older theories and attitudes is preserved in our own legal code and in public opinion.

One could divide the various theories into those which try to express something about the cause or causes of the taboo, and those which avoid the need for a cause and go on to examine the functioning of the taboo and its place in the social structure. Let us call the former 'causality theories' and the latter 'functional theories'. It is only recently that examinations from the functional viewpoint have taken into account sociological, psychological and ethno-anthropological aspects. This has contributed greatly to an understanding of the complex connection between the taboo and the functioning of a living society.

Degeneration and the mystique of inbreeding

At the beginning of the nineteenth century, as in earlier epochs, the objections to incestuous unions were still of a predominantly ethical, social and religious nature. Towards the end of the same century a biological argument for prohibition came increasingly to be heard. The Frenchman de Maistre believed he had found negative hereditary effects of incest and inbreeding, and Dugard, as well as medical research, seemed to support this view (Huth, 1887). Even if, according to Huth, Burton in his *Anatomy of Melancholy* (1640) had drawn attention to the negative hereditary effects of inbreeding, the idea was still new and had not occurred anywhere in our society before the sixteenth century (Levi-Strauss, 1966). L. H. Morgan (1877) was convinced that prehistoric man had recognised the damaging effects of such unions, and had therefore forbidden marriage between blood relatives. Looked at closely, this attempted explanation was not a well-formulated theory but only some observations within the framework of anthropological and historical researches into human 'prehistoric societies'. L. H. Morgan was convinced that the new kind of marriage 'which brought together in a marital relationship unrelated persons ... had a significant effect on society' in the sense that a positive psychological selection process was exercised.

The assumption upon which Morgan constructed his 'theory' – namely that incest and inbreeding as such caused psychobiological harm to descendants – has been disproved by contemporary research into human genetics (see Chapter Three, p. 75 ff.). But this alone would be no objection to Morgan's concept. Why should man not originally have had the same false conception of causality which today underlies wide circles of public opinion, and makes law-makers base the prohibition of incest on hereditary–biological grounds? The decisive objection is this – taking the degeneration hypothesis *ad absurdum*: that in many primitive cultures the incest ban applies to sociological relationships, and not merely to biological ones. On this point it has been established by some well-known figures in ethnology (Malinowski, 1929, for example) that there are groups with highly complicated exogamy precepts, who are completely unaware of the causal connection between sexual intercourse and pregnancy. It is therefore hardly credible that in such societies the cause of the prohibition is to be found in the wish to guard against the biological degeneration of the tribe, if the tribe does not even recognise the physiology of fatherhood. Moreover we should not forget that man has employed since the end of the Palaeolithic period endogamous methods of reproduction, which plants and domestic animals had perfected to an increasing degree. If we assume that man was aware of the results of this method and was capable, as is accepted, of a reasoned judgement of the matter, then how has he come to conclusions in the field of human relationships which stand in contradiction to events in the plant and animal world around him, upon which his whole well-being depends? (Levi-Strauss, 1966, p. 91.)

The degeneration argument has turned out in the long term

to be untenable, yet it has asserted itself in anthropology right up to the turn of the century, and is implicit in the confused auxiliary theories of Westermarck (1902). They are as far removed from the empiricism and status of scientific discoveries as was Pope Gregory I's belief that marriages between relations were forbidden, because, amongst other things, such marriages remained sterile.

An equally unsound hypothesis was put forward by the French sociologist Durkheim (1898). Durkheim's explanation of the incest taboo is part of his theory of totemism. In his view the rule about exogamy is connected with totemism, and the former is a product of the totem taboo. Through studying Australian tribes he came to the conclusion that the natives regarded 'blood' as a vital principle and – prisoners of superstitious thought – believed that inbreeding between members of the same name-giving totem was a great sin or a crime, since the totem was of the same blood as the man or the clan to which he belonged. With respect to unavoidable defloration, and also to menstruation, the 'blood ban' forbade sexual intercourse with any woman who belonged to the same totem or clan. The man had therefore to avoid all women of his own totem. Exogamy was thus made a necessary consequence of the totem laws.

The American anthropologist L. A. White (1963) proves this theory to be ethnologically totally inadequate since the incest taboo is far more widespread than totemism. The former is universal, the latter is not. Thus the Durkheim hypothesis shows itself to be a generalisation based on facts observable only amongst a limited number of tribal cultures. Over and above this, however, the theory hardly seems capable of explaining the many different definitions of the incest ban made by various tribal cultures (for a thorough critique see Levi-Strauss, 1966, pp. 98-9).

The kernel of Durkheim's theory of the destructive, fear-ridden, magical power of blood-mixing is reflected in the irrational thoughts of some German lawyers, who speak of 'unnatural bloodmixings' (introduction to a German penal code book, 1909) or say that 'the mixture of the same seed is against nature' (Villnow, quoted by Jäger, 1957, p. 57). Magical thought and an incest taboo are here revealed as two corresponding variables whose dark origins seem immune to rational criticism.

The 'blood tie' and sexual neutralisation

One of the most popular theories which even today seems to have wide public credibility is that of an aversion to incest, an aversion to sexual relations within the circle of the immediate family, which is 'somehow' natural to man. This is the theory of a 'blood tie' in a negative sense, an instinctive defence against incest. 'Instinctive' in this context means the same as inherited, innate. The most important adherents of this theory are the anthropologists Hobhouse (1912) and Lowie (1920). Today it no longer has any scientific following since it does not withstand empirical testing. The critical objections to it are numerous, and comparative ethnological research which points up the connections between exogamy and totemism has undermined the concept of a biologically based prohibition.

Here are just two of the most weighty counter-arguments: if the aversion to incest were inborn and thus universal it would be hard to understand why human societies have developed such strict prohibitions. Why then should legal steps be taken against something which everyone 'naturally' avoids? Second, it can hardly be assumed that an instinctive feeling for blood relationships is in a position to distinguish between the different definitions and legal qualifications of incest which vary from society to society and from country to country.

A theory hardly more tenable, whose very premises are false, is that of 'acquired aversion' of Westermarck (1902), with which Ellis (1932) is essentially in agreement. This could also be called the theory of sexual neutralisation, since the nub of it rests in the postulation that people who have grown up together and live in close contact with each other – meaning as a rule children, parents, and brothers and sisters – develop a mutual 'blunting of the libido', i.e. a sexual and erotic indifference (Westermarck 1909, pp. 40–3). The hypothesis of the 'blunting of the libido' through familiarity does not prevent Westermarck from simultaneously assuming once again an 'inborn antipathy' for incest and, behind the aversion, the existence of a 'law of natural selection', as well as an instinct regulator: 'And it is here . . . that we find a completely satisfactory explanation for the aversion towards incest; not because man at an earlier stage of development recognised the damaging effects of marriages to close relatives, but because the law of natural selection must have worked unerringly. . . . Thus an instinct could develop which was strong enough as a rule to avoid harmful unions' (1902, pp. 352-3).

Quite apart from the fact that psychoanalysis has found man's incestuous fantasies and tendencies to be a universal phenomenon (and this has not been proved of the 'instinctive' aversion), there are many societies whose attitudes contradict Westermarck's theories. Thus there is for example the Asande proverb: 'The search for a woman begins with the sister' (Levi-Strauss, 1966, p. 95). Freud (1964, p. 138) says somewhat ironically of Westermarck's concept that such an instinct would hardly go so far astray as to affect not merely 'blood relatives harmful for procreation but one's close household companions and friends'. And Frazer (1910, p. 97) thinks that it is 'not easy to see why such a deeply rooted instinct should need legal reinforcement. . . . The law usually only forbids people that which they would do under pressure of their drives. What Nature itself forbids and punishes, the law should not need to forbid and punish. . . . Thus, instead of concluding from the legal prohibition of incest that there is a natural aversion to incest, we should rather realise that there is a natural tendency to incest and that, if the law represses this drive as it represses other natural drives, then the basis for this is in civilised man's insight into the possible harm to society that might result from the satisfaction of this natural tendency.' Frazer's argument needs no commentary. It is in full agreement with psychoanalytical experience. Recently the anthropologist Ford (1968) and the psychologist Beach (1968) emphasised that close blood-relationship is no barrier to erotic sexual attraction. H. Schelsky (1965, p. 92) has, moreover, quite rightly pointed out that Westermarck's explanation leads to a vicious circle since he takes 'the stability of sexually neutralised family life as cause of the neutralisation itself.'

Politico-economic interests

The notion that the ban on incest could originally have been enforced to serve man's politico-economic interests is by no means new. Even St Augustine, the most important of the Fathers of the Catholic Church, explained in his *De Civitatis Dei* that the ban served the spread of human social intercourse and the formation of larger social groups. Similar theories were expounded by the Christian scholar Thomas Aquinas (1225-74), who saw the ban on marriage between close relatives as preventing the growth of narrow, sectional interests and, at the same time, as multiplying kinships. Luther (1483-1546) gave this basic theory a definite economic twist. He believed that marriage between relatives was well known to be forbidden not 'for the sake of conscience, but to prevent bad examples amongst the avaricious peasants; they would take their nearest blood relative for the sake of material gain'.

Yet it was only at the end of the nineteenth century that this sociological or politico-economic aspect of the ban on incest was first taken up by the anthropologists. E. B. Tylor (1889) was really the first anthropologist to ascribe to the exogamy rule and the incest taboo a significant role in the development of the culture, since – as he thought – until the existence of a ban on marriage within the group no progressive development towards larger societies through alliance with other social units seemed to be possible. He saw in exogamy an early method of political self-perpetuation, and a means of increasing the chances of survival. Most present-day anthropologists and sociologists agree with Tylor that bans on incest are in each case dependent upon the exogamy rules which a society exhibits. The negative side of the commandment to marry outside a certain group or social relationship is secondarily the ban on any sexual relations at all within this environment. H. Schelsky (1965, p. 89) has given this formulation completely in the sense of Tylor: 'The ban on incest is only the negative side of a social commandment, exogamy, which is required in all societies in order to spread beyond the family unit *and reach and secure the social structure and co-operative links and associations.*'

Margaret Mead (1959, p. 52) offers an impressive example of

this in her cultural-anthropological field surveys. She took extraordinary pains to discover the attitude towards incest of the Arapesh (a Polynesian tribe). When she finally succeeded in putting the question to some of the older men she received the following answer: 'What, you want to marry your sister? Are you not quite right in the head? Don't you want any in-laws? Can't you see that you can gain at least two in-laws if you marry another man's sister and another man marries your sister? With whom will you go hunting and till the fields, and who can you visit?'

In more recent times the American anthropologist L. A. White (1963) has extended the Tylor theory of a high degree of social self-interest and method of increasing the chances of survival into a kind of *theory of politico-economic co-operation*.

L. A. White proceeds from the premise that a basic fact of life for both men and animals is the fight for existence. The necessary precondition for existence and survival in a human group is co-operation. From the primeval beginnings of mankind it has been a matter of life and death in 'borderline situations'. White now assumes that in the course of the process of evolution – from the lower to the higher primates – the first co-operative group was the family. It was characterised by a completely new element, namely by an economic factor which had been introduced by the acquisition of articulate human speech. The first human family was based not, as with the animals, solely upon sexual attraction, but on mutual help, support and obligations in all areas necessary to life. But economic profit and well-being within the family are limited, and thus a way had to be found of overcoming the narrow social confines of the intrafamily stage of co-operation in favour of a more expansive and economically and protectively more effective interfamily co-operation. That meant a ban on marriage within the family nucleus, and from this resulted compulsory exogamy – a developmental tendency completely in opposition to the nature of the lower primates. The marriages between families, and later between larger units, became contracts, and the individual choice of partner finally became the business of the whole group.

Thus, according to White, the ban on incest has an economic motive at its base, an economic motive which came into play within mankind's process of biosocial evolution, when the faculty of speech developed and brought about the 'centrifugal' social tendencies of the family nucleus. Thus it follows that the exogamy rules are rooted in the crystallisation process of a particular social system rather than the result of conscious consideration on the part of the individual. For White, who seeks to support his theory with the results of socio-anthropological research (Radcliffe-Brown, 1930; Ogburn, 1933, and others), exogamy is a result of the incest taboo, and not the converse. The variable nature of the definitions of incest, that is the stretching of the taboo to cover various degrees of relationship in various cultures, he explains by the specific, circumstantial conditions under which co-operation has been or is being put into effect in the culture concerned. He is also of the opinion that even today the exogamy rules and the ban on incest still fulfil a necessary regulative function in our social life.

Independently of White, Levi-Strauss (1949), and, in conjunction with him, Schelsky (1955), have developed similar theories. The two last-named authors stress, however, the 'insight into the primary nature of exogamy as a command inducing a higher degree of sociability' and the 'subsequent significance of the ban on incest as the neutralisation of sexual relations between blood relatives' (Schelsky, 1965, p. 90). All the same, Levi-Strauss traces out the 'whole rationalised casuistry of blood and social relationships, exogamy and endogamy rules, in primitive societies' (Schelsky, 1965, p. 91) somewhat differently from White, namely through the institutionalisation of exchanging women and the consequent forced renunciation by the family of the biological and social fact of possessing the woman.

But is exogamy, and with it the incest taboo, only a simple, practical question of alternatives with a politico-economic significance? Is it conceivable that in all the many different isolated societies a group could develop which would have the social insight and the power to carry through its decisions? Let us leave the answer to these questions to those whose theories are based on a synthesis of the many different aspects of the problem which we have already touched on, and who, from newly discovered vantage points, seem together to be coming nearer to a solution to the taboo mystery.

Oedipus and patricide

One of the most notable, though most contested, theories on the incest taboo comes from Freud (1913). Injustice has been done time and again to the arguments of *Totem and Taboo* by reducing them to all too simple formulas, and ignoring Freud's fertile psychological ideas. Freud's theory is an attempt to apply the methods and findings of psychoanalysis to as yet unsolved problems of folk-psychology or cultural anthropology. To this degree it is in some ways an anthropological theory of culture. It contains thoughts which stem from various sources: partly ethnological and anthropological material which was available at the beginning of the twentieth century, predominantly that of Frazer (1910), but in particular the hypotheses of Smith (1889) on the religion of the Semites and their sacrificial ceremony, the totem-feast; partly the conjectures of Darwin (1859) that the first human society had consisted of one or several groups led by one despotic, all-powerful man; and finally his own thoughts from his psychoanalytical experiences with neurotic patients, in which Freud pointed to, amongst other things, the parallels between animal phobias in children and certain traits of totemism. The theory then is based in the final analysis on a highly complicated synthesis of the psychoanalytical theory of pregenital infantile sexuality, whose focal point is the oedipus complex, with Darwin's concept of primeval tribes and Smith's conclusions from his analysis of the totem-feast.

The *phylogenetic* theory of the incest taboo and the fear of incest is, however, hardly comprehensible without an exposition of certain basic traits from the psychoanalytical theory of the *ontogenetic* development of man's psychosexuality.

We will therefore attempt first of all to give a sketch of its basic outlines before we attempt a psychoanalytical explanation of the evolution of the incest taboo.

The beginnings of the formation of psychoanalytical theories are closely connected with, amongst other things, the theme of incest. The still incompletely developed analytical technique was almost Freud's undoing when, at the turn of the century, he believed his patients' fantasies of incestuous seduction and looked upon them as actual occurrences. But he soon saw his mistake, and concluded from his experience with neurotic patients that no such sexual seduction by the parent of the opposite sex had ever taken place, but that such descriptions represented an expression of repressed infantile incest-wishes, constantly to be encountered in the patients' dreams and associations. This interpretation was the point at which the *oedipus complex* was born, subsequently to become the nucleus of psychoanalytical teaching on neuroses, and at the same time an essential component of Freud's sexual theories.

Freud generalised his therapeutic experiences and postulated that the child at a certain age regularly develops a sexual interest in the parent of the opposite sex, and that towards the parent of the same sex feelings of hatred and jealousy unfold which, in their turn, call forth feelings of anxiety and guilt. He regarded this as a general psychological phenomenon which occurs in the third, pregenital phase of psychosexual development ('phallic phase') during which the child of about five associates his awakening, preferably genital, excitements with incest-wishes directed at his parents. The oedipus wish cannot, however, be fulfilled, the child's incest-wishes must be suppressed, since the child's physiological genital organisation has not yet matured: 'The early flowering of infantile sex life was, because its wishes were incompatible with reality and its infantile stage of development inadequate, condemned to disappear. In the most serious cases this phenomenon was accompanied by deeply painful emotions, anxieties and feelings of guilt. The loss of love and the failure left behind a lasting injury to the self-esteem, a kind of narcissistic scar . . . ' (Freud, Vol. XIII, p. 19). In the course of further development the child's psychosexual strivings associated with the oedipus complex become 'partially desexualised and sublimated . . . and partly restricted in their direction and changed into tender impulses' (Vol. XIII, p. 399). The oedipus complex *in boys* is submerged by the (subjectively experienced) 'threat of castration', the 'super-ego' as a (more or less subconsciously) accepted social-ethical requirement by the parents (conscience) comes into its own, and emotional relations with both parents are gradually 'normalised' again on a higher psychosexual level of personality. *In girls* it is the very 'castration-complex' which prepares the oedipal situation.

Under the influence of 'penis envy' the girl is driven out of her initially close relationship with her mother, and runs into the oedipal situation 'like a ship into a safe harbour'. She makes her mother responsible for the fact that she has no penis, never forgives her this injurious negligence, and transfers her penis-wish to her father; this wish is in its turn soon replaced by the wish to have a child by the father. For the girl it is at this juncture – according to Freud – that the oedipal situation begins, characterised as it is by rivalry and hostility, which reject the mother, and a tender, positive relationship with the father, coloured by incest-wishes. This situation is in addition characterised by another specifically sexual feature: the 'indefinitely long' duration and the late, and then only incomplete, 'dismantling' of the oedipus complex (Vol. XV, p. 138).

To sum up our extremely simplified presentation of what Freud was postulating, we can make the following abridged version:

1. The oedipus complex, as a far-reaching unconscious or highly subconscious psychological phenomenon, embraces all the child's psychosexual and psychosocial relations with both parents. It gives a specific character to one particular stage of the child's psychosexual development, and is connected with conflicts arising from guilt-laden ambivalence and anxieties; its final overcoming is the result of the formation of the individual conscience as a psychological representation ('super-ego'). This latter is of great significance for man's socialisation in the sense of his recognition and acceptance of social and ethical norms and values. To this process also belongs *the giving up of the incest-wish,* which is accompanied by the erection of an incest barrier in the sense of restraint and aversion. Freud considers this barrier to be general in application. He offers a sociological explanation by pointing to the fact that the respect for this barrier is predominantly a *cultural demand of society,* 'which has to defend itself against the damaging of its interests by the family', interests 'which it needs for the production of higher social units' (Vol. V, p. 127).

2. The development and overcoming of the oedipal phase is different for both sexes. For girls it is of longer duration, more complicated and – in contrast to boys – is only much later resolved.

Our task in what follows will be to point up the above-mentioned connections between the oedipus complex and conscience ('the super-ego') on the one side, and the incest taboo on the other, from a *phylogenetic* point of view. Freud considers the oedipus complex an unavoidable stage in the development of the individual, having its roots in matters biological.

He was of the opinion that the oedipus complex, though it is experienced individually by most people, is nevertheless 'a phenomenon conditioned and brought about by heredity' (Vol. XIII, p. 396), a phylogenetic scheme carried within people, an outcome of man's cultural history (Vol. XIII, p. 155). It is no great step from this phylogenetic speculation to the concept of the super-ego as one of man's given phylogenetic qualities. Whether or not the oedipus complex is one of the basic preconditions for the formation of the conscience or the super-ego, this latter is for Freud a phenomenon which was first acquired and then inherited, and therefore equally phylogenetic: 'What the biology and the destiny of the human kind have created and left behind in the id is taken over by the formation of the ideal of the ego, and by this means is re-experienced individually. The ego-ideal (or the super-ego) has, as a result of the course of its development, the richest connection with the phylogenetic acquisitions, the archaic inheritance, of the individual. What had in the life of the individual soul belonged to the depths becomes through the process of ideal-forming in the human soul the highest quality, according to our sense of values' (Vol. XIII, p. 265). Freud held fast – in the words of Bally (1961) – 'to the idealistic chimera of the natural man'.

What significance then does the (psycho-) genetic theory of the individual development of the oedipus complex and the super-ego have for our understanding of the incest taboo? A twofold one: first, the super-ego is not only inherently the result of the individual's particular present experiences in his encounters with the world around him, but it is also the very 'bearer of tradition, of all the unchanging values which have in this way been transplanted across the generations . . . in the ideologies of the super-ego lives the past . . .' (Vol XV, p. 73). Second, and this seems to us significant in this connection, the conscience is in our day and age precisely that part of the human psyche which stands nearest to the taboo, that is, from the point of view of ontogenesis, of the individual development of the super-ego, also stands near to the incest taboo, which is none other than a *command of the conscience*. In this respect Freud talks directly about a *taboo-conscience* and describes the ban on incest as 'probably the oldest form in which we encounter conscience' (1964 edition, p. 78). The conscience is, however, the 'inner perception of the rejection of certain wish-impulses which arise in us', which must be understood as the (repressed) unconscious half of another tendency channelled in the opposite direction, in the sense of 'ambivalence'. The dialectic of these psychodynamic motives is most clearly expressed in the oedipus complex. The taboo-ban arises, just like the conscience, from an ambivalence of feelings, in quite specific interpersonal relationships, when this ambivalence is inherent. The breaking of the taboo as an order of the conscience normally gives rise to guilt feelings, regardless of whether this contravention has a factual or, as in the case of the oedipus complex, a purely psychological (wish) reality.

The incest taboo could accordingly also be psychologically defined as an emphatic prohibition of the object of a violent, unconscious (psychosexual) desire or, as Freud says, 'Kant's categorical imperative', which 'desires to work by compulsion and rejects any kind of conscious motivation' (1964, p. 30). Yet the psychological derivation of the incest taboo, which stands or falls with the oedipus theory, did not satisfy Freud. He sought historical and anthropological evidence which would enable him at the same time to construct an explanation of the cultural-historical origins of the taboo.

We have seen that Freud derives the individual aversion towards incest from the conditions of the oedipus complex, and that he sums up respect for the incest barrier as the response to a socio-cultural demand. In fact both these are also at the centre of the phylogenetic theory of the origin of the incest taboo. The oedipus complex is the (psychological) key to the connection which anthropologists and sociologists earlier suspected existed between totemism (probably the first primitive religion) and exogamy. In other words: totemism and exogamy form the two halves of the oedipus complex. How did Freud reach this conclusion?

Both the taboo-rules of totemism, not to kill the totem and

not to have sexual intercourse with any woman who belongs to the same totem, coincide with the two integral parts of the oedipus complex, to remove the father and marry the mother; that is, they correspond to the two 'original wishes' of the child at the oedipal stage (1964, p. 148). From the analysis of animal phobias in children, in which the tender–hostile conflict of feelings (ambivalence conflict) towards one parent, mostly towards the father, are transferred to an animal ('father-surrogate'), Freud concluded the following: the similarity in basic characteristics of the totemist system, in particular of the sacrificial ritual, with its immediately obvious ambivalence of feelings towards the sacrificial animal, as well as the identification with it (the otherwise revered totem animal, the subject of a taboo, symbol of the Great Father, is once a year, with the participation of all the members of the tribe, ceremoniously killed, torn to pieces and then mourned), is none other than an action forbidden the individual, a taboo that can only be broken 'with justification' by the collective. This was the result of Freud's attempt to equate the totem animal (the totemistic 'Great Father' of the 'primitive' tribe) with the father and, from this basis, to derive the taboo, the ambivalence of feelings, and the identification from the processes of the oedipus complex (1964, p. 157).

From consideration of all these aspects, together with Darwin's hypothesis on the original state of human society, Freud found it possible to come to a deeper understanding of the taboo, i.e. of its historical origin.

According to Darwin, man in his primeval condition lived in small tribes, and each of these was under the control of a single, strong, violent and jealous man-animal, who, like many of the larger animals, refused his growing son-rivals' incest and kept the wives for himself. According to Freud, one day this group of brothers plotted together, killed the father, tore him to pieces, and 'so made an end to the father-dominated tribe':

'The mighty Great Father had certainly been the object of fear and envy for each one of the crowd of brothers. Now, with the act of dismembering him, they carried out a process of identification, they each received a piece of his strength. The totem-feast, perhaps mankind's first festivities, may be the repetition and the commemorative celebration of this criminal act, from which so many things had their beginnings, social organisations, moral restrictions and religion' (1964, pp. 158–159). But what became of the remaining 'brother-clan'? Freud assumes that, controlled by feelings of ambivalence towards the father, and placed in a difficult situation by strife and rivalry after the latter's death, the group drifted into a condition where the ambivalence was even stronger. Remorse and posthumous obedience to the murdered father made the brothers have nothing to do with the 'liberated' wives. They saved their organisation by imposing a ban on incest. 'Thus from the sons' consciousness of guilt they created the two fundamental taboos of totemism, which had to correspond precisely to the two suppressed wishes of the oedipus complex' – the sparing of the totem animal, an attempt to assuage the burning sense of guilt, and the ban on incest, a piece of posthumous obedience and at the same time a necessary rule of practical social significance (1964, pp. 160–1).

Thus there exists, in Freud's view, a close connection between incest and a *simultaneous origin of totemism and exogamy (and therefore of the incest taboo)*. In the oedipus complex there meet together the 'beginnings of religion, morals, society and art' (1964, p. 174), and at the start of this process of cultural formation stands the revolt of the sons against the father, patricide, nurtured by the conflicts of ambivalence. Freud saw in the ban on incest the basis of society and morality, the childhood beginnings of cultural development. He was completely aware that this whole theory was based on a highly disputable assumption, namely that there exists a 'mass psyche', that there is 'a continuity in mankind's emotional life'. Freud was convinced, though, that if the 'psychological processes of one generation are not transplanted to the succeeding one then each of its attitudes towards life must be worked out anew' (1964, p. 175).

What is there for, and what against, Freud's point of view? There is no proof of any primeval 'undisguised sexual condition' of the human species (Bally, 1961) in early or primeval history, indeed it is probably impossible to prove. And this is no less true of the ontogenetic–phylogenetic parallelism, which culminates in the derivation of exogamy and the incest taboo from 'a single concrete point', the oedipus complex, and is no more – in this author's view – than a highly disputable theoretical analogy. The same objection could be made against the postulated connection between totemism and exogamy (incest taboo) as against Durkheim's theory: totemism is not universal. Freud was very well aware of the fact that the high degree of convergence in his theory 'cannot make us blind to the uncertainty of our postulations and the difficulties surrounding our results' (1964, p. 175). If, however, the historical-phylogenetic derivation of the incest taboo appears questionable, what is left of Freud's point of view?

Perhaps the most significant section of this theory is the psychoanalytical revelation of the incest taboo as the result of a prohibition arising, in its turn, from a set of quite specific conflicts of ambivalence. Traces of the ambivalent attitudes towards the object affected by the taboo are evident in the double meaning of the word taboo itself, which denotes at the same time 'holy' and 'unclean', 'dangerous'. The close psychological relationship between the incest taboo and conscience can hardly be denied, and what Freud was the first to recognise as the functional significance of the taboo, i.e. as a cultural requirement with an original socially vitalising content, also remains unchallenged to this day (König, 1964; Schelsky, 1965; and others). In addition to this the 'aversion' or 'blockage' regarding incest can be regarded as an individual (culturally dependent) acquisition which is of extensive psychological significance within the framework of the process of socialisation and the formation of the personality. Admittedly, this aspect is closely linked to Freud's sexual theory, especially to the oedipus concept, and one will have to ask oneself exactly how matters stand with regard to it. One frequently occurring misrepresentation of Freud's sexual theory need not be discussed here: 'Psychosexuality was so widely defined, that it was never synonymous with "sex" ' (Rapaport, 1959, p. 51). The development of psychosexuality in children is a discovery verified by the direct observation of babies and children (Erikson, 1950 and 1953; Spitz, 1957; and others), and the oedipus complex or its equivalent is either held to be universal (Linton, 1956) or it is at least regarded, now as before, as the central conflict in our Western sphere of culture (Alexander, 1956). At the same time, one must take into account anyhow that – according to present-day attitudes – the concept of the oedipal conflict (as a psychodynamic phenomenon at a specific stage of the child's psychosexual development) also embraces certain psychosocial behavioural tendencies, and denotes as well a specific psychosexual and psychosocial crisis in the development of the personality. The character and overcoming of this crisis are also dependent on the cultural system prevalent at the time (Erikson, 1953, 1957 a, 1957 b).

Functions of the taboo

Faced with this disappointing analysis of the incest taboo and the general impotence of contemporary sociology and anthropology, a few experts recognised that no solution to the problem could be produced through unilateral biological, psychological or historical-anthropological forms of observation (e.g. Linton, 1936). In a voluminous work in 1949, Levi-Strauss puts the question whether the origin of the taboo is not to be found rather in the 'constant actual and empirically demonstrable functions, than in a vague and hypothetical schema' (1966, p. 101). The American sociologist Talcott Parsons (1954) has taken up these ideas and, with the discoveries of psychoanalysis in mind, has developed a modern theory of the *structural and functional significance of the incest taboo*.

Parsons (1964, pp. 109–16) proceeds from the view that the *family nucleus* (the living together in marriage of man and wife with their offspring) is a phenomenon which is universal and appears in all human societies, but which is never independent of the society. The incest taboo, which Parsons considers one of the most important traits of all human societies, possesses a constant element, namely the family nucleus. Its basic essential traits consist of the fact that (*a*) it represents a 'self-dissolving group', (*b*) its members are granted 'a high degree of diffuse emotionality', (*c*) more than all other social groupings it allows 'an institutionalised place in its structure to overt erotic attraction and satisfaction'. It has certain obligations and tasks, not only as far as its members are concerned, but also in respect of society.

Amongst the *primary internal functions* is the responsible duty of the parents to provide optimal conditions in order to guarantee the necessary long process of socialisation of the child and to guide its personality development. One further internal primary function, and an essential precondition for the socialisation of the growing young person, is the 'continued maintenance of a certain emotional equilibrium' by all the members of the family. These two primary functions can only be adequately fulfilled if the psychosexual organisation of the family nucleus is intact. Amongst the most well-known traits of what Parsons calls 'erotic organisation of the family' is, apart from the 'married couple's monopoly of genital eroticism' the 'positive institutionalising of the pregenital eroticism' within the framework of the mother–child relationship, and the placing of a taboo on any open expression of sexuality between 'post-oedipal' children and the parents, as well as between brothers and sisters once puberty has begun. The structure of the family nucleus, above all its psychosexual organisation, is thus characterised by '*a systematic combination of controlled expression and regulated prohibition*'. The '*incest-taboo is only a very important negative aspect of these more general rules*' (Parsons, 1964, p. 115).

In order to make our arguments so far more readily understandable, we shall now attempt to point up some connections between the family as a vehicle for the child's socialisation and the 'positive institutionalisation' of pregenital psychosexuality.

From the purely physiological stage common initially to any social relationship there develops step by step the first social relationship of the child to its environment, the first 'object-relationship' (Freud, Vol. V). In this first 'object-relationship', the 'duality' of the mother–child relationship (Simmel, 1908), lies the seed of every higher social development. Whether the latter is successful or not is essentially dependent on whether the mother is in a position adequately to satisfy the child's pregenital psychosexual needs, that is, its psychological needs and abilities which are linked in part to the maturing of its organs. Those malformations of the first object-relationship in early childhood which were examined by Spitz (1957) and the results of which can be psychological function disturbances and psychogenic and psychosomatic illnesses, leave no doubt that childhood psychosexuality is a decisive psychobiological component of the development of the personality, and an indispensable instrument for the socialisation of the child. Whether there emerges from it a mature personality and member of the community, 'capable of functioning' socially, depends in essence on the relationships within the family, and, in early childhood especially, on the mutual relationships between mother and child. Parsons (1964, p. 128) illustrates this process quite clearly when he writes: 'The erotic tie linking the child to the mother therefore represents the "rope" with which she pulls it up from the lower level to the higher in the difficult "mountain climb" of growing up. As, however, the bonds linking him to this "rope" remain sensitive, since his interest in them is not extinguished (but only suppressed!) a lasting channel continues to exist connecting the child with his infantile system of motivation which is still active. Serious disturbance in the balance of the personality can continually open this channel. This is, in general, what is meant by "regression", and the erotic behavioural patterns of childhood constantly play an important role in regressive tendencies.' The 'positive institutionalisation of pregenital eroticism' within the framework of the mother–child relationship, which Parsons considers a universal sociological feature of the psychosexual organisation of the family, makes allowance for the material which we have just quoted.

Now the satisfaction of childhood psychosexual needs by the surrounding world of the family is instrumental in an important way in the process of coming to social maturity. Unlimited satisfaction, however, stands to an equal extent in the way both of the development of the personality and the interests of society. Each new step in the development of the personality leaves behind a residue of those psychosexual components, which have indeed been of essential significance for the taking of that step, but may hinder further development of the personality if they are allowed to remain active. This is why in certain circumstances infantile psychosexual needs must be denied. They concern at first, independent of the sex of the child, the need for dependence on the mother, which – if they are encouraged or strengthened by the mother's own regressive needs – make more difficult or even prevent the child's development of independence and self-dependence. Moreover, these denials affect above all else the incestuous wishes which also arise during the 'oedipal phase', and can later restrict the extra-family choice of partner if they are reinforced and fixed by the parents' inadequate behaviour.

If, therefore, the family represents an organised framework for the positive utilisation of pregenital psychosexuality to build up the child's personality, then – according to Parsons (1964, p. 134) – the incest taboo in its negative aspect must be regarded as a mechanism which prevents this positive utilisation from 'getting out of hand'. What does this mean? We shall attempt to elucidate Parsons' theory with the help of a schematic diagram (Fig. 1).

A society makes certain specific demands on its members, regardless of whether this society is structured around the family unit, as in most primitive cultures, or not. Amongst these expectations and demands are (1) the assumption of extra-family 'supra-personal' roles, without whose adequate fulfilment the society does not function. According to Parsons the nature of this role is characterised by the complete subordination of 'erotic interests' to other interests; (2) the ability of the adult personality to establish new, independent family nuclei. It is important for society that the family nucleus is not a self-perpetuating unit (1964, p. 121).

The psychological preconditions and motivations for the fulfilment of both these social functions are acquired in the process of the development of the personality, and are integrative facets of socialisation: apart from the aspect of the heterosexual choice of partner, socialisation is 'aimed at the goal of establishing at least a precedence if not a complete monopoly of normal genital-erotic attraction over all other possibilities: the choice of object outside the family and the stability of object-orientation are included in this' (1964, p. 129). In this respect the incest taboo proves to be a regulator (or mechanism) of the process of socialisation, preventing the parents from retaining any power of attraction for the child. At the same time it contributes towards ensuring that the awakening genital-sexual interest shown by the young person growing up is directed towards persons of the opposite sex and the same generation outside his own family.

One of the most important steps in this direction is the adoption of the given biological, sexual role, a learning process of psychological self-categorisation, which begins with the oedipal

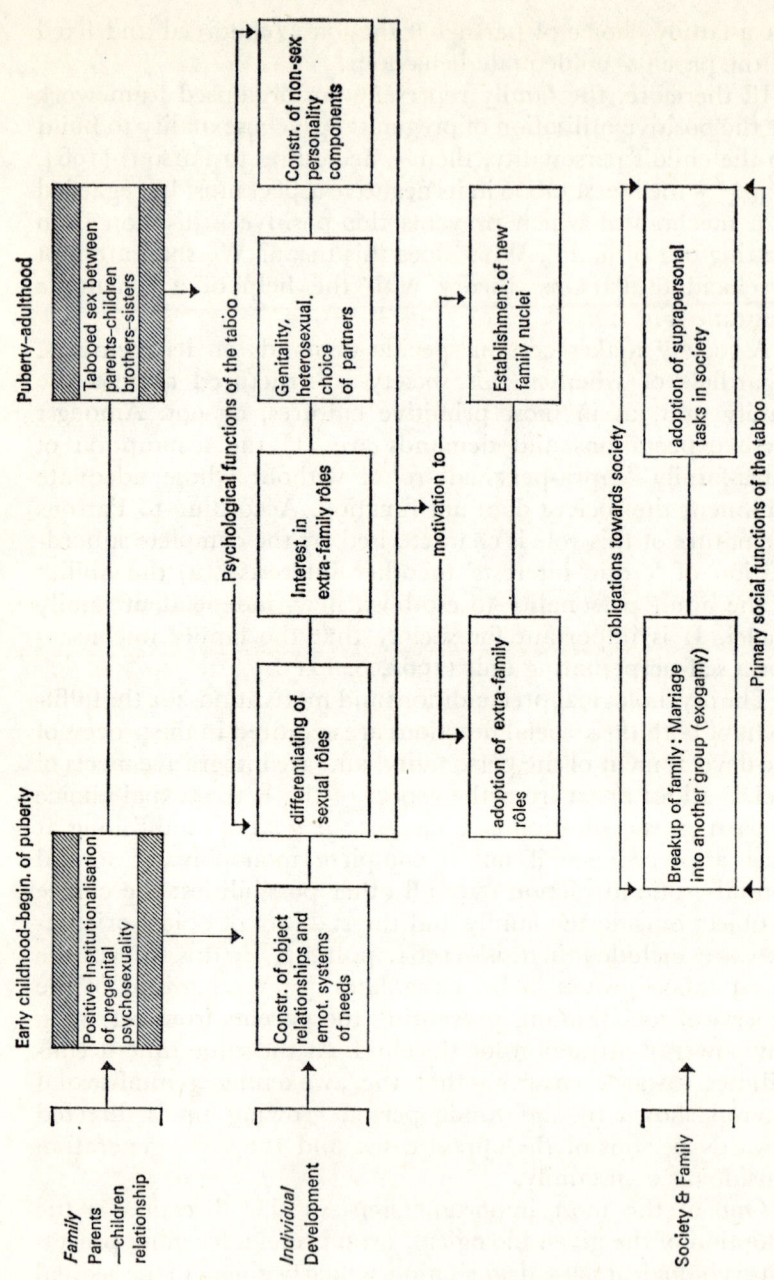

Figure 1.

phase and passes through critical stages in puberty and adolescence (Erikson, 1956). Parsons has pointed to the fact that in this process an essential role is played not only by the relinquishing of the pregenital needs and interests directed at the parents, under the 'pressure' of the incest taboo, but also by the associated diverting of the child's primary interests into relationships with friends of the same sex and approximately the same age. By this means there is established 'a solidarity between people of the same sex reaching out beyond the family', and there is a stronger motivation towards psychological differentiating between the sexual roles (1964, p. 131). Moreover, the 'non-erotic components' of the personality structure (the formation of the super-ego: see previous section) which arise in part out of oedipal conflicts, form a dam against regressive needs and wishes which are still present, and are especially easily reactivated under the influence of sexual maturing during puberty.

The incest problem in its aspect of psychosexual development of the personality thus moves into a much more extensive sphere, namely that of the 'structuring of the motivations of the personality in time and in relation to the choice of object' (1964, p. 128). In this connection the incest taboo may be regarded as a mechanism which makes an essential contribution to this structuring. For the (sociologically) adult personality, remarks Parsons(1964, p. 133), incest-wishes then represent the prototype of regression. 'They are the path to the reactivation of the primitive layers of the personality structure.'

In order to achieve *the adoption and carrying out of extra-family roles and functions* socialisation aims at motivating the maturing personality correspondingly and developing its capabilities. The incest taboo in its infantile dependency wishes, and in its positive aspect (as the obligation of the sociologically mature individual to leave his own family), is a basic mechanism for the development of a sense of independence and orientation in extra-family roles, in puberty and at the end of adolescence. That is why Parsons interprets incest or the incestuous marriage – as do Fortune (1932) and Levi-Strauss (1949) – as a social phenomenon of regression, as a result of which the individual negates those responsibilities upon whose fulfilment and practice the supra-family structures of the society rest.

With this theory Parsons has characterised both the psychological and the social functions of the incest taboo, and illustrated in what manifold ways the taboo 'is linked with the functioning of every living society' (1964, p. 134). The question which nevertheless must finally be put is whether the meaning of the taboo is not in its turn dependent on the given social structure of a society. Parsons represents the view that the incest taboo has a politico-economic function important to life in those societies in which blood-relationship is the basis of group-forming (the prototype for this is the tribe). Yet the incest taboo still loses this originally vital social significance in societies whose social structure is not built on blood-relationship and whose economic, political and religious functions are taken care of by an 'anonymous' apparatus. This applies to modern industrial society in which blood-relationship stretching beyond the nucleic family is today of no further social weight (Parsons, 1964; Schelsky, 1965). Nevertheless the incest taboo still possesses, independently of the type of social system, a twofold value: it fulfils important *psychological functions* in connection with the individual general development of the maturing personality, a development which is universally achieved, from birth to maturity, within the family nucleus. Closely connected with these are the *social functions* of the taboo under the influence of which there take place the break-up of the family of origin and the setting up of new family nuclei, as well as the adoption of roles not conditioned by the family.

With his theory Parsons has left open the question as to the origin of the incest taboo and reduced the 'problem' to the analysis of the functional significance of the taboo within the framework of the interdependence of the personality processes and social systems.

3. The law and criminal statistics on incest

In this chapter we shall be concerned with the legal norms affecting incest, with their motivation, with the sanctions connected with infringements of the legal norm, and with the frequency of incest relationships. In the course of this we shall pose the question of whether the formulation of the laws regulating the problem of incest is guided by 'common sense' – together with its implications of 'healthy public opinion' – or whether it takes as a criterion for its codification a critical and rational attitude based upon modern scientific knowledge.

Historical survey

The laws of Ancient Rome did indeed – as has already been mentioned – punish incest, but not as a crime in itself, only in connection with certain marriage laws. To that extent it was primarily a failure to respect the marriage laws, a kind of 'offence of personal status' (Maurach, 1964), and a transgression of the religious ordinances (Mommsen, 1899). The ban on marriage between relatives at that time extended to cover the sixth degree of relationship.

As the centuries elapsed, the Catholic Church, and later the Calvinism and Puritanism of the Protestant Church, exerted a strong influence on the temporal formulation of laws on sexual offences in general and on incest in particular. In the 'Canon Laws' based upon the Bolognese lectures of the monk Gratianus, a distinction was made, as early as 1431, between the incestuous transgression against religious ordinances and 'incest according to natural law' (Meyer, 1888; Marcuse, 1915; Többen, 1925).

The *Constitutio Criminalis Carolina* (CCC) of Charles V, 1532, talks in Article 117 of 'Immodesty' with stepdaughter, daughter-in-law and stepmother, but all the same leaves vague the definition of incest and its punishment, a fact which led subsequently to many contested interpretations (Maurach, 1964; Mezger and Blei, 1964).

The Age of Enlightenment witnessed strong criticism of prevailing legal formulations and cast strong doubt upon the punishable nature of incest (Welzel, 1965; Mezger and Blei, 1964).

In both the *Allgemeine Landrecht* (1794) of the Prussian States (ALR II 20, 1033/1047), and the *Bavarian Legal Code* of 1813, there are exhaustive regulations for the punishment of incest (Maurach, 1964). The basis for the present-day situation is the *Prussian Legal Code* of 1851 (§ 141). In the suggestions for reform of the Prussian legal code 'a basic re-examination' of the punishment of the crime had been announced as early as 1845. But the suggestion that incest should only be punished 'in cases of public nuisance and injury to the rights of a third person', remained the demand of a few progressive legal experts till well into the twentieth century (Mittermaier, 1906).

Comparative legal observation

The definition of incest, the motivations behind the legal formulations, and the threat of punishment for incestuous acts, are characterised across the centuries and from state to state by their variability. This lack of uniformity is reflected at the same time in official uncertainty in behaviour and attitudes towards the offence, as well as in the dependence upon culture and epoch of the judgement of punishable nature and reasons for protection. In this respect nothing has changed even today.

The French philosopher, mathematician and physicist, Pascal, noted down the following sentences in his solitude at Port-Royal in the middle of the seventeenth century: 'Three degrees of latitude nearer to the pole and the whole of legal knowledge is turned upside down, a single degree of longitude determines the truth. . . . What laughable justice that has a river as a frontier. This side of the Pyrenees truth, the other side falsehood. . . . Custom alone makes the Law; that it has been handed down is its only justification; it is the mystical basis of its authority. Anyone who tries to trace it back to a true basis, will eventually have to repeal it. . . . He who seeks the motivation (of a law, or legal formulation) will find it to be so weak and insignificant, that he will wonder at its lack of justification, unless he is accustomed to recognising man's insane prejudices' (*Pensées*, 294, published posthumously, 1669).

There is no easier way of providing confirmation for Pascal's sentence about 'the justice which has a river as a border' than by merely juxtaposing some European and non-European legal norms on incest. What in Luxemburg is not punished (that goes for all forms of incest) is, on the other side of the Moselle, in the Federal Republic of Germany, punished with corrective training of up to five years or with up to two years in prison, and what others can 'get away with' with a 500-dollar fine or at the most six months in prison, means for American citizens of Louisiana ten to twenty years, and in California up to fifty years of penal servitude. In this age of quick communications, of mass information media, and of constant fresh technological discoveries, this state of affairs seems distinctly grotesque and arbitrary.

In some countries of Europe the prevailing laws and legal definitions for a section of sexual offences are regarded either as *outmoded* or *divorced from reality* or as *insufficient* or *ineffectual* (Middendorff, 1959). This is true of incest also.

Thus for example, in Luxemburg, Portugal, and Turkey, all types of incest phenomena are unpunished. In states like Belgium, Holland and France, on the other hand, incest is not punished as a separate offence, but as part of 'indecent offences with children under age'. In Italy the offence is only prosecuted when a 'public nuisance' is deemed to have occurred, and the Spanish legal authorities try only the male partner in brother–sister incest. In England, before a prosecution can take place the agreement of the Lord Chief Justice is needed, and in Switzerland – as in the Romance countries and the Netherlands – the offence is classed together with indecent acts with dependents or indecency with children. In Denmark's legal code incest is today no longer treated as a sexual offence, but as a transgression against the family, and is limited to members of the family in immediate ascending and descending order, and to brothers and sisters. Only the Scandinavian countries, Sweden and Norway, have – like the Federal Republic of Germany – retained the laws dealing with incest without amendment even if the criteria of relationship for those concerned, the measure of threatened punishment and the punishable age-limit for young offenders, do vary(Plaut, 1960; Bauer, 1963; Sturup, 1963).

Official opinion in Belgium is that the law should only intervene when there is incontrovertible evidence to prove that what has been committed is against the public interest, 'whilst immoral sexual behaviour within the family must be left to the judgement of social ethics or religion' (Plaut, 1960, p. 345). It is worth noting in this connection also that – as Bader (1959) has pointed out – today it is above all in the Romance countries that an attitude of far greater legal tolerance towards incest is adopted that in other European countries.

There is no uniformity in Europe concerning the object which the laws on incest are designed to protect. In some countries this is given as 'general morality', in others 'the purity of the family'. 'Protection of youth' is also quoted in this context as well as such vague and emotive motives as 'racial hygiene' and 'the dignity of man'. The taboo sanctions of some countries are limited to the very closest relationships, in other lands by contrast there is even an attempt to protect in-law relationships. Also subject to this variance are the penalties, which vary from one to ten years prison or reform home.

Conditions in the United States of America are not very different. In each state of the Union the contracting of marriages between parents and children, brothers and sisters, grandparents and grandchildren, uncles and nieces, as well as between aunts and nephews, is placed under a fundamental ban, and in twenty-one states this ban is extended to include the contracting of marriages with first cousins (e.g. in Pennsylvania), yet the penalties vary greatly from state to state. In some, incestuous marriage is punished just as rigorously as incestuous sexual offences outside marriage; in other states, however, the offences are punished in different ways. Eleven states penalise incest as an extra-marital sexual offence only, the remainder both marriage between close relatives and the act of incest itself. Three states have separate penalties for incestuous marriage and the offence of extra-marital incest, and the latter carries the heavier penalties (Masters, 1963).

In Georgia, for example, incestuous marriages are punished by one to three years in prison, whereas the same kind of union as a sexual offence can carry a sentence of one to twenty years. In eighteen states the maximum penalty for incestuous sexual offences does not exceed ten years, but in New Mexico penalties of up to fifty years in prison are still retained (Masters, 1963; Weinberg, 1963). In most of the United States only one penalty is applied to the person committing incest, irrespective of the degree of relationship. In a few states there are two penalties, as for example in North Carolina, where the male partner in uncle–niece relationships is punished more lightly than in father–daughter unions. In West Virginia marriages between cousins are annulled, but the partners are not punished. There is a similar double attitude of the law towards the sexes. In most states only the male partner can expect sanctions, but some have penalties for both sexes. In Tennessee, for example, the daughter is punished if she 'puts up with the incest for several months', and in Texas a daughter is regarded as an accomplice if she 'makes up to her father' (Weinberg, 1963, p. 27). So-called 'unwitting' incest is also prosecuted, even if the nature of the penalty in such cases is much less severe (Masters, 1963).

In the face of such variation in the formulation of the law, the causes for which should be sought in just as great a variance in motivation, it is hardly surprising that even in the USA critical voices have been raised. The American penal law expert Brenner and the psychiatrist Caprio have stated that the law on incest in the USA is based upon 'Biblical prohibitions' (1964, p. 218). In this connection Masters writes that it is 'the business of religions to judge what is "sinful", not what is lawful'(1963, p. 68). An impressive example of the 'moral indignation about incest offences which affects American juries in such cases' is supplied by Middendorff (1959, p. 53). Of eighty-nine cases of incest in Wisconsin the male was punished for rape in more than half of them, and not for incest, since rape in the USA carries a higher penalty (Eliott, 1952).

Federal Republic of Germany

The basis for the present formulation is § 141 of the Prussian Legal Code of 1851, which was taken over in essence by the Legal Code of 1871 and came into effect for the whole of the German Reich in 1872. In section 13 of the present-day legal code, which deals with sexual offences under the vague heading of 'transgressions and crimes against morality' (§ 173 to § 184b), even the legal conditions of the so-called 'defamation of the blood' are retained (§ 173) – a designation which can be justified neither by its content of untruth nor by its derivation from Roman Law (Maurach, 1964). The text of the law runs:

'I. Cohabitation between relatives of ascending or descending order will be punished in the first instance with corrective detention up to five years in the last instance with up to two years imprisonment.
II. Cohabitation between brother and sister will be punished with up to two years imprisonment, as will the cohabitation of relations by marriage, of ascending and descending line, if the marriage upon which the relationship is based is in being at the time of the act.
III. In addition to terms of imprisonment a sentence of deprivation of civic rights can also be passed.
IV. Relations and in-laws in the descending order of relationship will remain unpunished if they have not completed their eighteenth year.
V. In the case of cohabitation between relations by marriage the court may ignore the penalty if a marriage household was no longer extant at the time of the deed. Prosecution will not proceed if there is evidence of the lifting of the marriage ban on in-laws by virtue of an annulment.'

So that some of what is discussed below may be more comprehensible to the reader we must just briefly explore formal legalistic concepts such as *Definition of the offence, Culpability* and *Penalty*. In this we shall stick essentially to the best-known German legal textbooks and commentaries (Maurach, 1964; Welzel, 1965; Mezger and Blei, 1964, 1966; Schönke and Schröder, 1965).

The law distinguishes between incest in the narrower sense (§ 173, sections I and II, 1), i.e., *true incest* (only of cases where a blood-relationship is involved) and *not true incest* (only of cases involving in-laws of ascending and descending relationship: § 173, section II, 2, section V). In the case of adoption relationships § 173, section II, 2, is not applicable. Apart from these considerations the *decisive definition* of the offence is cohabitation, i.e., 'Any union of the sexual parts, irrespective of the degree to which the male organ penetrates the female sexual organ' (Judgement of the Federal Court of Justice 26.7.1961). All other sexual activities (stroking, masturbation, coitus-like acts, etc.) do not fall within this definition, i.e. they cannot be considered as incest.

To which the following must be added: if this decision of the Federal Court of Justice – to restrict incest to this narrow definition of cohabitation – is designed, amongst other things, to guard against conception (Kohlhaas 1961, BI. 1563) then this does not at all accord with medical experience. Coitus-like activities (for instance, physical manipulation restricted to the thighs) can equally well result in pregnancy (Wallis, 1965).

In the *New Legal Proposals* of 1960 incest is included under § 192 with all the other legal statutes for the protection of the family, marriage, and the person, to be precise, in the twelfth sub-section of a special chapter entitled 'Punishable acts against the marriage, the family, and the person' (Proposal 1960, p. 321).

The inclusion of incest under the above heading is justified by concluding that the act is an offence not only against 'morality in a sexual sense but also most of all against the physical and moral health of the family' (Prop. 1960, p. 321). This 'regard for etiquette' leaves no doubt that one of the aims of the reformers was to take into account the protection of 'the basis of moral order or average moral sensibilities' (Prop. 1960, p. 315). The definition of the offence in § 192 was taken unchanged in its essentials from the law as it stood, save that cohabitation between those related by marriage was no longer regarded as 'an offence against the blood' since it did not represent a 'criminal act', only an 'immoral' one (Notes 1959, p. 363). As before, juvenile relatives in the descending order of relationship are not punished, although the age of responsibility in this respect was lowered from eighteen to sixteen (Prop. 1962, p. 92). As far as the exemption from punishment of incest between brother and sister where both were juveniles was concerned, the legal commission could reach no firm decision.

According to the proposals for a new Legal Code Book (Prop. 1960, Prop. 1962), incest *is considered one of he most serious crimes known by the law* (Prop. 1960, p. 322). The penalty for relatives of the ascending order of relationship was even strengthened. The argument for this runs: 'Taking into account the obviously very serious nature of some acts the maximum sentence of corrective detention ... has been increased to ten years' (Draft law, 1960, p. 322).

W. Hochheimer (1963, p. 101), points to the 'highly emotional tone' of this proposal and criticises it with reforming zeal: 'A case which may be seen by the legislators as "obviously serious" will in future be more severely punished! And what do the legislators mean when they talk of "less serious cases," for which they prescribe one to five years imprisonment in the proposal? Answer: "Single acts of incest which have their origin in overcrowded living conditions" (Draft law, 1960, p. 322). Do the reformers seriously believe that the sole cause of incest is overcrowded living conditions? What scientific findings are there to justify the view that, for example, a father's single act of sexual intercourse with his fifteen-year-old daughter has less far-reaching psychological effects on the girl than a fourteen-year-long incestuous relationship between father and daughter which is based, to no small degree, on the voluntary surrender of the girl in a free sexual choice? What are the criteria for a "less serious" case – the frequency of the act, the cause or causes of the act or the psychological damage to the juvenile? It is equally questionable why there should be no allowance made for "less serious cases" with the possibility of a milder prison sentence in cases where the child involved was under sixteen at the time of the act (Draft bill, 1960, p. 322). The setting of this age limit is not easy to understand in view of the earlier sexual maturity of present-day youth' (cf. Hochheimer, 1963). Or is the setting of this age limit a tacit reflection of the reformers' assumption that the possibilities of psychological damage are generally greater with a fourteen-year-old, for example, than with a sixteen-year-old? These are only a few of the very many questions which arise from the debatable basic premises of the new draft legislation.

The treatment of incest as a special kind of offence still survives despite the attacks of many eminent German critics. According to the existing law of the Federal Republic and the new legal proposals, incest is a *serious criminal offence*. The question will have to be asked as to whether – as far as incest is concerned – Pascal's phrase about custom being the sole basis for the law has any truth in it, and whether one can agree with the assumption of the legal expert Jäger (1957) that 'an obvious schism' has arisen between the penal law and the empirical sciences. This will be the subject of our discussions in the section which follows.

Motivation behind existing penal legislation in Germany: Statute 173

In this century there has been no lack of scientifically based analyses of the ideas and aims behind the German penal laws on sex. Mittermaier (1906), Hiller (1926), Sieverts and Hardwig (1955), Jäger (1957), Bader (1959), Middendorff (1959), Bauer (1963) – these are only a few of the progressively minded legal experts who have not avoided speaking out frankly in the clash about the statutes concerning incest. There are quite concrete grounds for this.

German laws on sex stem – apart from quite insignificant emendations – from past centuries. And it can now hardly be denied that during this time, as a result of rapid strides in science and technology, quite a few things in man's way of life and thinking have changed, 'and it is indeed difficult to grasp why the ethics, taboos and, more to the point, the norms of sexual behaviour should form an exception to the general and constant process of change and the metamorphosis of all living things' (Jäger, 1957, p. 35). More than anyone else Dader has pointed to this 'area of tension' between sexual order and legal order: 'Whilst man's sexual ethics and sense of values have undergone a change since the beginning of this century, the generally prevailing law of the land is a bastion of the long eroded moral code of the bourgeois era' (1950, pp. 214–17). Despite the verifiable change in sexual and ethical attitudes and approaches, and the ever-increasing number of discoveries about them in the field of the behavioural sciences, our legal penal code holds fast to its legislative conception, not only of fighting anti-social and injurious forms of activity, but also of protecting and preserving a certain (long-changed) sexual ethical set of norms. And there is one further aspect which evokes a rational-critical analysis: the discoveries of the behavioural sciences, which indicate the dangers arising from the increasing penetration of all spheres of life by collectivist and ideological elements. In this connection **Jäger** (1957) argues that emotional, collective psychological, i.e. at first sight no longer completely definable, influences can also have an effect on the process of law-making. Therefore we will also have to put the question as to whether in the promulgatory act of the incest statutes the massive use of force 'is only the result of cool reasoning, and thus leads of necessity to the most meaningful social solutions' (Jäger, 1957, p. 2), or whether there is an admixture here of thoughts which are irrational and empirically untenable.

If one assembles all the motives behind § 173 and classifies them according to an ordered table of relationship, then it emerges that the basis of the legal norm consists of several very heterogeneous trains of thought. From the point of view of their relationship to the empirical and non-empirical sciences these motives can be divided into two large groups:

1. The group of *empirical-rational motives*, arising from the idea of the (direct or indirect) injurious effects of incest.
2. The group of motives with *irrational tendencies*, which are characterised by notions of the ethical or religious abnormality of the offence. Whilst the motives belonging to the first group have a validity which is verifiable by various empirical sciences, the sources of those in the second group can be revealed with the help of cultural historical and socio-anthropological methods of examination. The division which now follows gives a survey of the various grounds current today which support the classification of incest as a special kind of act.

Empirical-rational motives: 1. *The notion of hereditary biological safeguards* which – as Jäger (1957) has pointed out – is frequently mixed with motives of quite a different kind, but which can, all the same, be checked with the aid of modern human genetic research, psychopathology and psychology. 2. *The notion of safeguards in social hygiene*. This concerns 'the destructive effect on the family' of the offence and relates – illogically and unpsychologically – only to 'cohabitation' and not to 'indecent acts' within the family. This motive can be checked also, as far as its validity is concerned, with the aid of social psychology within the framework of legal psychology and psychiatry. 3. *The notion of psycho-hygienic safeguards* which takes into account – primarily – the safeguarding of minor dependants from psychological harm, and can be subsumed under the title 'protection of young people', which also – according to Jäger (1957, p. 53) – includes the safeguarding of sexual self-determination as well as of the 'rights of upbringing and protection'. The question of the harm done to under-age victims of incest is very much a field for psychological and medical research.

Motives with irrational tendencies: 1. The notion of the ethical and religious abnormality of incest in which the law takes it upon itself to preserve *'the moral order'* and *'sexual morals'*. These points of view include a mixture of ideas about order whose origins are partly obscure and archaic. Here there is a wide field of research for moral theology, cultural philosophy and anthropology, sociology and psychology; 2. *The concept of moral protection of the family.* It occurs in conjunction with such different issues as, for example, 'purity' or 'moral health and "sexually free sphere" of the family'. Here also the concept applies only to proved cohabitation and not to mere 'indecency'.

The grounds for the law expounded in the above section will now be subjected to analysis in what follows.

a) *Hereditary biological motives*

The question of the injurious effects on after-growth and health, brought about by incest, has long exercised the minds of biologists, medical experts, legal experts, philosophers, psychologists and anthropologists. But it was only in the twentieth century that 'physical health', hereditary biological protection, became one of the most important motives for the punishment of incest (RG. 57, 140). Right up until the present day it has played a role in the adoption of the status of a special offence. In very general terms it can be said that there is even today a widespread view that the 'abhorrence of incest' can be traced back to a natural tendency towards 'keeping the race healthy'. In this sense the norm of prohibition appears as an expression of a legal measure peculiar to human biology. Regardless of the fact that the theory of an innate 'abhorrence of incest' or 'incest barrier' has long been disproved by the behavioural sciences, the accent here is on 'keeping the family healthy' and 'keeping the race healthy' which suggests that incest entails a danger for the progeny of such unions.

There can be no doubt that health is amongst the elementary individual rights which call for protection, a conclusion which – as Jäger (1957) explains – could be arrived at by analogy with offences concerning bodily harm. Incest also brings up the question of indirect damage to the health of the children of such unions. Yet a biological protection is also conceivable as a measure of protection against after-growth harm in succeeding generations, i.e. as a protection against direct harm. In this latter context H. Jäger has elucidated in no uncertain manner the dangerous and inhuman sides of National-Socialist racial strategy. As early as 1933 incest was dealt with in the Prussian Ministry of Justice memorandum on National Socialist penal law in the chapter 'Attacks on the family', under the title 'Endangering the blood'. The main aims of this legal persecution later became racial and political. (*Nationalsozialistisches Strafrecht. Denkschrift des Preussischen Justizministeriums*' [National Socialist penal law. Memorandum of the Prussian Ministry of Justice] 1933, p. 68.)

How do matters stand, then, with these dangers? What scientifically relevant factors can be introduced to support or refute a biological justification of these incest statutes?

If one goes into the question of which specialist literature is cited by the law-maker or by those legal experts who go along with a hereditary biological motivation for the incest statutes, then it will be established that they rely predominantly on legal-psychiatric examinations from the twenties and thirties of this century. In fact the findings of that period frequently provided a biologically, psychopathologically and socially unfavourable picture of those involved in incest and their families, so that even some of the most outstanding researchers saw in them an argument for the hereditary-biological motivation.

The psychiatrist Marcuse had, however, as early as 1915, expressed the opinion that the idea of a direct biologically harmful effect of incest on posterity was scientifically unfounded. Marcuse drew his conclusions mainly from the medical and biological research into families carried out by Lundborg (1913) on an interrelated community of Swedish peasants numbering over 2,000 persons. Lundborg came to the conclusion that 'degenerate progeny' in this community were not the result of consanguinity (blood-relationship) as such, but more the outcome of negative inherited material. Marcuse thus represented the opinion that legal intervention was only justified in cases where 'an action gave rise directly to serious dangers, but not when, as in the case of incest, these dangers were really quite remote, only indirectly caused and thus rare'(1915, pp. 7 and 71). This attitude, which appears so extraordinarily modern, was later challenged by other psychiatrists. E. Wülffen (1921) pointed to the appearance of negative inherited features which were encouraged by incest and saw in this a 'not unimportant' part of the motivation behind the legal norm. H. Többen (1925) did indeed take into account the psychiatric findings of Kraepelin (1914) and Bleuler (1918), according to which no danger to the health of progeny existed, yet he pronounced himself in favour of a deterrent penalty 'of the most serious kind' on the basis of his own research materials. E. H. Rosenfeld (1926) postulated 'penal measures' on grounds of racial and hereditary protection, and he appealed to the law-makers: 'The state must take a real interest in the protection of society against poor and sickly progeny and give this interest in a qualitative population policy legal status and protection' (1926, pp. 46–7). Together with Marcuse (1915), Sieverts and Hardwig (1955), one could oppose this view with the fact that the law-maker in other instances – one has only to think of the problems surrounding § 218 (abortion) in cases of pregnancy as a result of sexual assault – does not appear over-interested in the production of healthy progeny. As early as 1937 Eber was writing, basing himself on his criminal-psychological and medical examinations, 'that it is not the mentally sick type, nor the weak-witted, nor the hypersexual or sexually abnormal man, nor the man with the most inferior character, who is dominant amongst those committing incest' (1937, p. 263). In recent times the psychiatrist Wagner (1953) has given an emphatic warning against generalising on the findings of examinations of incestuous couples and their families (e.g. Schwab, 1938). The most recent investigations show that those committing incest include some whose personalities are psychologically comparatively normal or, as Gerchow puts it on the basis of his intensive examinations – they include 'a group that is fundamentally normal' (1965, p. 45). Other writers (Finke and Zeugner 1934, and others have also come to similar results. If one were to extract the essence of the most recent psychiatric research into incest then it can best be expressed in Gerchow's words: 'Over the whole question we can bring proof to bear, *for it is beyond all doubt, that it is not any eugenic policy which is in the foreground . . .*' (1955, p. 180).

What results, then, are produced by *modern human genetic* (i.e. hereditary biological) *research*? What conclusions if any does it offer us on the risks of incestuous unions or – in the wider sense – marriage between relatives?

Quite apart from the concrete results of examinations, geneticists, even of the standing of a Verschuer or a Stern, do not disdain to use as evidence examples of incest taken from an anthropological view of history. They recall the law of the princely households of the pre-Columbian Incas, that the blood should be kept 'pure' by brother-sister marriages – a command that was obeyed through the course of fourteen generations, with no sign of degeneration. O. von Verschuer (1934) points to the dynasty of the Ptolemies in Ancient Egypt, which, after several generations of repeated brother-sister incest, produced Cleopatra, without there being any physical or intellectual defects in evidence. The American geneticist Stern (1960) produces as examples Toulouse-Lautrec and John Ruskin who were both offspring of marriages between cousins. With regard to Lautrec's deformed legs Stern remarked that they 'were probably the result of a dominant inherited *osteogenesis imperfecta* (incomplete bone-formation because of low calcium deposits) and had nothing to do with the blood relationship of his parents' (1960, p. 391).

Nowadays human geneticists are generally agreed that incest or inbreeding in itself causes no inherited damage in offspring (von Verschuer, 1959; Stern, 1960; Vogel, 1961; Saller, 1965). Even American experts who reject marriage between relations by pointing to the danger of diseased recessive genes becoming homozygote (hereditarily equal), are prepared to agree that 'Incest *per se* is not responsible for unfavourable phenomena in organic formation' (Stern, 1960, p. 391).

All the same a certain amount of support for the idea of the biologically negative results of incest can be drawn from the fact that sickly children are not infrequently the offspring of marriages between relatives. W. Lenz (1962) comes to the conclusion that, in general terms, children from marriages between relatives are twice as likely to have mental and physical anomalies as those from marriages between non-relatives. Verschuer, however, believes that a higher risk of danger exists only for, in general, children from those marriages which exhibit a situation of stress within the family, 'thus leading one to fear that recessive diseased tendencies will become homozygote or that there will be a conjuncture of negative secondary tendencies' (1959, p. 354). Yet the latter case can occur outside marriages between relatives. Although occasional recessive inherited defects can result particularly from marriages between relatives, it would be wrong, according to von Verschuer, to generalise from such findings and apply them willy-nilly to all marriages between relatives (1959, p. 354). In this connection the hereditary-pathological surveys by Hanhart (1956) are noteworthy. In them he presents findings based on thirty-three years' research into isolated communities. These show great differences between the various areas of inbreeding in Switzerland. As well as parishes with high frequencies of recessive hereditary illnesses, there are others which show no increased frequency of illnesses, despite a high degree of inbreeding. The insights gained from genetic research do, however, provide some understanding of the often contradictory effects of inbreeding which sometimes appear in the least desirable phenotypes or even in normal or above-average constitutions. In this respect C. Stern expounds the theory that such diverse effects 'can be traced back in part to the differing initial states of the two original partners who might have been carriers of either favourable or unfavourable recessive genes' (1960, p. 391). Verschuer comments on Hanhart's findings and believes that they would show that the (already existing) amount of unhealthy hereditary natural traits amongst the population is of quite decisive significance (1959, p. 58).

In recent times the human geneticist and anthropologist K. Saller (1965) has addressed himself to this problem on the basis of an hereditary-biological examination of three children who were the products of father–daughter incest. All the children were at the time of the examination at an age where an hereditary, biological, anthropological, clinical and psychopathological estimation of the eventual harmful effects could be given with the greatest degree of certainty. Saller comes to the decision that in 'all three cases nothing in the children's physical or mental make-up' could be established 'which would in any way have lifted them above the peculiarities common to their age group or social milieu' (1965, p. 2106). On the question of harmful effects Saller expresses himself in agreement with other human genetics researchers: no damaging effects of incest *per se* can be established on the basis of what findings are to hand. The *manifestation of recessive hereditary tendencies* through homozygotisation *can effect positive as well as negative physical and psychological peculiarities*. With regard to the issue of the legal and penal attitude to incest the expert sums up by saying: 'The findings argue beyond any doubt for the pardoning of incest . . .' (1965, p. 2106).

So far as the consequences for genetic counselling which might develop from these research findings are concerned, the experts do not really seem to be of one mind. The American human geneticists are basically against marriages between relatives (von Verschuer 1959). W. Lenz (1962) considers it urgent to make clear the risks involved if a recessive hereditary disease is present in close relatives, and Vogel considers the statistical proof of an increased threat of danger insufficient 'to justify in some way dissuading individual couples during eugenic counselling from entering into marriages with relatives'. This question would only arise when – for example as the result of the birth of a child unequivocally the object of recessive hereditary diseases – it can be proved, 'that both partners are heterozygote for the same recessive gene' (1961, p. 574).

The upshot of this is that we can say that, according to the most recent psychiatric and human-genetic research findings, the hereditary-biological motivation of the legal norm has become *doubtful*.

Because of lack of information, or for other reasons, many penal law experts cannot and do not share this opinion (Sturm, 1959; Mezger and Blei, 1964; Maurach, 1964; Schönke and Schröder, 1965; and others). They represent the point of view that 'true incest . . . should be punished in the interests of population eugenics' (Hellmer, 1961, p. 314) or that 'harmful tendencies are seldom absent from the circles of those who commit incest, so that the eugenic side of things is of particular importance in cases of genuine incest' (Mezger and Blei, 1964, p. 76). Modern teaching on penal law, on the other hand, considers the hereditary biological justification for the incest statutes to be 'extremely questionable and rationally unsound' (Sieverts and Hardwig, 1955, p. 613; and Jäger, 1957; Bauer, 1963). According to the conception of injury to personal rights subscribed to by the above (Jäger, 1957, pp. 18–28) the effects of incest are not 'typical of the deed itself'; the health of posterity is *not directly injured* by incest and any threat to progeny even from 'inbreeding' over a lengthy period is *dependent on certain biological preconditions*. Yet if there is not scientific proof of any threat to health as a result of incest, then the statutes can no longer be justified from a hereditary-biological point of view, and the punishment of the offence must be based upon other motives.

b) *Protection of the family*

Apart from the biological point of view, credence is also given to various motives involving the protection of the family. These include on the one hand ideas of social hygiene and on the other the moral aspect.

The *social hygienic* point of view refers primarily to the stability of the family unit. It is continually pointed out that incest has a highly disruptive effect on the family (Sturm in *Niederschriften*, 1959, pp. 357–8, 363; and Maurach, 1964; Schönke and Schröder, 1965, and others). Just as in the case of the hereditary-biological motivation basis, great reliance is placed on 'experience from legal practice' and on legal-psychiatric examinations carried out some time before.

More recent surveys show a quite different state of affairs. Above all the forensic expert Gerchow (1955, 1965) has been able to show that in the majority of cases incest is not the cause but the result of a disturbed family make-up. That would mean that cause and effects are the wrong way round in the setting up of the law (§ 173) and that there is an attempt to protect something which has already been 'destroyed'. We shall come back to this point and discuss it more extensively in the light of the findings of our own surveys.

Since Marcuse (1915) legal experts (Mittermaier, 1906; Hiller, 1926; Jäger, 1957; and others) and psychiatrists (Gerchow, 1965) have pointed to the fact that in many cases the law produces exactly what it is trying to prevent, namely the destruction of the last remains of a family which is externally and economically still intact and which has – in many cases – remained conflict-free, in spite of the incest (cf. Gerchow, 1965). The establishment of this fact is not made in a vacuum, and it would be an over-hasty judgement to see in it an argument for the liberalisation of incestuous promiscuity. The material difficulties after the dissolution of the marriage, and the emotional sufferings and conflicts of the members of the family during and after legal prosecution, are only a few of the familiar factors concerned here. In view of the fact that this type of case is not uncommon it can hardly be assumed that penal legislation actually helps to achieve 'family harmony' (Welzel, 1954, p. 325). As early as 1915 Marcuse was writing that the legal prosecution 'often (represented) only a violent assault on family harmony' which poisoned the family psyche and 'in the process (led) not to the upholding but to the threatening of the just interests of the state' (1915, p. 73). Even if – in view of the present-day stage of research – one does not need to share Marcuse's idea of 'undisturbed family harmony' in incest families, the fact cannot really be doubted that a serious intervention as a result of the legal proceedings can in many cases lead to a complete dissolution of the family with all the bitter consequences this entails. It is nevertheless interesting that in the *ratio legis* to the French Penal Code it is precisely the possibility of harm as a result of the legal process which is produced as a ground for the non-punishment of incest; in Germany punishment to guard against endangering the common interest, in France no punishment in order to guard against endangering the public interest (Wilhelm, 1911).

Yet if empirically *no relevant social hygienic points of departure* can be established, we must turn – leaving aside the very important psychohygienic motives affecting the protection of dependent minors – to moral grounds for motivation. In fact the legal entity that is allegedly to be protected in cases of incest takes refuge increasingly in definitions such as 'attitudes having regard to morality' (Kohlrausch and Lange, 1961, p. 414).

Amongst the *moral motives*, which are constantly connected with the protection of the family, two aspects can be isolated, though they frequently appear mixed together: 1) 'family purity' or 'the moral health' of the family (Welzel, 1965; Maurach, 1964; Schönke and Schröder, 1965; amongst others), and 2) The 'sex-free sphere' within the family (Mezger and Blei, 1964; Welzel, 1965; Kohlrausch and Lange, 1961; Sturm in *Niederschriften*, 1959). If one now looks at both these aspects alongside the two rational motives we have already considered, the social-hygienic and the hereditary-biological, then one will involuntarily be reminded of the words of Jäger: 'We must thus suspect in the penal law other motives than the protection of personal legal rights. It looks as though the law can be traced back to quite disparate sources, as though mixed together in its norms were modern social considerations and archaic concepts and values, as though the sensible were mixed with the hardly explicable' (1957, p. 5).

It must first of all be pointed out that the principle of 'family purity' and 'area of non-sexual relationships' is inconsistently applied, if – in conformity with the definition of incest – under § 173 only 'cohabitation' is punished and not other 'indecent acts' within the family. A similar inconsistency is expressed in the varying degrees of punishment applied. It is not clear at all why, for example, the 'family purity' should be less sullied by an incestuous relationship between stepfather and stepdaughter than by the same relationship between a father and his natural daughter.

Apart from this, unprejudiced legal experts are of the opinion, as far as the concept of 'purity' is concerned, that 'immoral activities' which are not at the same time harmful, never possess legal status (Jäger, 1957; and others). The concept of 'purity' is here a category of sexual ethics, whose roots can be traced back to socio-cultural taboos, conventions, religious commandments and even to magical and mythical ideas as well. Already at the beginning of this century the legal expert Wilhelm (1910) was pointing out the danger which – under the guise of the basic ethical attitude of the state – is inherent in the legal treatment of incest: namely the assumption that the legal repression is justified simply by the moral prescription of these sexual relationships. Wilhelm stresses the irrational basis of this fact when he writes: 'the strength of the moral indignation is partly derived from older religious attitudes according to which sexual lapses, and in particular those activities which went against the basic drives of the majority, such as ... incest, represented such accursed sinnings against nature and God that the avenging arm of the judge had to intervene against such shameless filth' (1910, p. 820). Wilhelm sees in such attempts at justification on 'state grounds' nothing more than 'moralising tendencies' and, as far as incest is concerned, 'feelings of disgust and repulsion which are reflected in the penal law and provide the stimuli for the penalties laid down' (1910, p. 820).

In the first chapter we showed how ambivalent and how emotively conditioned is man's attitude to the incest taboo, and how magical-mystical and magical-religious attitudes can be deeply rooted in the fear of rationally unfounded or unproven results of incest. Yet where a great deal of fear of irrational threats comes into play, the prejudices are transformed into great taboos, which are strongly upheld in the law. In this connection prejudice can be defined absolutely by Mitscherlich's 'an habitual judgement without sufficient foundation,' (1963, p. 367). If, however, 'habit alone creates the law' (Pascal) and the latter turns out to be an habitual judgement without sufficient foundation, then in the legal bases for the incest statutes which we have discussed above there is an habitual prejudice.

This is true also for the motive of the 'area of non-sexual-relationships', a concept which is ill-suited to the characterisation of an object of protection and represents more of a negative paraphrase of the definition of the act (Jäger, 1957). The motive and the concept of an 'area of non-sexual relationships' are, even viewed from the standpoint of the psychological reality of the family (cf. Chap. II, Section 5), hardly suited to form an integral part of the *ratio legis*. This motivation completely by-passes all the empirical discoveries of present-day behavioural science and creates – together with the moralising tendencies which are behind it – at most confusion. As a basis for the law the concept proves to be psychologically the result of the projection of unfulfilled and unfulfillable needs for purity and metaphysical transfiguration, the original emotional point of origin of which was the sentimentally nurtured idea of the 'asexuality' of the child – indeed this still seems to be the case. As an analogy to the 'purity' and 'asexuality' of the child there arose the idea of protecting the 'purity' and 'area of non-sexual relationships' of the family.

It is a truism that ethical attachments cannot be maintained by penal threats. It is also debatable whether it is the task of the state to suppose an object for protection in cases when it is only the fear of having its basic ethical attitudes misunderstood, that causes it to apply a penal threat. G. Simson (1966, p. 11), points to the fact that the fear of misunderstanding has been placed in the way of meaningful legal progress: 'As soon as one wished to stop hanging thieves, cutting off deceivers' tongues, and drowning adulteresses it would immediately be objected that the law-maker might thus be misunderstood, people would think that he now held property, truth and marital fidelity in less high esteem than before.'

Moreover, it has been shown by experience abroad in removing from the statutes offences which are still punishable in Germany, e.g. adultery, that the feared effects on 'public consciousness' or, a 'healthy public attitude' have been minimal (Simson, 1966; Lackner, 1966).

Our earlier surveys of the underlying motivation have shown that, to use Jäger's words, 'the motives behind the punishment of incest leave us all at sea'. Jäger comes to the conclusion: 'As a result I would consider the punishment of incest to be one of those atavisms, cultic and sacramental remnants, whose purpose and meaning, as Bader says, have long been lost to us. It thus seems to me to be more than questionable whether we are really justified in trying retrospectively to build into the legal norm a rational protective purpose. Perhaps a single exception could be made, under the heading of protection of young people . . .' (1957, p. 67).

c) *Protection of young people*

In fact the notion of protecting young people and, in connection with it, what we had earlier called the psychohygienic motive, seems to be the most essential aspect to be considered in the question of the punishment of incest. Abuse of authority and interference in the sphere of sexual self-determination would equally be two factors to be considered.

Jäger has contributed greatly to explaining the aims of the protective legislation in § 174, No. 1 (protection of dependent minors) and § 176 I, No. 3 (protection of young persons) of the German legal code, so that in this sphere we shall rely upon his expositions (1957, pp. 46–56). These few indications make it clear that, in tackling the question of protection of the victims, we are already outside the bounds of § 173. In fact we agree with Bauer (1963) that both the most frequent and the most serious cases of incest are covered by other legislation; for example, by the provisions covering the sexual protection of young persons. Jäger (1957, p. 118) therefore suggests for the future leaving incest unpunished, but creating *a special legislation for the protection of minors*, 'which – like French and Dutch Law – makes incest between ascendants and descendants still under age an offence. The extension of the age of protection to twenty-one years seems to be required both by the special dangers inherent in the situation as well as by the legal age of majority.'

Criminal statistics

Whilst it can be said with certainty that incest occurs in all Western societies, only very unsatisfactory and barely comparable data on the frequency of its occurrence are available. The reasons for this are of various kinds. The unknown figure is probably high, higher than is generally thought. The criminologist von Hentig (1964) estimates that over 90 per cent of all cases of incest in the Western world go undetected. Kinsey, on the other hand, is of the opinion that heterosexual incest plays a greater role 'in the thoughts of doctors and welfare workers' than in reality. The assertions of some psychoanalysts that incest is very widespread do not correspond with the findings of their own surveys (1963, p. 505). All other estimates of the unknown figure vary between these two extreme poles. However high the figure may be, in fact there are good grounds for thinking that it is not as small as Kinsey is inclined to conclude from the findings of his examination (Masters, 1963; Flügel, 1935; Weinberg, 1963; Marcuse, 1908; Riemer, 1936). The sociologist König (1963, p. 340) talks of a veil of secrecy which the family draws around the occurrence, and von Hentig (1964, p. 118) is hinting at the same thing when he speaks of the 'protective dynamics' of the family group. Fear of the total economic and social collapse of the family, which would seriously affect the wife and children, fear that the whole family will be discriminated against by those around them, and shyness if any of their sexual affairs become known – these are only some of the causes which König and von Hentig introduce to explain the unknown figure. Not infrequently, however, it is the 'unnaturalness' of the act which makes it inconceivable, against all feeling, and therefore unlikely, and thus leads to a rejection of the victim's revelations. Cases in which this rejection by the victim's mother or even, according to von Hentig (1964), by the courts, are known in the literature on the subject and correspond to our own experiences, as we shall see later.

The difficulties in an international comparison of official statistics on incest arise from the variations in law-making, definitions of incest, and penal measures, in the individual states and countries concerned. If, all the same, we cast a cursory glance over the official incest statistics, then we do so with all the reservations and qualifications which arise from the factors we have just touched upon above.

a) Earlier and more recent official statistics

German Reich and Federal Republic: between 1895 and 1906 the annual number of those convicted of incest by courts in the German Reich ran at 381 (min.) to 534 (max.) persons; i.e. 1·0 to 1·3 for every 100,000 under the courts' jurisdiction (Marcuse, 1915, pp. 57–8). As with all other sexual offences, during the First World War the conviction figures dropped from 1·10 (1913) to 0·55 persons in 1919. Yet by 1921 the figure was rising rapidly from 1·58 to reach 2·13 by 1925, subsequently to show a falling, but none the less fluctuating, tendency between (max.) 1·70 (1927) and 1·23 (1935) (Marcuse, 1915; Exner, 1938). A similar development could be observed after the Second World War. Since about 1950 the number of those convicted of incest by courts in the Federal Republic has almost continuously been falling from 436 to 111 people in 1965 (see Fig. 2).

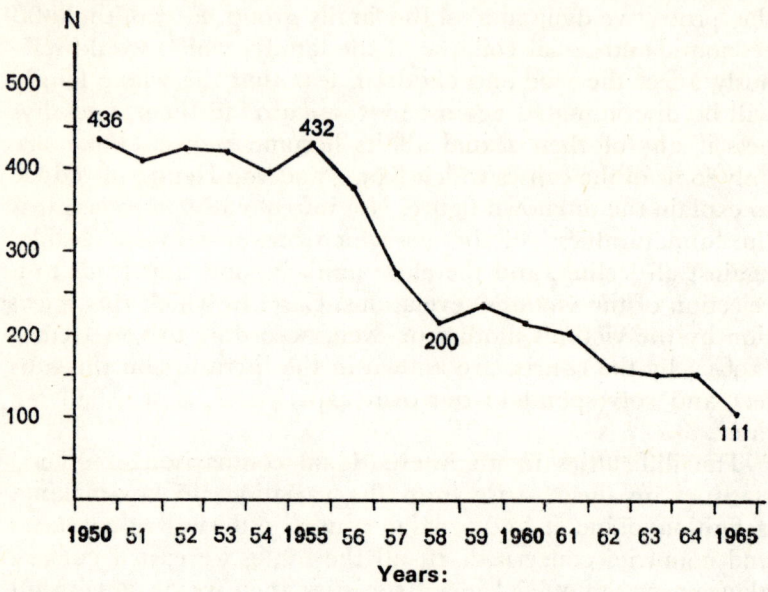

Figure 2. The number of persons convicted under para. 173 of the German Penal Code between 1950 and 1965 (from West German official statistics).

The causes of these fluctuations and the recent decreasing trend (the number of all sexual offences has fallen in recent times) can only be surmised at. The greatest part of the number of those convicted in recent years has – as might be expected – been composed of adults with around seventy-five per cent (1965) to ninety-five per cent (1953). All the same, there is still a yearly number of between five per cent and almost thirty per cent (1960, 1965) of adolescents (eighteen to twenty-one) and young people (fourteen to eighteen) convicted of incest. What is remarkable is the high percentage of convicted girls and women. It rates between approximately a quarter and a third to a half of all cases (1962).

Amongst the states of the Federal Republic with the highest (officially recorded) absolute figures for incest are North-Rhine Westphalia, with, for example, 115 (1954) or 109 (1955) convicted persons, Baden-Wurttemberg with seventy-six (1954) or ninety-five (1955), and Bavaria with eighty-one (1954) or seventy-three (1955), at the head of the table, whilst northern Schleswig-Holstein with seven (1954) or twenty-one (1955) and the Hanseatic City of Bremen (1954: 5, 1955: 2) and Hamburg (1954: 11, 1955: 13) show the lowest figures (Federal Bureau of Statistics, Wiesbaden). Admittedly these comparisons must be accepted with considerable qualifications, because we are not dealing here with crime figures for incest, and the absolute figures produced depend upon the size of the population of the Federal State concerned.

British Commonwealth (England, Wales, Scotland, Canada, New Zealand and Australia): A similar long-term fluctuation to that observed in Germany is described by Weinberg (1963, pp. 37–8) for the British Commonwealth. With 9·0 convictions per million inhabitants in 1937 New Zealand had the highest frequency of incest offences within the Commonwealth, whilst Canada with 5·1 and Scotland with 3·9 convictions per 1,000,000 came considerably lower. England and Wales, although at that time the most thickly populated country, showed, with 1·4, the lowest crime figures for incest. However, between 1905 and 1936, both countries had relatively speaking the highest average quota of legally convicted incest offences in the British Commonwealth: 36·27 of every 1,000 offenders of all criminal categories. Measured over the same period Canada followed second with 1·47, Scotland with 1·09 and New Zealand with only 0·79 persons (out of 1,000 offenders of all criminal categories).

United States of America: In 1910 the average number of convicted incest offenders in the USA was 1·2 persons per million inhabitants, in 1920 it was 1·9 and in 1930 1·1 (Weinberg 1963, pp. 38–9). According to Masters (1963), the present-day figure for convicted incest offenders in the USA has settled at around 2 persons per million.

In Sweden until 1935 there was a yearly average of thirty persons convicted, or 0·73 persons per million inhabitants (Riemer, 1936, p. 86). Unfortunately no more recent data are available to us. The following evidence may be provided about Denmark: of 3,175 sexual offenders, convicted and subjected to a psychiatric examination between 1929 and 1939, 428 were incest offenders, that is 13·5 per cent (Christiansen and colleagues, 1965, p. 60). In 1938 of 100,000 male persons (over fourteen years of age) in Danish cities five, and in 1955 a further three were incest offenders, whilst in small towns over the same period the frequency rose from nine to sixteen, and in country areas fell from twenty-one to fourteen (Stürüp 1960). Quite obviously there is here a certain interdependence between the number of inhabitants and the frequency of convictions, which need not necessarily, however, reflect any certain connection between the number of inhabitants and the actual incidence of incest. From the official statistics for Austria we have reckoned out an average conviction frequency of 29·2 persons for the period from 1959 to 1963. What is striking here is once again the high number of convicted females, sometimes in some years making up even over half of all those convicted of incest (official statistics for Austria).

Even if, on the basis of the enormous variations in penal law, legal methods of prosecution, age of responsibility, and administration of official statistics (crime figures), there can hardly be any question of possibilities of relevant comparison, nevertheless the statistics from the individual countries do show that with incest convictions are made in only a minority of cases.

b) *Nature and degree of penalties*

Under the law in the Federal Republic of Germany the two penalties for incest are prison and corrective training. The official statistics show that the number of people who were committed to reform institutions because of incest between 1951 and 1954 was equivalent to 3·4 to 4·4 per cent of all people sent to such institutions over the period in question (Statistics of the Federal Republic of Germany 1954, p. 23). Further, according to these statistics, on average, in the four years quoted, 106–7 received reform institution sentences for incest. Roughly twenty-five per cent to thirty-three per cent of the people in Western Germany sentenced under § 173 were as a rule sent to reform institutions, and in the cases of roughly thirty-three per cent of these people German courts imposed sentences exceeding two years (Frankel and Jeschek 1959, p. 23).

c) *Frequency of recidivism*

The results of surveys so far available on the frequency of recidivism amongst incest offenders all agree in essential details. They show that the recidivism rate *is relatively low*, both in the absolute sense and also in comparison with other sexual offences. Of 3,175 Danish sexual offenders who were convicted between 1929 and 1939 13·5 per cent (428) had committed incest. The recidivism calculated for an observation period of twelve to twenty-four years on 2,934 sexual offenders, was, for all criminal offences, 24·3 per cent (N=714), for sexual offences 10·6 per cent and for all forms of incest together only 2 per cent (N=14). Christiansen and colleagues (1965, pp. 57–84) established that the greatest danger of recidivism existed in cases of father–daughter incest (1·3 per cent), whilst the figures for stepfather–stepdaughter incest (0·6 per cent) and for brothers and sisters (0·1 per cent) seemed to be much lower. In addition, the American researches of Glueck (1952, 1955) reach the conclusion that (amongst 1,146 sexual offenders) persons committing incest and persons committing sexual offences against children show the lowest figures for reversion (Reckless, 1961, p. 105). The recidivism rate of 2 per cent worked out by Christiansen and his colleagues for male incest offenders corresponds, in round terms, with the quota of 2·3 per cent established by Langeluddeke for 1,036 emasculated sex offenders (1964, p. 93).

Yet even these results can only convey an impression. Age factors, sampling, and length of the observation period are basic variables influencing the statistical findings. More well-founded surveys are needed before we can pass any reliable judgement.

92 Incest

d) Forms of incest

According to most authors, father–daughter and stepfather–stepdaughter incest are recognised as the two forms of incest most frequently recorded in Western civilisation. This surmise draws extensive support from various psychopathological and sociological surveys. Next in order is incest between brother and sister whilst mother–son incest would appear to occur very rarely (Weinberg, 1963; Masters, 1963; Caprio and Brenner, 1961; and others). Combined forms of incest, as, for example, father–daughter and simultaneously father–son incest, are equally rare and, according to the findings of Weinberg (1963), occur predominantly in sexually promiscuous families. Forms of incest which extend beyond the relationships of the basic family nucleus (e.g. uncle–niece) may not be considered here, since in such cases the legal definitions vary from country to country and often no longer even count as incest. S. K. Weinberg expresses the view that brother–sister incest is dominant in primitive tribes, whilst father–daughter incest, on the other hand, occupies only second place, and in these groups too mother–son incest seems to play only a subordinate role. In addition there are yet other, mostly combined forms of incest. These, however, are primarily of sexological interest and occur rarely; they will be dealt with in Chapter Eight (p.196). 'Incest and abnormal sexual behaviour' (p. 196).

The spread of incest amongst the various social strata will be dealt with more extensively at a later stage and with reference to the findings of our own surveys.

4. Family sociology, psychology and psychopathology of incest

In the chapters which follow we shall be engaged in exploring the social and family milieu, against the background of which incestuous relationships develop, the personality and behavioural forms of the incest partners, as well as the effects of incest. In so doing we shall take into account, apart from the findings of our own research, other works which have a bearing on the subject – in so far as these were accessible to us.

1. Definition of the problems and methodology

While cultural anthropology, sociology and psychoanalysis have contributed in some ways to an understanding of the incest taboo and incestuous fantasies, incestuous behaviour has remained the stepchild of sexological research. If one examines briefly writings on the subject over the past forty or fifty years one will be surprised at their small number compared with those dealing with research into other forms and groups of 'deviant' sexual behaviour (forms of behaviour which contravene the norms and expectations pertaining in a social system; Cohen, 1959). And there are specialists who, on examining incest, have fallen into the trap of their own moral value judgements or become imprisoned in an impasse of one-sided explanations. In view of these last two factors we have a general responsibility to give unbiased information and to take into account as wide a selection of relevant facts as possible.

Tasks

In previous scientific expositions the offender's psychopathology (i.e. predominantly that of the male incest partner) and the question of the causative factors in the incest relationship were given prime importance. Most works base themselves on cases from forensic medicine, especially from legal psychiatric practice, and have as their object of study the most frequent type of case, father–daughter or stepfather–stepdaughter incest. The research worker's attempts to explain the offence can be divided into several groups according to the different emphasis put on the results of his investigations and theories:

Amongst the *biologically orientated attempts at explanation* there is hardly one which does not make some isolated abnormal phenomenon responsible for creating the incestuous relationship. Whilst at the start of this century there were still a large number of scientists who believed that it was above all the mentally sick who committed incest (Wülffen, 1910; Rohleder 1912; and others), there were those who later adopted the view that a certain (genotypical) condition associated with the constitution, the so-called 'incestoid', is by far the most frequent cause of such behaviour (von Hentig, 1925). Reflections of this idea can still be seen today in the hypothesis of a certain inner readiness for incest as a function of (congenital) character structure (Wagner, 1953). Some experts, in contrast, see the cause as *an unusually strong sexual impulse* (hypersexuality) on the part of the male incest partner (Krafft-Ebing, 1894; Sonden, 1936; Schwab, 1938; and others). Frequently also a disproportionate role is ascribed to innate or acquired *intelligence defects* (Holder 1949; Schwab 1938; Plaut 1960; and others).

The second group of attempts at explanation is centred around *environmental influences*. *Lack of living space* (Kay, 1894; Fink, 1899; Bloch, 1916; Marcuse, 1915; Flügel, 1935; and others), or other economic needs (Marcuse, 1915; and others) are seen as decisive factors. Alcohol also is given great significance as a motivating force (Forel, 1905; Wülffen, 1910; Birnbaum, 1921; Többen, 1925; and others), and finally the lasting or temporary sexual *inaccessibility of the offender's wife* is regarded as a decisive factor (Rosenfeld, 1926).

Since the highly fruitful work by the Swede Riemer (1936) the interest of incest researchers in the social-psychological side of the question has been much broadened. The point of view which looked for a unilateral causality was abandoned in favour of a *multi-dimensional method of examination* at the same time as

Family sociology, psychology and psychopathology of incest 95

incest came to be regarded as the coming together and the working together of various psychological, psychopathological and social-psychological factors (Finke and Zeugner, 1934; Wagner, 1953; Gerchow, 1955, 1965). With the development of this process the situation inside the family before the start of incest has come more and more to be the focal point of interest (Gerchow, 1955, 1965; Rinehart, 1961; Gebhard and colleagues, 1965). Personality and behaviour as far as the most under-age incest partners are concerned have so far, however, hardly been systematically examined at all.

The multi-dimensional method of examination, which is amongst the essential tasks of this part of the book, has several levels:

1. A detailed description of the social characteristics of the family background.
2. An examination of the psychological and psychopathological aspects of the personality of the parents in incest families (especially that of the male incest partner) as well as the psychosocial and sexual relationships between the married couple before the start of incest.
3. An examination of the development and personality of the (mostly) under-age female incest partners (daughters, stepdaughters).
4. An analysis of the factors predisposing towards, stimulating, maintaining and ending incestuous relationships, and a consideration of the personality and modes of behaviour of the incest partners (the dynamics of interaction, i.e. the interacting influence on the individual's behavioural patterns).
5. A description of the effects of incest on family and incest partners, especially on the female partner.
6. An analysis of the relationship between incest as a sexually deviant form of behaviour and other forms of abnormal sexuality.

At all these levels there are numerous individual questions which will be dealt with within the framework of the chapter in question. In the foreground of our examination is – following the statistics quoted in the previous chapter – the most frequent form of incest, sexual relations between father and daughter, stepfather and stepdaughter. Other forms of sexual contact will also be brought in, including those which do not come under § 173 of the Law of the Federal Republic (complete intercourse). In addition there will also be some examination of the rarer forms of incest as for example between mother and son, father and son, as well as hetero-homosexual and other combinations.

Terminology

In specialist writing dealing with sexual offences, especially those committed against children, the concepts 'victim' and 'offender' have become well established. For want of better concepts we find ourselves forced to use them in our turn. One should, however, be fully aware that both words easily arouse associations which contain moral and emotional preconceptions and are capable of blurring the edges of any factual or neutral judgement. For this reason we would like both concepts to be understood as free of value judgements.

All sexual acts between near relatives, which in some way contravene the legal code, will here be referred to as incestuous or incest relationships, irrespective of whether it is a question of the so-called 'indecent acts' with dependent minors (§ 174, section 1, Statute Law Book), or coital relationships (§ 173, SLB). In contrast to that of the legal formulas our terminology proceeds from a psychological and psychopathological point of view and not from the physically localised direction of the sexual activities. To this extent we are – for reasons to be explained later – accepting the views of more recent research into incest (Gerchow, 1955; Rennert, 1958; Plaut, 1960).

The survey material and methods

Our findings are based on a *total of seventy-eight cases* (number of offender–victim relationships) which came before German courts.

The group of victims consists of seventy-six female (N = 71) and male (N = 5) witnesses who, at the time of the main legal proceedings, were still under age or already adult (the higher number of actual offender–victim relationships can be explained by cases in which incestuous relationships existed between the victim and both parents). In eighty-five per cent (N = 66) of these cases sexual relations arose between father and daughter (N = 34) and between stepfather and stepdaughter (N = 32). Sixteen per cent of the cases (N = 12) were divided up amongst the other forms of incest (see Table 1). Incest in the legal sense (according to § 173, SLB) was present in fifty-one per cent of cases (N = 40), whilst forty-nine per cent (N = 38) of the sexual relationships fulfilled the necessary preponderance of characteristics stipulated by § 174, para. 1, SLB.

TABLE I Distribution of the social relationships of offenders to victims. N = 78 (number of victims N = 76)

Social relationship: offender–victim	N	%
Father–daughter	34 ⎫ 66	44 ⎫ 85
Stepfather–stepdaughter	32 ⎭	41 ⎭
Father–son	4	5
Mother–son	3	4
Mother–daughter	1	1
Grandfather–granddaughter	4	5
Total	78	100

The *victims* were at the time of the main legal proceedings (or the forensic psychological examination) between the ages of three and sixty-six. The main group of seventy female victims had a median age of 15·56 ± 4·47 (the most frequent age was seventeen).

The *total group of offenders* consisted of sixty-seven men (N = 63) and women (N = 4). The lower number of offenders may be explained by the fact that in some cases the father or stepfather was carrying on more than one incestuous relationship. Sixty offenders were convicted in accordance with the law (§ 173, para. 1 or 2, § 174, para. 1, some also under § 176, 1, sub-section 3, and very occasionally also under § 177, para. 1, § 181, para. 1, sub-section 2, or with § 175 (*a*), sub-section 3, SLB). Two further offenders committed suicide (after receiving the bill of indictment) and in five cases the offenders were acquitted for lack of evidence (the dependants had used their right to withhold testimony in the main proceedings). Sentences totalling sixty-eight years and four months penal servitude were passed on twenty-one men and one woman, and thirty-four men and three women received prison sentences totalling fifty-seven years eleven months. The shortest penal servitude sentence was eighteen months, the longest six years, whilst the prison sentences ranged between six months and three and a half years.

The *basis of the material* consisted of fifty-five expert opinions as to the credibility of the victims. In a further twenty-one cases in which the offenders made full confessions, ancillary documentary material was used as and when it was to hand (legal documents, school reports on the victims, foster reports, reports from the youth probation service, and gynaecological evidence). Psychiatric reports on the legal responsibility and personality of the offenders were omitted from the documentary material (with the exception of two opinions by offenders on themselves). The methods used in reporting on the victims include a comprehensive personality and intelligence examination using the techniques of modern psychodiagnostics (tests), also an exhaustive series of questions as to the course of the incest and the family (for a fuller description of the methodology: Müller-Lückmann, 1963; Hiltmann, 1956, 1960). In order to elucidate the victim's physiological and psychological development (biographical anamnesia), as well as the social and internal situation of the family, still other sources of information were drawn upon (questioning of the victim's mother, the offender, official records). The evaluation of the whole was carried out from the point of view of description and phenomenology and by means of statistical-mathematical analysis (detailed description of statistical methods: Mittenecker, 1960; Hofstätter and Wendt, 1966). Lack of space forces us to omit any really extensive descriptions of these methods.

Limitations and qualifications

Our material covers all the most important forms of incest with the exception of brother–sister incest. For this reason we shall only be able to touch very briefly on this form in 'Emotional partnership and free relationship' (p. 205).

Another limitation on the binding nature of the results of our survey is caused by the nature of the material: the survey group (sample) is indeed, as we shall proceed to show, representative of forensic reality (cases convicted under the law) as far as the age of victims and offenders at the start of incest and their social origin are concerned, but our statements cannot be generalised to cover the actual incidence of the forms of incest being dealt with.

We can only make vague assumptions about the amount of unknowns as well as the age, education and social origin of those involved in cases in medical practice, or which are recorded in non-official sources.

2. Forms of sexual contact, age of incest partners and duration of the sexual relations

The connection between the forms of sexual contact practised in sexual offences and the age of the victim and the offender has in recent times increasingly become the object of criminological and sexological research (Matthes, 1961; Gebhard and colleagues, 1965; Schonfelder, 1968; and others). It is of criminal/political and sexual scientific interest. The information we shall give in this chapter provides essential points of reference for all subsequent conclusions.

Forms of sexual contact. Sexual activity in a sexual offence involving two persons can take on many different forms. These range from acts which do not necessarily include any physical contact (e.g. exhibition of the genitals) to coitus. In incestuous relationships, a stage of physical contact between the partners is always reached. Our own survey and the findings of other research show that *in incest the various forms of genital contact are dominant.*

The most frequent occurrence is coitus, as opposed to non-genital contacts (physical manipulation restricted to the thighs, breasts, mouth) which are very rare. This situation is elaborated in Fig. 3 and by a comparison of our own findings with the latest American Kinsey Institute Survey results.

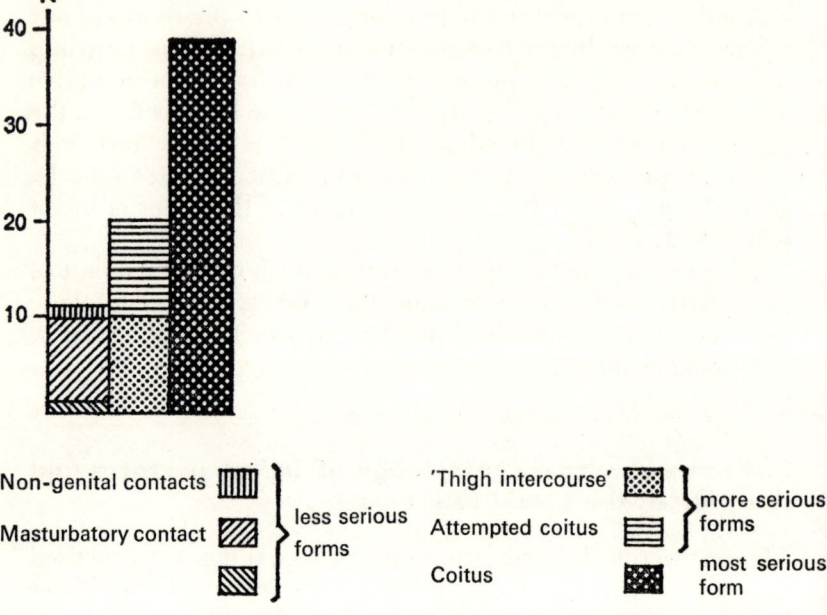

Figure 3. Forms of sexual contact: results of own survey main group N = 70

In our material (father–daughter, stepfather–daughter, grandfather–daughter) coital relationships (fifty-five per cent) or attempts at coitus (fourteen per cent) arose in almost seventy per cent of cases. In those cases where 'thigh pressing' was the most intimate form of contact it was not always possible to ascertain whether attempted coitus or coitus had not actually occurred (this aspect was not researched by Gebhard and colleagues). It is worth noting that oral–genital contact (mouth intercourse) is the most difficult to establish – probably because this kind of sexual stimulation is subject to a taboo of silence, both on the man's and the victim's part, and is generally regarded as 'perverted'. Even if oral–genital contacts were registered in our survey material, especially in coital relations of some duration, this form of sexual contact seemed to us to involve so many imponderables that we did not produce it as a special category in our table (Gebhard and colleagues quote a figure of only nineteen per cent). In relationships where masturbation was the most intimate form (fourteen per cent) there are an equal number of unilateral as well as mutual acts.

TABLE 2 Forms of sexual contact: findings in our own survey and American ones (Gebhard 1965, p. 819)

	Coitus	Attempted coitus	'Thigh intercourse'	Masturbation contacts	Oral–genital	Non-genital	No. in group
Own survey %	55	14	14	14	(see text)	1	70
	69						
Gebhard %	49	5	(see text)	25	19	3	170
	54						

NB: Percentage figures have been rounded down or up. In all cases only the most intimate form is recorded.

In addition to the forms of contact in heterosexual partnerships dealt with here there are, in our survey material, several homosexual relationships of a masturbatory, oral– and anal–genital kind which we will examine in the chapter 'Incest and abnormal sexual behaviour' (p. 196 f.). In the same chapter we shall deal with hetero-homosexual forms of incest, more especially with trioles (three-sided intercourse) and other abnormal sexual practices.

Age of incest partners at start of incest

a) Victims. The frequency of coital relationships might lead one to suspect that the girls are at an age when, from the point of view of physical maturity, the anatomical prerequisites for this form of sexual contact are already present. The average age of the female incest victim in our survey group is 12·3 years, and the most represented age is the (completed) thirteenth year. Roughly two-thirds were between their tenth and sixteenth years of life (nine years to 15·6 years), the youngest girl was six at the start of incest and the oldest nineteen. Comparable surveys in Germany, Sweden and the USA have produced similar results (cf. Table 3).

TABLE 3 Average age of female incest victims at the start of incest: earlier and more recent research

	Többen (1925) G	Plaut (1960) G	Sonden (1936) SW	Weinberg (1963) USA	Tamm (1965) G	Gebhard and Co. (1965) USA
Average age in years	13·1	15·0	14·0	15·3	12·9	13·0
Size of survey (N)	66	101	137	159	39	171

Note: G = Germany; SW = Sweden

Our research and that of the Kinsey Institute (Gebhard and colleagues, 1965, pp. 770, 772) show that incestuous relationships with girls before the (completed) seventh year of life and after the age of nineteen occur very rarely (six per cent or eight per cent, and none three per cent). Non-incestuous heterosexual offences and cases of rape on girls under seven are, however, by no means so rare (Gebhard and colleagues, 1965, p. 770). Mohr and colleagues (1962, p. 258) established that the preferred age for victims of non-incestuous heterosexual sexual offences lay between six and eleven. From the research findings it may be concluded that daughters and stepdaughters should preferably be, at the start of an incestuous relationship, at a stage in life in which sexual maturity is just beginning or is already in progress (see p. 105).

b) Offenders. Among the most well established of the findings of present-day incest research are the data on the age of the male offenders, more especially of the fathers and stepfathers. They are *on average in their fifth decade*, i.e. between forty and forty-nine (Többen, 1925; von Hentig and Viernstein, 1925; Finke and Zeugner, 1934; Sonden, 1936; Eber, 1937; Wagner, 1953; Gerchow, 1955; Nürnberger, 1955; Plaut, 1960; Weinberg, 1963; Gebhard and colleagues, 1965; and others).

The males in our survey group were of an average age of 40·7, and about two-thirds were between thirty-three and forty-eight. The fathers in fact were on average slightly older (41·5) than the stepfathers (forty), though the difference is not statistically significant. The youngest offender was twenty-seven and the oldest sixty-six. As far as average age is concerned our findings agree very nearly with the figures, reached on the basis of a larger sample, of 41·0 in Germany (Schwab, 1938) and 39·6 in the USA (Gebhard and colleagues, 1965). A division into intervals of the age data from our survey and that of Plaut (1960) demonstrates the frequency concentration of cases (roughly eighty-three per cent to eighty-seven per cent: see Fig. 4).

Our findings agree fairly well with other survey results especially the latest ones in the USA, in showing that (*a*) fathers and stepfathers commit incest *relatively late in life*, (*b*) at the start of incest the offenders are at an age when, generally speaking, a man is *still in full possession of his sexual impulses* (up to the end of their thirties incest was committed by, according to Plaut, roughly fifty per cent, according to Gebhard fifty-one per cent to seventy per cent, in our group roughly fifty-six per cent). American researchers explain the relatively late stage (agewise) at which the legal offence is committed by the fact that this group has spent a good part of its life in a normal heterosexual partnership (marriage) and in building up a family, while this is far less the case with other groups of sexual offenders. Only thirty-one per cent of exhibitionists, twenty-four per cent of voyeurs, five per cent to sixteen per cent of homosexuals, twenty-eight to thirty-three per cent of heterosexual rapists, and twenty-nine per cent to

104 *Incest*

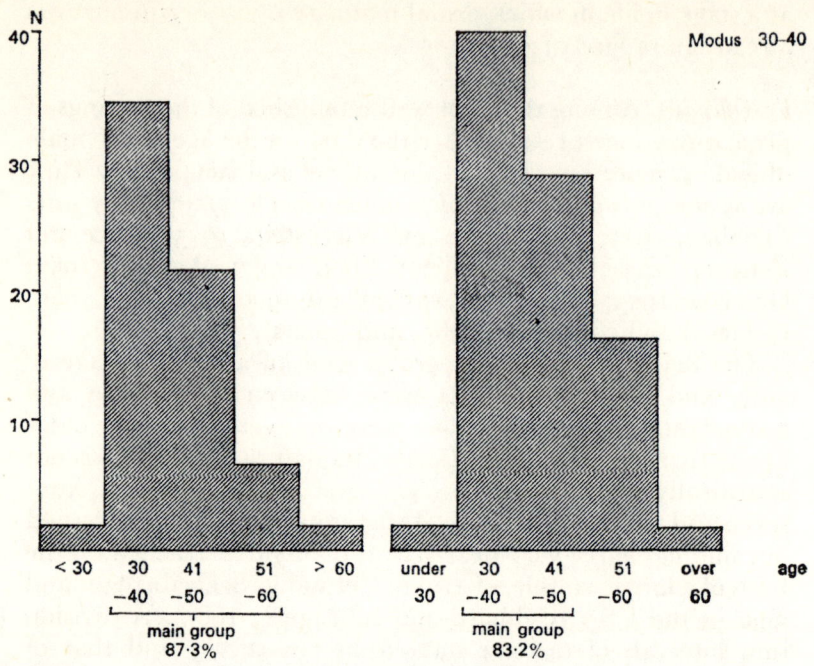

Figure 4. Distribution of age of incest offenders at the start of incest: Findings of Plaut (1960, pp. 94–5) and our own survey.

Note: Plaut's group N = 83: our group N = 63.

thirty-one per cent of heterosexual offenders (where violence was not involved) were married at the time of the offence, and a relatively high percentage of these groups had never been married (see Gebhard and colleagues, 1965, p. 698). So long as there are no exact comparative surveys of legally or sexologically clearly defined test samples, we will have to base ourselves on the American researches of Gebhard and colleagues, according to which incest offenders are one of the three groups of sexual delinquents whose ages are highest at the beginning of the offence (1965, p. 747). Violent non-incestuous offences against girls (rape or attempted rape) and violent and non-violent sexual offences against girls in puberty (twelve- to fifteen-year-olds) are in contrast committed by essentially younger men (average ages: 24·5 to 31·7 and 23·2 to 24·7 years).

Relationship between age of victim at start of incest, biological maturity and forms of sexual contact

The young girl's progress to sexual maturity – coupled with development – is not only expressed in the shape of the first period (menarch) but also in the external aspects of bodily build. According to Tanner the *development of the female breast-bud*, with a significant protuberance and rounding of the breast and the nipple, may in general be regarded as the *first sign of genuine puberty* (1962, p. 49). These specific stages of this development lie today between the eleventh and twelfth years (second and third stage). It is at about the same time that there most likely begins the pubertal development of the uterus and the vagina (abrupt change in the reactive qualities of the vaginal mucous membrane from pre-pubic to adult). These biological processes, especially the development of the breast-bud, are as a rule observable even before the menarch begins, though both phenomena are temporally highly correlated (Nicolson and Hanley, 1953; Deming, 1957).

In our survey material there are various indications that the sexual approaches of the father or stepfather are frequently motivated by the changes in the shape of the body coupled with the process of sexual coming to maturity, especially the development of the daughter's or stepdaughter's breasts. In this connection we shall have later to examine whether there is a possible interaction to be found between the daughter's physical 'attraction' for the father, caused by her growing maturity, arising from the same causes (see Chapter Seven, p. 169).

At the start of the incestuous relationships approximately seventy-six per cent ($N = 53$) of the female partners were at an age at which today the menarch sets in with a statistically significant frequency (from the eleventh year on: Steuer, 1965). About thirty-four per cent ($N = 24$) were at the average age of development of the breast-buds (eleven to twelve/thirteen years), and forty-two per cent ($N = 29$) were, at the beginning of sexual contacts, at a phase in life (beyond the age of thirteen) in which this development has as a rule already taken place. Purely from the point of view of age these signs of maturity were only not relevant (statistically) for twenty-four per cent ($N = 17$). The fact that in the case of two girls in this latter small group the menarch had already set in at the age of nine or ten, merely indicates the breadth of individual variation possible in the biological maturing process.

Of the forty-eight girls with verifiable data on the menarch (almost seventy per cent of the survey group) in roughly seventy-three per cent of cases (N = 35) the menarch had already happened, and in twenty-seven per cent (N = 13) it had not yet appeared. A further eight per cent (N = 5) were at an age (sixteen to seventeen) at which in the present-day female population the menarch had happened in ninety-five per cent and more cases (Steuer 1965), while for the remainder of the survey group (approx. twenty-two per cent) no certain information was available. The average age at menarch in our group was 12·2, the most frequent twelve (twenty-one girls). According to the view of German and foreign surveys the average age at menarch amongst the female population today lies between twelve and a half and thirteen and a half (Reynolds and Wines, 1949; Deming, 1957; Winter, 1958; Scott, 1961; Tanner, 1962; Steuer, 1965). Even if, because of the gaps in information in our material, we can only supply evidence on individual menarch timing for a section of the girls whose age suggested they were approaching sexual maturity, it was nevertheless possible, by means of other information, to throw a good deal of light on the temporal role of the maturing factors. Where it was relatively easy to classify temporally statements by the victim about the sudden interest shown by the male partner in the female breast, or statements by the male about the sexual attraction proceeding from the victim's 'physical development', we were enabled to determine the connections between biological maturity factors and the beginning of incest (for examples: see p. 169 f.).

In fact there is a very *close connection between signs of biological maturity* (development of the breasts, menarch) *and the age of the victim at the start of incest* (ten years). Thus it will come as no surprise that, when the forms of sexual contact are examined, in cases of completed incest coitus occurs more often after the menarch than before, whereas in uncompleted incest the sexual activities tend rather to take place before the menarch. Whether the non-coital forms of contact are merely sexual activities brought to a head in the early stages of completed incest by the discovery of the relationship, or should be considered as something completely separate, will be explored at a later stage (see Chapter Eight, p. 196).

Also worth noting is the set of *relationships between certain sexual forms of contact and the age of the victim at the start of* incest.

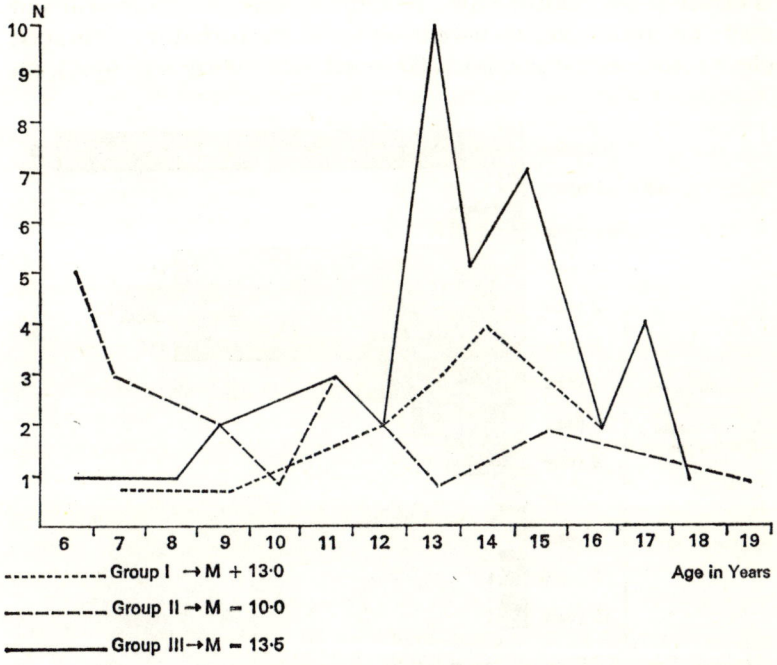

Figure 5. Diagram of distribution of age of victim at the start of incest: groups of sexual forms of contact. N = 70.

Note: Group I = Masturbatory contacts; Group II = 'thigh intercourse'; Group III = coitus.

Yet they seem obviously not to be specific to incest, but to reflect only a general criminological factor in sexual offences against girls under age: girls, with whom coitus-type activities took place ('thigh intercourse', attempted coitus) are younger (average age: ten years) than girls with whom there were predominantly masturbatory contacts (average age: thirteen years) or coitus (average age: 13·5 years). Fig. 5 sets out these findings. The age differences between these groups of sexual forms of contact have been statistically checked (t-test, five per cent level).

I. Matthes (1961) was able with a larger group (N = 813) of female victims, of predominantly non-incestuous sexual offences, to point to very similar patterns (frequency concentration of coitus-type activities: six- to nine-year-old girls; of coitus: fourteen-year-olds; of masturbatory contacts: eleven- to twelve-year-olds). Gerhard and colleagues (1965), on

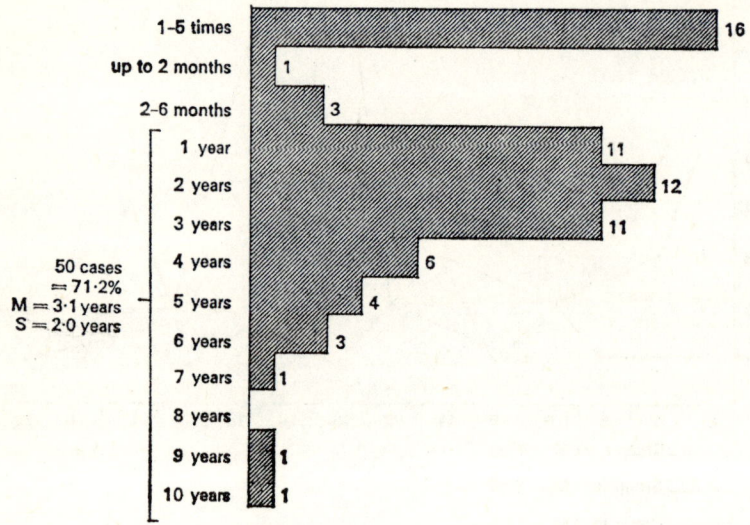

Figure 6. Length of incestuous relations. N = 70.

interviewing 1,356 convicted sexual offenders, came to the conclusion that coitus is far more frequently performed with twelve- to fifteen-year-old girls (two-thirds of the cases), and especially in incestuous relationships, while in non-violent sexual offences against children under the age of eleven non-coital forms of contact dominate.

Whether, considering that the girls are still children when coitus-type forms of contact take place, the victim's signs of biological maturity play any role at all as 'stimuli' of the male's behaviour can only be judged in individual cases. It is nevertheless conceivable that amongst offenders who are related to the girl and those who are not and who practise these forms of contact, there are frequently those who prefer precisely those girls whose secondary sexual distinguishing features (breasts, pubic hair) are still not developed (cf. Chapter Eight, p. 196 f.).

Duration of the sexual relations and victim's age at the end of incest

In roughly seventy-one per cent of cases (N = 50) the sexual relations between the incest partners went on for one year or more, whereas in approximately twenty-nine per cent (N = 20) we are dealing with either isolated acts or activities of relatively short duration, say up to six months (see Fig. 6). The concentration of incestuous relations on the period of one year or longer is already well known (Finke and Zeugner, 1934; Tamm, 1965). In contrast to this, non-incestuous heterosexual offences on girls under age are dominated by isolated acts or relationships of short duration, of between one and six months (Wegener, 1953; Lange, 1956). In our material, amongst relationships lasting one year and more, coitus occurs most frequently (sixty-four per cent) as the most intimate form of sexual contact, and amongst the coital relationships cases lasting one year and more are predominant (eighty-two per cent). For longer incestuous relationships (>1 year) we have achieved an *average duration* of 3·1 years (frequency peak at two years), a finding which coincides fairly well with the average figure of 3·3 years produced by Tamm (1965). Fig. 6 shows that nevertheless incestuous relationships of more than three years' duration are no rarity (twenty-three per cent).

The cases which offer the most worthwhile information on incestuous relationships are precisely those which last longer. As Fig. 7 shows, these girls were on average in their sixteenth year at the end of sexual relations and were most often seventeen. The youngest victim was seven at the end of incest, and the oldest was already twenty-two years old. There was, however, a noticeable and statistically significant (five per cent level) difference in this connection between completed and uncompleted incest: girls who had coitus were on average two years older when the incest ended than those who were involved in masturbatory or coitus-type acts or attempted coitus. By what

110 *Incest*

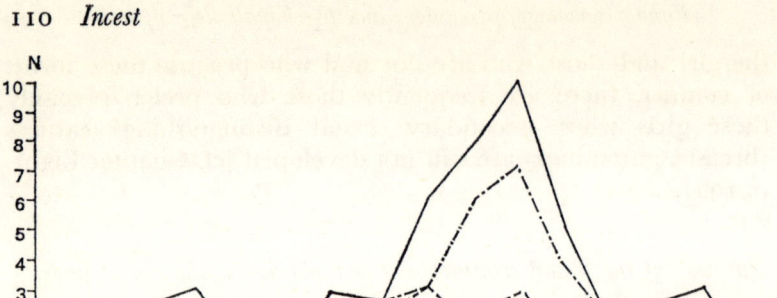

Figure 7. Distribution of age of female incest victims at the end of incest (cases lasting one year or more). N = 50.

social or psychological factors this difference is brought about will have to be explored later.

On the whole it can at all events be said that girls involved in the more lengthy incestuous relationships are, at the end of these latter, at an age (sixteen to eighteen), as a rule, when not only extra-family social orientation (professional training and job adjustment) but also psychosexual partner-orientation (friendship, engagement) begin to play an important role.

3. Social characteristics of the family milieu

In this chapter we will be dealing with the most varied sociological aspects of the family milieu in which incest develops (father–daughter/stepfather–stepdaughter). We shall also touch upon criminological factors, in so far as they contribute to the characterising of the given social conditions.

Introductory remarks on family sociology

In connection with the workings of the incest taboo we have already indicated above (see p. 58 f.) the significance of the family nucleus for the *socialisation of the child* and the *formation of the personality* of the child as it grows up. In western industrial societies the family has a further basic function to fulfil: the *stabilisation of the adult personality* (Parsons and Bales, 1955).

According to the views of American sociologists, the adult personality only unfolds fully in its relationship to the succeeding generation. F. Specht (1967, p. 39) has given renewed emphasis to the fact that the stabilisation of the adult personality depends to a great extent upon 'how far the family can cope with its task of socialisation'. Even if sociological surveys of families made in the last decade have shown clearly that the long-held view of the family as the unique moulder of social personality is no longer sufficient (König, 1955; Schelsky, 1957; Riesman and colleagues, 1958; and others), present-day sociologists and psychologists are nevertheless unanimous in believing that the family lays the first essential basis for the formation of personality.

A threat to the family and the carrying out of its functions may arise when 1) the family unit with its 'group character' is broken by the separation, divorce or death of the parents, 2) the intimacy of the family 'togetherness' is destroyed, for example by a broken marriage (König, 1955). In both cases we shall refer to a disturbance of the (internal or external) family constitution or to *disorganisation* (König, 1964). Illegitimate motherhood, i.e. the extra-marital birth of a child, or the fact that a member of the family comes before the courts, may also be included amongst the symptoms of this disorganisation.

Social stratum and financial circumstances

By social stratum is meant a number of people who consider each other of equal value and feel themselves as being higher or lower than other sections of the population (König, 1962; Bolte, 1964). This feeling of belonging to a particular social stratum is extensively linked to the social prestige dependent upon a list of professions in order of 'importance' (prestige/respect for a certain profession) (Mayntz, 1958). The division into social strata is thus based on certain categories of professions (strata system).

Our research agrees more or less closely with earlier surveys on incest by showing that families in which incestuous relations are officially recognised as existing are *predominantly amongst the lower social strata* of the population. According to the strata system of Janowitz (1958), which allows for sufficient differentiation between lower and middle strata for the Federal German Republic, roughly ninety-one per cent of the families in our material belong to the two lower social strata, i.e. the fathers are trained workers, skilled workers, independent craftsmen (upper lower stratum: sixty-two per cent) and semi-skilled or unskilled workers (lower lower stratum: roughly twenty-nine per cent). *The middle stratum,* i.e. office workers with jobs involving small to medium degrees of responsibility, middle rank and lower rank salaried employees, and self-employed (lower middle stratum) is little represented with about nine per cent, and the *upper social stratum* is not represented at all. When compared with the distribution of occupational groups amongst the social strata of the population of the Federal Republic, these findings show that the incest offenders in our group come to a far greater extent from the lower social stratum than one would have expected from the population distribution (roughly fifty-two per cent). The middle stratum, on the other hand, is comparatively under-represented (nine per cent as opposed to forty-three per cent of population of Federal Germany).

Other surveys also give documentary evidence of a strong representation of the broad lower social stratum (Finke and Zeugner, 1934; Schwab, 1938; Nürnberger, 1955; Plaut, 1960). Analogous conditions pertain in the USA (roughly comparable with our middle stratum: 4·5 per cent to twelve per cent; upper stratum nought per cent to two per cent, according to Gebhard and colleagues, 1965).

Compared with other results of earlier surveys, however, a notable difference is expressed in our results, a difference which has also been observed by American writers (Gebhard and colleagues, 1965). It is in fact in the large increase of skilled and specialist workers as compared with earlier periods. It is quite conceivable that this developing tendency can be traced to the 'exodus of the unskilled' (Dahrendorf, 1956) as a result of the change in working methods associated with technological progress. Nevertheless surveys in the past forty years indicate a *remarkable stability to one specific stratum* in officially notified cases of incest. It should not immediately be concluded from this that the most common form of incest, that between father and daughter or stepfather and stepdaughter, is also actually more common in strata of the population which have the lowest social prestige. The presumably high number of unknowns makes one hesitate to reach such generalised conclusions.

Moreover today one is no longer justified in concluding that because a person belongs to a lower social stratum his essential basic economic needs are not met. The idea, which can still be found in the latest textbooks on criminal jurisdiction, that incest is 'born of poverty and need' (Mezger and Blei, 1966, p. 83) is taken from surveys conducted thirty to fifty years ago and is thus no longer applicable. The earlier works (Marcuse, 1915; Többen, 1935; Schwab, 1938; and others) which use material collated at times of economic depression and socio-political upheaval, only serve to illustrate the degree to which the results then achieved were historically dependent.

As will be seen from Table 4, roughly twenty-eight per cent of the fathers in our survey group earned DM 800 a month or more (up to DM 2,000). A further thirty-two per cent, with a monthly income from the main breadwinner of DM 600 to DM 800, were within the scale on the cost of living index of a 'medium working-class family' (four people) for the years 1958 to 1962 (DM 570 or DM 669 to DN 750; from *'Statistisches Jahrbuch'* 1962, p. 416; 1965, p. 473). In thirty-nine per cent of cases, nevertheless, the monthly income of the main earner fell below, or only just matched, the cost of living for the year concerned. Now it must be added that in ninety-five per cent of cases the father of the family was the chief earner, but that roughly forty per cent of the wives could, by full- or part-time work, improve the family budget by amounts varying between DM 100 and DM 400. If one takes this fact into account then only twenty-three per cent of the cases we examined had a monthly income below the cost of living necessary for a 'medium working-class family'. Some of these families were receiving supplementary maintenance from the state.

Altogether seventy-seven per cent of the families lived in 'comfortable' financial circumstances. Even though it is hard to compare the standard of living in the USA with that in Germany, it is nevertheless worth pointing out that the research group at the

TABLE 4 Monthly income of the main earner

	Income groups: DM per month				
	600	600–799	800–999	1000–1199	1200
abs.	23	19	13	3	1
%	39	32	21	5	2

NB: Of a total of sixty-two male offenders the financial circumstances of fifty-nine could be clearly established (plus one man of independent means who was kept by his wife); period of observation 1960 to 1965.

Kinsey Institute, using a sample more than twice the size (147 incest offenders), came to similar results (the socio-economic status of seventy to seventy-seven per cent of the cases fell within the upper working class to upper middle class income group, with the majority coming broadly from the 'middle classes' – fifty-five to sixty-eight per cent; Gebhard and colleagues, 1965, p. 53).

Size of family and living conditions

The *average number of children* of the sixty-two families in our material is 3·48 – a figure which is essentially lower than the average number given in other writings on incest (see Table 5). *Families with two children* formed the *highest percentage* (roughly twenty-six per cent) and seventy-two per cent had one to four children (ninety-seven per cent in the Federal Republic). The number with more than five children, on the other hand, is very small (ten per cent). Nevertheless, though our statistics show that families in which incestuous relationships arise are altogether larger, i.e. have more children than the average number per family in the Federal Republic (1·8), they are, however, not as large as one might have expected on the basis of earlier German and the latest American research on incest. It is quite conceivable that our findings already reflect the general decrease in the size of the family (number of children) amongst the population as a whole (cf. Mackenroth, 1955; Wagner and Planck, 1957; Pflanz, 1962).

This hypothesis is plausible in so far as the latest American results (Weinberg, 1955, 1963; Gebhard and colleagues, 1965) are taken – as far as the year of birth of the incest offenders is concerned – from comparatively much older material (sixty-three to one hundred per cent alone of all Gebhard's incest offenders were born before 1919). Apart from this, the average number of children per family in the USA is greater (Weinberg 1963). This temporal factor must therefore be taken into account, and one must treat with some reserve the commonly held notion that incestuous families are predominantly those with many children (Kay, 1864; Flügel, 1935; Schwab, 1938).

Also on the periods when the research is done is the information about living conditions and accommodation. Whereas the established 'bad' living conditions in times of economic depression were once held to be typical of those in which incest occurs (Marcuse, 1915; Többen, 1925; Nürnberger, 1955) and in fact they really only reflected a general situation of need amongst the lower social strata of that period, Weinberg in the USA and Plaut (1960) in Germany have in particular been able to put in a proper perspective the overrated factor of living accommodation.

The *majority* of the families in our survey (seventy-nine per cent) were living in two- or three-roomed accommodation. Only two families were living in a camp, and one owned its own house.

From the person–room ratio it emerges that a *good half of the families* (roughly fifty-three per cent) lived in *relatively favourable accommodation* (less than two and more than one, or less than one person per living room). In fourteen per cent of cases, however, the accommodation situation was 'critical' since three or more people were forced to use one room. When compared with the state of living conditions in West Germany in 1960 (*Statistisches Jahrbuch*. 1963, p. 273) the 'critical' cases are over-represented in our material (fourteen per cent as against 0·3 per cent in West Germany as a whole), the 'very favourable' ones (up to one person per room) are very greatly under-represented (twelve per cent as against fifty-three per cent). Although this comparison, which can only be made with considerable limitations,

TABLE 5 Distribution of the frequency of numbers of children per family, average numbers of children: in our own survey, previous incest research, and comparative figures for West Germany

No. of children in family	Frequency distribution of children per family in own survey (absolute figures)	%	In West Germany	Average figure (M)	Other incest research comparative figures from various authors
1	9	14	10	3·5	G: own research
2	16	26	28	1·8	G: *Statist. Jahrbuch.* (1965)
3	11	18	25	4·3	USA: Gebhard (1965)
4	9	14		(3·0)	USA: Gebhard (1965)
5	11	18		(5·0)	USA: Gebhard (1965)
6	2	3		(5·0)	USA: Gebhard (1965)
7	1	2		5·0	G: Finke and Zeugner (1934)
8	0	0		5·5	G: v. Hentig (1925)
9	0	0		5·2	USA: Weinberg (1955, 1963)
10	2	3			
11	0	0			
12	1	2			

NB: G = Germany. Families: N = 62.

shows that living conditions in incestuous families seem on the whole to be unfavourable, one cannot take living conditions in West Germany from 1955 to 1965 as indicating a true situation of need, if in seventy-eight per cent of the cases one to less than three people shared one room. S. K. Weinberg (1963), basing himself on his sociological surveys in the USA, came to the same conclusions (in thirty-three per cent of cases there was less than one person to a room, in sixty-seven per cent 1·39 per room).

Education, occupation, attitude to other members of family and previous criminal record of incest offenders

The fathers in our survey group had almost all (ninety-three per cent) been to *Volksschule* (primary and junior school), a lesser number (five per cent) had secondary or middle-school education, and one was illiterate (two per cent). All the same only ninety per cent went through school in a regular way, while roughly ten per cent did not finish *Volksschule* (eight per cent), or did not go to school at all (two per cent). Altogether fifteen per cent had difficulties at *Volksschule*, i.e. they had to stay down and repeat one or two classes.

Because of the different educational system in the USA a comparison with American incest research is only possible with a great many reservations. Nevertheless a certain correspondence seems to exist to the extent that the American researchers also found a low percentage with higher education (four per cent in Weinberg, five to eight per cent in Gebhard and colleagues). According to the American research, incest offenders do not differ, as far as education is concerned, from other groups of sexual offenders with the exception of homosexuals who show a somewhat higher level of education (Gebhard and colleagues 1965).

Taken as a whole, these results seem to testify against the 'mental inferiority' of incest offenders which has been so often emphasised in writings on the subject (Forel, 1905; Wülffen, 1910; Rohleder, 1912; Sonden, 1936; Schwab, 1938; Holder, 1949; Plaut, 1960).

Almost seventy per cent had learnt a trade (specialist workers, craftsmen, and ordinary to middle-grade salaried

TABLE 6   Occupations of incest offenders

Glazier	Comptroller	Paint-sprayer
Electrician	Driving instructor	Carpet-layer
Welder	Navigator (ship's)	Machinist
Decorator	Lighterman	Roof-tiler
Tinsmith	Upholsterer	Carpenter
Master baker	Iron-moulder	Waiter
Demolition worker	Type-setter	Cook
Turner	Slaughterer	Publican
Locksmith	Mason	Chemist
Gardener	Ship's captain	Commercial assistant
Bank clerk	Technician	Seaman
Musician	Scrap-metal dealer	Unskilled labourer

employees), twenty-nine per cent were unskilled or trained workers, and one of those concerned practised a self-employed trade. Table 6 presents a picture of the various occupations.

The Kinsey Institute Research Group (Gebhard and colleagues 1965) made a most interesting discovery. They compared the group of incest offenders with eight other groups of sexual offenders and came to the conclusion that, at the time of committing the offence, incest offenders showed the *highest quota of married men/women* (eighty-seven per cent) and that these marriages were – to judge from the frequency of the breakdown of marriages and petitioning for divorce – at least *externally the most stable* (fifty-eight per cent had up to that time been married only once). To be sure, the relatively high ratio of separations (in our survey forty-eight per cent, in that of Gebhard and colleagues forty-one per cent) even if partly dictated by other factors in the composition of the group, could indicate 'a far-reaching crisis in society at large' (König) and show that a section of these incest offenders had personality problems and difficulties in choosing partners (cf. 'Personalities and interpersonal

TABLE 7   Marital status of incest offenders at the time of the offence, and past record of marriage/divorce: own results and those of Kinsey Group (Gebhard and colleagues, 1965, pp. 216, 236, 258, 578, 754)

Sources	N	Status at time of offence		Record of marriage/divorce		
		M. %	div./wid./sep. %	Married once %	twice %	three times %
Gebhard and Co. 1965	173	87	13	58	26	15
Own survey	58	96	7	52	29	29

Total of quantifiable cases of marriage/divorce recorded in the American survey: N = 143.

relationships of the married couples' [p. 124 f.]. As Table 7 shows, the results of our survey do not coincide absolutely with American findings but approximate to them well enough.

The image which society in general has of sexual offenders is probably formed by, amongst other things, the particular nature of the sexual offence and by the preconceived attitudes of public opinion towards the taboo or legal norm which has been contravened. Such a contravention succeeds in overshadowing all factors present in the offender's life up to that point – even those of his actions which could be given a positive value. Amongst society's reactions to sexually deviant forms of behaviour there are also to be found, in most cases, opinions which reflect certain stereotyped ideas, i.e. a combination of personal characteristics which often have a doubtful basis in truth tend to be confidently expected of every member of a particular sexually deviant group. This is the point at which one finds prejudices forming, a process in which, in Germany, popular magazines like *Bild-Zeitung* play a not inconsiderable role.

Is the incest offender a 'criminal'? On the basis of differentiated criminological analyses in the latest German and American research it can be stated that *as a rule incest has nothing to do with other areas of criminality* (Gerchow, 1955, 1965; Gebhard and colleagues, 1965; own survey).

The figures of those with previous criminal records (percentage of those previously sentenced by courts of law) vary between thirty-two per cent (Finke and Zeugner, 1934), thirty-five to forty per cent (Wagner, 1953), forty-four per cent (Gerchow, 1955), and forty-six per cent (own survey) in Germany and forty-nine per cent in the USA (Weinberg, 1963). A more detailed examination of the sentences and a comparison with other groups of sexual offenders shows, however, the following:
1) There were amongst the incest offenders a great many who, at the time of the offence, had only one previous conviction for a casual or petty offence (traffic offences; drunk in charge of a car; one instance of theft many years before, vagrancy, disturbing the peace, etc.: fourteen per cent in our own survey, twenty-five to thirty-four per cent petty offences and twenty-one to forty-four per cent single previous convictions in Gebhard and colleagues). 2) Compared with other groups incest offenders had the lowest 'disposition to crime', measured in terms of convictions per person (Gebhard and colleagues, 1965, p. 724). 3) The nature of the previous convictions makes it clear that (*a*) amongs-

incest offenders there is an extremely small tendency to acts of violence against the person (own survey: fourteen per cent of all previous convictions; Gebhard and colleagues: eight to fourteen per cent of those previously convicted) – this tendency is lower than in all other groups of sexual offenders except homosexuals (Gebhard and colleagues, 1965, p. 727); (*b*) amongst incest offenders there is an extremely low number with previous convictions for sexual offences in general and sexual crimes of violence in particular (own survey: 1·5 per cent; Gebhard and colleagues: 1·3 per cent); and (*c*) amongst incest offenders there is the lowest record of juvenile crime (seven to nine per cent according to Gebhard and colleagues 1965, p. 721). 4) Although, after homosexuals, incest offenders commit the least number of crimes against property, this kind of offence is predominant amongst such people (in our material sixty-nine per cent) or can be included amongst the punishable acts most frequently committed by incest offenders (eighteen to thirty-one per cent of those previously convicted in Gebhard and colleagues).

An exhaustive analysis of our material shows that only twenty-six per cent of the cases were criminologically 'unusual' and amongst that number there were some with seven or as many as sixteen previous convictions who could certainly be classed as 'criminal'. This is in contrast, according to the present-day state of research, to roughly three-quarters of the incest offenders who had either committed no crime up to the time of the discovery of the offence (more than half), or, from the manner and frequency of their previous convictions (a quarter), could not be classed as criminologically unusual.

The wives: age, frequency of divorce, illegitimate births, criminal activities

If one disregards the figures for divorce, which are partly conditioned by sampling factors, then there are sociologically and criminologically no remarkable outstanding features amongst the wives, unless it is the relatively high proportion of women with illegitimate children (there are no comparative data amongst other writings on incest).

The majority of the wives (eighty-three per cent) were

younger than their husbands, a smaller number (seventeen per cent) were mostly one or two years older (two women were eleven/seventeen years older respectively). Similar findings (eleven per cent older wives) were arrived at by P. Plaut (1960).

The number of husbands already divorced before the marriage in which the incest occurred (forty-eight per cent), corresponded almost exactly to the number of wives who had been divorced one or more times, although amongst this number (forty-seven per cent) there were less who have been divorced twice (about seven per cent) than amongst the men (about nineteen per cent). It must nevertheless be said – in spite of possible errors of sampling – that the quota of divorces is relatively high, if one considers that the divorce figures since 1948 for the German Federal Republic have declined (1965: ten per cent) and that between 1948 and 1965 the twenty per cent mark has never been exceeded (*Statistische Jahrbücher* [Statistical Yearbooks 1960–7]).

TABLE 8   Frequency of divorce amongst the wives (N = 58)

	Total No. divorced	Divorced once	Divorced twice	First marriage	Married 2 or 3 times to offender
abs.	27	23	4	31	(8)
%	47	40	7	53	(14)

No information about one case.

The most notable fact to arise is the large number of women with pre-marital or extra-marital children (fifty-one per cent). Of a total of forty 'illegitimately' born children only in seventeen per cent of cases was the father subsequently the woman's husband.

Of virtually no significance is the register of previous convictions (only 5 per cent had previous convictions for petty theft). It is worth noting all the same that ten per cent of the women had spent their youth in foster institutions – mostly because of sexual delinquency.

Sociological characteristics of the victims

Two closely interconnected factors are of especial importance for the development of the young personality: *civil and legal status at birth* (marital/non-marital) and *the situation in the family during childhood* (complete or incomplete family).

In our material the incidence of illegitimate children amongst female incest victims – a total of thirty per cent, twenty-seven per cent born of unmarried parents and three per cent outside marriage – is significantly higher than the average in the comprehensive birth statistics for the Federal Republic (highest figures for illegitimate births in the Federal Republic 1946: sixteen per cent, followed by a drift down to 1966 with 4·6 per cent, from *Statistische Jahrbücher der BRD* 1946–67). This is equally the case if one takes into account the relationship between unmarried births and social stratum (according to von Harnack, 1958: thirteen per cent in the 'qualified' and twenty-six per cent in the 'unqualified' stratum of workers).

Even if illegitimate birth carries with it the possibility of unfavourable influences, it must be said that it does not automatically mean there is a poor outlook for the young person (Specht, 1967, p. 45). It is only the family situation which accompanies illegitimate childhood which is of decisive importance.

Roughly forty-three per cent of the girls and women in our survey group had up to the discovery of the incestuous relationships lived together with both their natural parents, while fifty-seven per cent had often lived for long periods alone with the mother, and later with a stepfather (forty-six per cent) or with a stepmother (eleven per cent), and in most cases had more or less consciously witnessed the break-up of their parents' marriage. In most of the families with step-parents there also existed step- or half-sisters or brothers (a total of thirty-nine), a situation which not infrequently contributed to the formation of rival groupings and limited the development of clear behavioural roles as well as of intrafamily social control (cf. Chapter Five, 'Personalities and interpersonal relationships of the married couples' [p. 124 f.].

Amongst the daughters and stepdaughters in our survey those who were *first-born* predominated (fifty-one per cent), thirteen per cent were only children. In agreement with the sociological research findings of Weinberg (1963), in the USA, we find that sexual relations arise predominantly with the *eldest* daughter/stepdaughter present in the house at the time (Weinberg sixty-four per cent; own survey seventy-three per cent). Only in those cases where the eldest daughter offered resistance, was already married, or no longer lived at home, did the father turn his attentions to the next youngest daughter (in Weinberg almost fifty per cent).

The fact that almost all the girls had been to *Volksschule* (primary/junior school) (ninety-one per cent in our survey group) testifies in the first place against the hitherto much-represented view of an accumulation of 'intellectually defective conditions' amongst female incest victims (Stelzner 1924; Holder 1949). Only three per cent had been to a school for backward children, and two per cent to upper or middle (secondary) school (cf. 'Personality of female incest victims' p. 146 f.). Most of the girls (fifty-seven per cent) were still at school during the period of the offence, fourteen per cent were already in a permanent job. In nineteen per cent of cases being at school and at work were both within the period of the offence (only ten per cent were at home all the time). At the time of the legal proceedings forty-seven per cent already had an employer, the majority of these girls (sixty-seven per cent) were employed as trainee or salaried staff, and the remainder were unskilled workers (about thirty per cent, see Table 9).

TABLE 9   Occupations of female incest victims (N = 33)

1. Manual worker
2. Salesgirl
3. Hairdresser
4. Commercial employee
5. Bookbinder
6. Chemist's assistant
7. Doctor's assistant
8. Tailor
9. Domestic employee
10. Office employee
11. Hotel employee
12. Commercial assistant
13. Architect
14. Commercial correspondent
15. Seamstress
16. Nursery school teacher
17. Secretary
18. Nurseryman's assistant

5. Personalities and interpersonal relationships of the married couples

Whereas in the last chapter we sketched out the social background of the family, in the present one we will be discussing the personalities of the married couples, that is of the person committing incest and his wife. This will involve the identification of certain (normal) psychological and psychopathological traits, as well as the various forms of behaviour in these people and their interpersonal relations. In cases of father–daughter incest it would be a mistake to try and explain the sexual relations from the personalities of the incest partners and the immediate circumstantial evidence, without going into the relationships of the people who help shape the 'family atmosphere'. In this respect we now face the question of whether the internal constitution of the family was still intact before the start of the incestuous relations.

Husband and family father

The stereotyped image which one has as a rule of people who commit incest is no different basically from the other simplistic clichés current about people who commit sexual offences: 'primitive people with limited judgement about ethics and morals, who have a strongly developed, unrestricted, demanding sexual urge, and who are spiritually weak characters'. Does this thoroughly negative image correspond with reality? What can be said today, on the basis of previous research, is that it is certainly no single recognisable type who commits incest. Instead their personalities – expressed in simplified terms – range from those who are mentally normal, unexceptional fathers who care for their family correctly, to those who are already changed by the excesses of alcoholism and whose capacity for rational self-control has been limited. Thus incest is committed not only by those who are 'psychologically abnormal', but also by people whose original condition is psychopathologically 'unexceptional' (Rennert, 1958, p. 260; Gerchow, 1955).

In the following sections we shall examine the various research results individually.

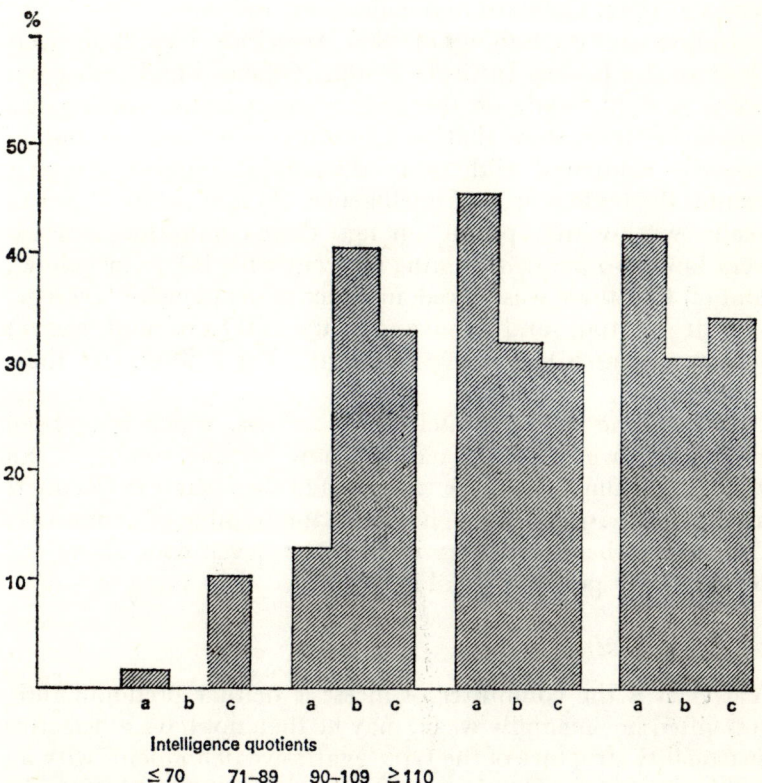

Figure 8. Distribution of the Intelligence quotients of incest offenders: as collated by Gebhard and colleagues. (1965, p. 679). N = 138.

Note: Intelligence quotients of 70 and below = 'weak-witted'; IQ 71 to 89 = 'slightly below average capabilities'; IQ 90 to 109 = 'average intelligence'; IQ 110 and above = 'above average intelligence'. a, b, c = three groups of people committing incest.

a) Intelligence

Whereas at the beginning of this century science accredited those who committed incest with being 'spiritually inferior' or 'spiritually and morally defective' (Forel, 1905; Wülffen, 1910; Rohleder, 1912), it had later to be accepted that the 'weak-witted' type was in no way dominant amongst these people (Eber, 1937). Now recent German, but more especially American, research in the last ten years has furnished conclusive proof of this (Mangus, 1953; Glueck, 1956; Mohr and colleagues, 1962; Gebhard and colleagues, 1965).

In line with the findings of other American research projects those of the Kinsey Institute groups (Gebhard and colleagues 1965, p. 679), made on the basis of comparative intelligence measuring tests, show that (*a*) committers of incest and homosexuals – compared with other sexually delinquent groups – exhibit the highest level of intelligence, (*b*) that the incidence of really 'weak-witted' people amongst those committing incest is very low (two per cent to nine per cent with IQ 70 or below), and (*c*) that there was a predominance of people with 'average' (IQ 91 to 109) and 'above average' (IQ 110 and above) talents (sixty to eighty-five per cent). Fig 8 illustrates these results.

Even if the German intelligence surveys, which have been mostly of an exploratory nature, show varying results, it can still be said that – with the exception of three surveys (Rennert 1958; Plaut, 1934; 1960) – here also the number of committers of incest of below average intelligence never rises above the level of forty per cent (see Fig. 9).

b) Aggressiveness

Yet even if the committer of incest is neither predominantly less gifted nor mentally weak, may he then not have a defective personality structure of the type 'aggressive delinquent, with an erotic strain' (von Hentig 1925)? What is the truth, what can be proved?

As we saw in the last chapter (see p. 119), as far as the period before the offence is concerned there is no ground for considering acts of violence an essential characteristic of this group of people. On the other hand psychopathological surveys have

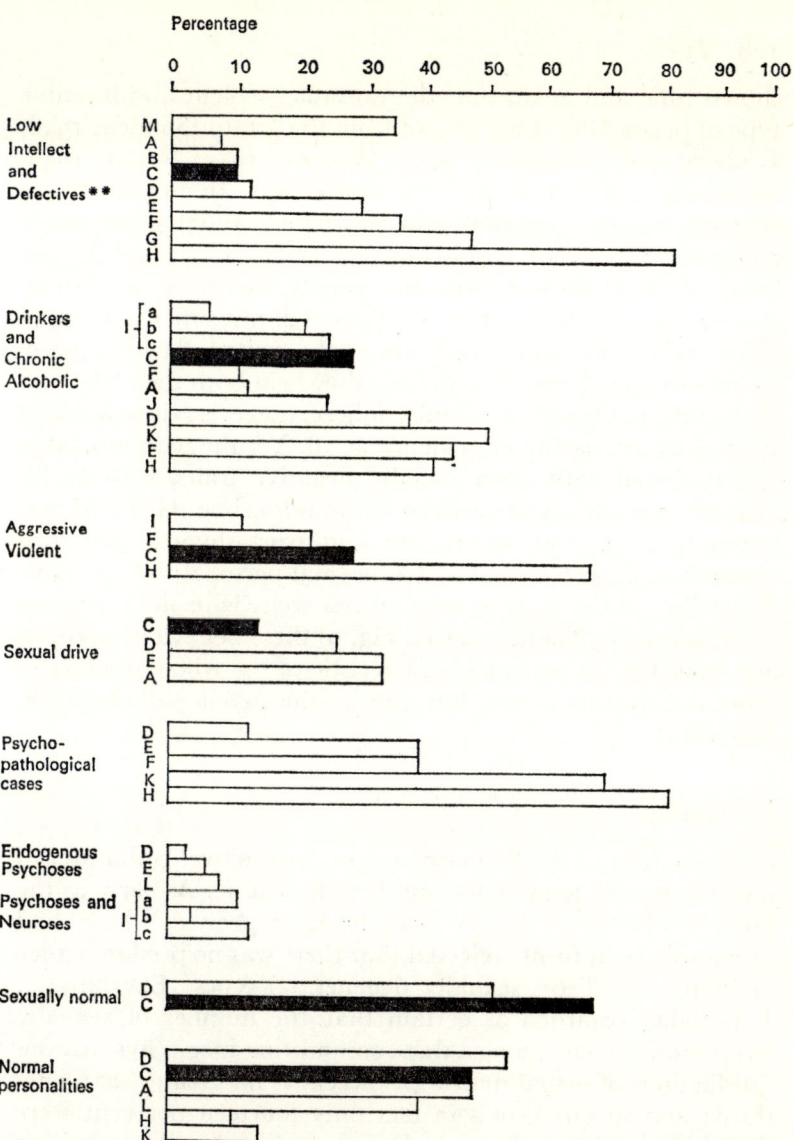

Figure 9. Psychopathological findings amongst incest offenders: collation according to my own researches and other literature.*

Notes: *Capital letters = works from which the findings are taken: A = Gerchow 1955, 1965 (N = 57), B = Wagner 1953 (N = 20), C = own findings (black columns), D = Schwab 1938 (N = 413), E = Többen 1925 (N = 30), F = Finke and Zeugner 1934 (N = 60), G = Rennert 1958 (N = 16), H = Plant 1960 (N = 83), I = Gebhard and colleagues 1965 a(N = 56), b(N=66), c(N=25), J = Sonden 1936 (N = 391), K = von Hentig 1925 (N = 24), L = Holder 1949 (N = 14), M = Eber (1937) (N = 100)—size of test sample occasionally given in parentheses.
** See (a) Intelligence (p. 93).

shown time and again that the unstable, violent and irascible type of personality is not absent from the group (Sonden, 1936; Kinberg and colleagues, 1943; Wagner, 1953; Szabo, 1958; Weinberg, 1963; and my own researches). In the American research survey (Gebhard and colleagues, 1965) there was a constant ten per cent, and in our material even twenty-nine per cent, of those fathers who are usually described as 'family tyrants' or despots (see Fig. 9). They will not suffer any opposition within the family, they are easily excited, flaring up and quick to anger. From time to time they beat both their wife and the children. Outside the family sphere, however, these forms of behaviour are hardly in evidence at all. Yet they are to a large extent linked with other socially negative traits, such as for example a tendency towards more serious crime (Gebhard and colleagues, 1965) or alcoholism and work-shyness (my own researches: cf. g) 'Normal and abnormal personalities', p. 132). According to the present stage of research (with the exception of the survey by Plaut, 1960, cf. Fig. 9) these behaviour patterns are, however, in no way characteristic of the whole number of those committing incest, but only of the psychopathologically abnormal.

c) *Sexuality*

Even the idea of the 'hypersexual' or 'instinctive' committer of incest is hardly tenable for any length of time. As early as the nineteen-thirties a theory was being expressed which had previously been firmly rejected that there was no predominance of 'hypersexual' or 'sexually degenerate' types (Eber, 1937). It is today regarded as certain that the number of sexually hyper-active men amongst those committing incest (five to seven satisfactions of sexual desires per week) is no greater than one-third; and in our group in fact only fourteen per cent were thus identified (see Fig. 9). It is therefore hardly surprising that the sexological researches of the American Kinsey Institute Group (Gebhard and colleagues, 1965) show that committers of incest, as opposed to most other groups of sexual offenders, homosexuals, and rapists of adult females, have, on average, the lowest frequency of satisfaction of sexual urges. Furthermore our surveys showed that the frequency of coitus by these men in their marriage is no higher than that in a control group of previously unconvicted married men of the same age (Gebhard and colleagues, 1965, p. 599). Neither could the Swiss psychiatrist Wyss (1967) establish any connection (statistically) between the sexual behaviour of incest offenders and increased sexual activity (at least seven satisfactions of urges per week over a lengthy period of time).

Admittedly this has still not taken into account everything about the general psychological and physiological constitution of these men. It is a fact that a fair number of the fathers and stepfathers are in their fifties and a smaller number in their sixties, and we must thus ask ourselves how matters stand with the initial symptoms of the ageing process, i.e. with the decrease in vitality and the associated loss in the dynamic of the sexual urge (libido and potency). Apart from some disturbances in potency brought about by illness (dystrophy) in some former German prisoners of war (Gerchow, 1953, 1955), the American surveys show – in addition to some transitory disturbances in potency caused by the effects of alcohol (twenty-eight per cent of the more elderly incest offenders) – a relatively low percentage (ten to fourteen per cent) of serious disturbances affecting the capacity for erection (Gebhard and colleagues, 1965, pp. 482–3), we ourselves found only three per cent. The results of the Kinsey Group surveys nevertheless leave no possible doubt that the number of serious as well as occasional (caused by toxic substances) disturbances in potency is highest amongst those committing incest, when these are compared to other groups of sexual offenders.

If neither 'hypersexuality' nor disturbances in potency are characteristic of incest offenders, then one might come to consider whether it is not a matter of 'weak sexual desires'. The latest Swiss surveys (Wyss, 1967, pp. 26, 48) reach the conclusion that incest offenders with less than one sexual satisfaction per week and a serious 'constitutionally conditioned lack of drive in all areas of vitality' are a rare occurrence. But all these findings say nothing about the sexual relations between these men and their wives, i.e. about the harmony or subjective satisfaction of the marital sexual relations (see p. 137).

d) Alcohol

If there is one especially prominent psychopathological characteristic of incest offenders then it is the relatively high percentage of 'chronic alcoholics' which marks off this group from other groups of sexual offenders (see Fig. 9). At least a fifth to a quarter are drinkers and (already addicted) chronic alcoholics (twenty-four per cent of our test material). Dependent on alcohol, some to the point of mania, disturbed in their relationship with the world around them, in particular with their family, these men at times also neglect their dependants from an economic point of view.

Earlier German surveys mention even higher figures of forty to forty-five per cent (Többen, 1925; von Hentig, 1925; Schwab, 1938). More recently in Switzerland, in dealing with 160 (unselected) paedophiliac sexual offenders of various categories, a closer connection has been established between 'chronic alcoholism' and the committing of incest (Wyss, 1967), and American research workers came to the conclusion that those committing incest, compared with other sexual offenders (homosexuals, exhibitionists, paedophiles, etc.), showed the greatest number of alcoholics (Apfelberg and Pfeffer, 1944; Frosh and Bromberg, 1939; Glueck, 1956; Gebhard and colleagues, 1965). Only the heterosexual rapists (whose victims were children) would appear with forty per cent addicted drinkers to outdo the incest offenders (Gebhard and colleagues 1965, pp. 147, 743).

Quite apart from the fact that the alcoholic is indeed for this reason in no way predominant among this sector of people, it would be a mistake to deduce from suitable cases a direct specific, causal connection between alcohol and incest: 'Alcohol as a group phenomenon seems to be of no greater significance in the predisposition to a sexual offence than in the predisposition to non-sexual criminal offences. The condition of being under the influence of alcohol does indeed encourage punishable behaviour, but still does not determine the form and manner of this behaviour' (Gebhard and colleagues, 1965, p. 740). At a later juncture we shall turn our attention to the criminogenous significance of alcohol in incest (see Chapter Seven, 'Predisposition', p. 170).

e) Psychopathy

'Psychopath' is not only a current term of abuse, but it is also a typological concept of classical psychiatry – as inexact as it is vague. Sometimes it is used to signify all quantitative deviations of personality (from an average norm), from which the respective person, or even society, is suffering (Schneider, 1959); at other times it is used to mean exaggerated instances of certain human characteristics, arranged according to certain 'psychopathic types' (Gruhle, 1922), and even to apply to such character types as can be arrived at by using the most predominant and usual kinds of reactions and attitudes as a basis (Kretschmer, 1955). At this point we come to the question of the natural tendencies which the term 'abnormal personality' suggests – a question which is answered firmly by many and evasively by some experts. One must agree with one of the foremost authorities in this field when he admits that: 'Some clinical terms which have been in use for a long time are in retreat . . . even the term "psychopath" is a little suspect and it will soon be a thing of the past' (Schneider, 1959, p. 36).

Faced with these uncertainties in the field of definition and differential diagnosis, it is not surprising if earlier researches offer a picture of complete discrepancy, and the figures of psychopathy of incest offenders vary between three per cent (Sonden, 1936), sixteen per cent (Schwab, 1938) and eighty-eight per cent (Plaut, 1934, 1960) (see Fig. 9). At all events we can hardly come to firm and binding conclusions on the basis of such findings.

f) Mental and emotional illnesses (*endogenous psychoses*)

The view, which is often widely held, that sexual offenders must be – in general terms – mentally ill, is frequently a response to the incomprehensible nature of what has happened. Yet, in fact, the majority of sexual offenders who are expertly examined show no sign of mental illness (Rasch, 1962), and it is precisely those who do who are the exceptional cases amongst the incest offenders (see Fig. 9: three to six per cent). This is equally true of the 'emotionally ill', of the manic-depressive kind. Amongst the sixty-seven offenders in our sample we found only one endogenous psychosis (confused sense of perception) of the manic-depressive variety (see Chapter Eight, p. 200).

The survey results of the American Kinsey Institute Group are not relevant in this respect, since they present incest offenders suspected of psychoses and neuroses as one group (Gebhard and colleagues, 1965; four to twelve per cent; see Fig. 9). Yet it is worth noting that some Anglo-American experts are of the opinion that schizophrenic patients are to a large extent obsessed with ideas of incest and that the incest-wish is often a precursor of schizophrenic psychoses (Fleck and Lidz, quoted from Kahn, 1965; Wahl, 1960).

g) *Normal and abnormal personalities*

But if it is 'not the mentally sick man, the half-wit, the hypersexual man, nor the sexually abnormal, nor the man whose character is most inferior, who predominates amongst those committing incest', as Eber (1937) showed over thirty years ago, then what is it that characterises the psychopathologically abnormal personality amongst those committing incest? How is it different from the normal personalities in this group, and how large is the number of these latter?

On the basis of previous experience this last question can be answered more easily than the first two. The most recent German research on incest has given the number of offenders whose 'initial condition was primarily normal' (Gerchow, 1955, 1965) or 'without mental or character disorders' (Schwab, 1938) as fifty per cent to almost sixty per cent. Brain damage and associated 'personality changes' are very rarely diagnosed neurologically or psychopathologically, and sometimes not at all (Nürnberger, 1955), and the most recent Swiss survey showed that those committing incest had a very low incidence of neurotic disorders in childhood (anxiety, stammering, *pavor nocturnus*, mother fixation, etc.), and of character or sexual neuroses when adult (Wyss, 1967). Our own material shows that fifty per cent are socially and psychopathologically quite normal fathers to their families (see Fig. 9). These facts show once again that consideration of the nature of the deed is no ground for any firm conclusions on the personality of the person committing it.

Our statistical analysis gives rise to the following picture of the most outstanding psychopathological behavioural traits of the fathers and stepfathers: *violent and irascible* (twenty-nine per cent; highest phi-correlation with the psychopathologically abnormal), *maladjusted at work* (twenty-three per cent: constantly changing jobs, unsatisfactory performance at work, and work-shy), alcoholics (twenty-four per cent), *previous criminal record* (forty-six per cent; but only the fourth highest phi-correlation with the psychopathologically abnormal), and *highly sexed* (fourteen per cent: five to seven or more sexual satisfactions per week). In fifty per cent of our cases these traits were present more or less strongly expressed and in various combinations.

The most clearly expressed is the combination of violent and irascible, i.e. unstable, aggressive forms of behaviour and an unhealthy dependence upon alcohol (phi-correl.: ·61***), dipsomania, and maladjustment at work (phi-correl.: ·56***) as well as of brutal-irascible behaviour and maladjustment at work (phi-correl: ·37**). Offenders with a previous criminal record often also prove to be maladjusted at work (phi-correl.: ·42**), and, finally, there is also a connection between instability at work and attempts at suicide (phi-correl.: ·30*). (*NB:* Significance levels: *** = 1%; ** = 2%; * = 5%.)

In order to illustrate this documentation we will now sketch briefly the most striking social and psychopathological features of a forty-year-old father of a family:

Case 39: The subject, an artisan, already twice married, was committed to prison for two and a half years for repeated incest and rape (of his daughter). He had been before the courts for theft on three previous occasions, was a jack-of-all-trades, and constantly changing his place of work. His attendance at his place of work was, at most, irregular. For five or six years past his consumption of alcohol had been rising steadily, and in the last two or three years he had been drinking six to ten bottles of beer a day. Under the influence of the alcohol his sexual desires were aroused and he demanded sexual intercourse with his wife almost daily, and at least five times a week. He liked to accompany the act with sadistic practices (whipping). Easily excited, he would suddenly flare up and become angry and then strike his wife and children violently, mostly when he was drunk, but also when sober. At other times he would be weeping and moaning as helplessly as a child

The man was physically healthy, normally sexed and lively, his intelligence was average, from a clinical neurological angle there were no pathological signs. Although the man most certainly had an abnormal personality it could not be given any psychiatric value-classification as an illness – he was pronounced to be fully responsible for his actions.

Although this case acts as an example for the most abnormal personalities, it is no model case which could cover all the variations and degrees of severity of the psychopathological behaviourial traits in this group. There is no such thing as *the* abnormal personality of the incest offender, just as there is no such thing as *the* incest offender. What can be said though – at least on the basis of our analyses – is that the abnormal incest offenders can be distinguished from the relatively speaking normal group by (*a*) *a reduced self-control* (forty-one per cent) of aggressive and/or oral, and/or sexual instinctive impulses, as well as (*b*) *lack of an ordered way of life or planning of their lives* (thirty-four per cent). In so far as there are any suspect forms of behaviour amongst the 'normal' incest offenders at all they never appear in a socialised form, and on closer examination of the individual case they lose their psychopathological importance altogether.

If one looks at the documentary material we have so far presented from the point of view of prejudice against sexual abnormalities, one will observe the following end result: the stereotyped picture of the incest offender, almost completely composed of socially negative, 'unhealthy' qualities, seems not only to be coloured by the manifest incomprehensibility of the incestuous act to the average mind, but is also probably the result of a generalisation of 'abnormal' and socially undesirable personality traits which are indeed observable in a section of the incest offenders, but not in the majority.

Wives and mothers

The life partner of the man who commits incest and the mother of the victim has hitherto had little time devoted to her in writings on the subject, with some exceptions (Schwab, 1938; Gerchow, 1955; Weinberg, 1963). Yet neither is the development of the victim's personality fully comprehensible nor can a measured judgement be passed on the 'incest situation' unless one considers the wife and mother, and her role in the marriage and in the family.

a) *Outstanding social and psychopathological features*

Generally speaking the personality picture of these women does not depart from that of the normally intelligent average woman of the lower social strata. Admittedly the breadth of variations is greater: the artistically active woman of sensibility and above average intelligence is as much represented as the promiscuous personality damaged by alcoholism or epilepsy who has hardly any relationship to her marriage and family. The *majority* offer no more crude social or psychopathological abnormalities than these, but many of the working wives (forty per cent) are worn out at work and physically overtaxed.

TABLE 10 Outstanding social and psychopathological features in wives of incest offenders: surveys by Schwab (1938) and our own survey

Schwab (1938, pp. 271–2)	%	Own survey	%
Sexual promiscuity	10	Sexual promiscuity	22
Sexually 'overexcitable'	6	Prostitutes	3
'Asocial by nature'	6	Child removed from care	8
'Bad housekeepers'	6	Unstable way of life	29
'Easily noticeable as "abnormal" characters'	14	Drinkers	5
Weak-witted	4	Previous criminal record	5
Having psychoses	2	Formerly in children's home	10
Epileptics	1	Epileptics	2
Total abnormal personalities	app. 25		app. 25

In a minority of cases, i.e. about a fifth to a quarter of these women, it is always possible to find forms of behaviour in their life history which are chiefly characterised by an *unsettled way of life* (twenty-nine per cent) and *promiscuity* (twenty-two per cent) (see the above table for details). Before their present marriage to the incest offender these women had mostly had no fixed abode, were frequently without a steady job, were bad housekeepers, and took little or no trouble over their children (at the time illegitimate) who were growing up in institutions or foster-homes. Some had been sexually delinquent in their youth (nine per cent), or had been taken into the care of the local authorities (ten per cent), a smaller group had previously been before the courts (five per cent), fallen victims of alcohol (five per cent) or become prostitutes (three per cent). While some had nevertheless succeeded in establishing a kind of stability in their marriage to the incest offender, the remainder continued to lead promiscuous lives and remained in various respects psychopathologically and socially abnormal (alcohol, epileptic changes in character, low capabilities).

b) *Physical illnesses*

The question of the state of health of the wife of the incest offender is not without importance. It is posed time and again because a physical illness can, under certain circumstances, exert an unfavourable influence on the married and family life, or the absence of the wife and mother (hospitalised, bed-ridden) caused by the illness may even encourage the start of incest in individual cases.

Thirty-three per cent of the wives in our survey had gone through physical illnesses before or during the period of incest, and this had more or less adversely affected their general well-being. Over half of these (nineteen per cent) suffered illnesses of a more serious nature (cancer of the stomach, epilepsy, heart diseases, lung tuberculosis, stomach ulcers, diseases of the lower abdomen, etc.), and in about sixteen per cent of cases the illness had a negative effect on sexual relations with the marriage partner (according to Schwab, 1938; Finke and Zeugner, 1934: fourteen per cent).

Now what significance do these findings have for the interpersonal relationships of the married couple and the forming of the family situation and 'atmosphere'? In the next section we will try to give an answer to this.

Internal situation in the family before incest

The family make-up before the beginning of incestuous relationships has increasingly become the focal point of research in the last thirty years. Swedish experts have already recognised that incestuous activities, together with some other kinds of behaviour, had to be analysed as an expression of certain attitudes towards family life (Riemer, 1936). In Germany it was above all Gerchow (1953, 1955) who saw in the structure of the marriage 'perhaps the most important and also most interesting hypotheses' for incest (1965, p. 43). Proceeding on the basis of present-day results from international surveys there can hardly be any more doubt as to the frequency of unstable, and crisis-ridden, marriages and disturbed family relationships before the start of incestuous relations (Gerchow, 1955; Szabo, 1958; Bromberg, 1948; Rinehart, 1961; Kahn, 1965; Gebhard and colleagues, 1965). The recognition of this fact is indeed hardly surprising, but it neither fits into the framework of one section of earlier incest research (Schwab, 1938; Többen, 1925; and others), nor does it support the contention of those who draw up the laws that incest alone disrupts the marriage and family order, and who think that penal legislation will protect this order, which was non-existent even before the incest began (see p. 81).

What, then, is the extent of the disrupted 'family order', what are its symptoms, and its causes? Statistical comparisons are problematic, since the definitions of 'disturbance' and 'disorganisation' of marriage and family life vary from source to source. Reliable sources quote the figures for 'disturbed' marriages, before the start of incest, as roughly fifty per cent to sixty-five per cent (see Table 11). Yet, in fact, the percentage of 'disturbed families' is greater still if one subjects the family situation to a differentiated socio-psychological analysis.

TABLE 11 Frequency of marriages already 'disturbed before the start of incest': comparison of sources

Authors	Eber (1937)	Gerchow (1955)	Szabo (1958)	Gebhard
%	56	51	50	66

In Gebhard and colleagues (1965, p. 218) figures covering the period before incest are only available for one group (fifty-six).

In our own survey we discovered symptoms of 'disorganisation' in eighty-eight per cent of cases; the symptoms were of various kinds and had various causes, but only twelve per cent could be described as relatively 'free of disturbance'. Admittedly here 'disorganisation' does not mean only the external, social destruction of the family (ten per cent), but also the kind of marriage which is merely a façade to the outside world, with more or less overtly expressed hostilities and a family atmosphere of constant tension, or it can also signify the complete interpersonal indifference of the married couple one to another (where tension is more or less absent), i.e. four per cent of cases. We will shortly examine the main causes of these symptoms by means of a catalogue (Table 12) and quote some individual cases as illustrations.

a) The married couple's social and emotional relations

In an overwhelming majority (seventy-six) of all cases ('disturbed' and 'disturbance-free' families) the family structure was formed by and bore the stamp of the dominating, though extremely varied, influence of the husband and father. In only nine per cent of cases was the wife at the head of the hierarchical system, controlling, in most cases, her soft, unstable and childishly dependent husband. There was also a relatively small percentage of the more democratically orientated families (twelve per cent), in which a couple, in view of their mutual solidarity, would not allow such overt bids for dominance as occurred in practically all the remaining cases. The most remarkable features of the predominantly father-centred family structure were, on the one hand, the discrepancy between the father's 'authoritarian' claim to leadership and his actual behaviour, and, on the other, the mother's inability or physical incapability of guaranteeing the (emotional) harmony or solidarity of the family. The symptomatic forms of this kind of family make-up, expressed as it is in very simplified terms, are just as variable as the processes of interaction and the causes which give rise to it. This will best be understood by examining the more prominent symptomatic forms and causes of family disorganisation given below (see Table 12).

TABLE 12 Main causes of disturbed marriages and family relationships before the beginning of incest (N = 58)

Disruptive factors, i.e. causes of disorganisation	N	%
Husbands		
Negative influence on marriage and family	30	51
'Family tyrant'	18	31
Violent and irascible	17	29
Drinker	14	24
Violent and drinker	11	19
Wives		
Negative influence on marriage and family	13	22
Drinker	3	5
Extra-marital relations	3 (7)	5 (12)
Behavioural traits indicating unsettled way of life	9	17
Drug taking	1	2
Physical illnesses	19	33
Both partners		
Negative influence on marriage and family	8	14
'Asocial'	6	10
Polarisation of relationships in family	6	10
Sexual problems caused by		
Wife's absence	17	31
Unsatisfactory sexual relations for husband	14	26
Restriction of sexual relations because of illness of wife	9	17

Because of incomplete information the factors of sexual disturbance are based only on N = 54. The division into categories is in all cases based on a consensus of two or at most three sources of information (father, mother, daughter). The multiple nature of most causes of disorganisation naturally leads to overlapping.

Amongst the causes of disorganisation is the *negative influence of the husband* on the shaping of the marriage and the family in the first place (fifty-one per cent). In this connection we must call to mind that group of psychopathologically abnormal fathers who constantly give rise to family tensions by their aggressive behaviour and their excessive consumption of alcohol. The *family tyrant* (thirty-one per cent) is recruited almost exclusively from this type of unstable personality, who, with his claim to possession and power, keeps the family in a state of fear and tension. These fathers, who are often quite incapable of relating their despotic claim to leadership to their social efforts for the family, tend towards abuses of authority of every conceivable kind, and they not infrequently endeavour to secure their dominant position by socially isolating the members of the family from the world outside. Swedish, American and French surveys have pointed time and again to the patriarchal position of such fathers, who set up a 'primitive family order' (Kinberg and colleagues, 1943; Bromberg, 1948; Wagner, 1953; Weinberg, 1963; Rinehart, 1961; Plaut, 1960; Gebhard and colleagues, 1965; and others).

The following case from our survey is in no way unique; yet it shows at the same time that men of this type can be completely normal in their jobs and outside their family.

Case 18: Subject: a forty-six-year-old man, at the start of incest married for twenty years (first marriage). At work (he was a middle-grade civil servant with a lifetime appointment) he was regarded as irreproachable. He had never been before the courts before, and was now sentenced to several years in prison for incest with his own daughter. He had lived for many years in his own one-family dwelling with his wife, who was somewhat younger, had a very simple personality make-up, and was constantly worried about the well-being of the family. The marriage and family life had suffered from the outset because of the man's personality: easily excited and irascible, he would beat his wife on the least pretext. He ruled despotically over all the members of the family and would not tolerate opposition. He would accuse his wife of lying and deceiving him before their marriage, and was constantly reproaching her, quite without reason, for being a bad housekeeper. Ten years before the incest began the wife had considered divorce several times when the husband's extra-marital relations came to light as a result of a sexual illness. The marriage became more and more tense and unharmonious, mainly because of the husband's developing taste for alcohol. The family situation had become increasingly tense in the years immediately before the incest as the wife tried to have her husband placed in a home for alcoholics. Then he began, quite groundlessly, to accuse his wife of having extra-marital relations. Moreover, he suspected his daughter, who was at the stage just before puberty, of having relations with men. Even before it came to incest he controlled his daughter's every word and action, tried to isolate her socially, examined her clothes for signs of sperm and became paranoically jealous.

It is clear that in such cases the character of the family is merely an outward façade, in which frequently economic necessity is the only motive for keeping the marriage going. Social disorganisation and breakdown is complete in those cases where *both partners* exert a negative influence on the shaping of the family (fourteen per cent). Incest under these mostly *asocial* conditions is only the last in a line of consequences of the total external and internal breakdown of the family.

Case 39: Subject: thirty-nine years old, skilled worker, for some years only occasionally employed because of bad health, already before the courts on two occasions, a violent drinker, temporarily on probation for drunkenness. The wife was some years younger and came from a family with lots of children and a 'bad name'. At the age of sixteen she had been in a home as a result of sexual delinquency and she had two illegitimate children by different men. She left them in institutions and foster-homes and did not worry about them. They were temporarily removed from her care by the authorities. The marriage developed unfavourably from the start. There was the burden of two other children born before the marriage (both of them were the husband's and they were later legitimised). The family lived in various camps, from which they were always being asked to move on, because the husband caused a scandal when he was drunk, and beat his wife and children. The wife had sexual intercourse with other men on several occasions. Sexual orgies involving the married couple and friends who were present took place even when the children were in the same room. Both man and wife had several times filed for divorce but had later withdrawn the petition. As a result, the parents had been deprived of control over their children. In the judicial justification for this decision it was stated: 'Relationships within the family . . . as observed by the youth authorities up to this point, have in all decent respects been completely destroyed, so that it would no longer be responsible to leave the children in this milieu.'

In this case from the very outset there was no question of a close emotional and social family relationship being formed. The parents, themselves victims of failures in socialisation, necessarily failed to perform the basic tasks for the family. The situation is exactly the same when the wife and mother, as a result of her promiscuity, alcoholism and unstable way of life, hinders the establishment of a firm family basis, and when even the most indulgent and forgiving husband capitulates (eight per cent).

Case 44: The subject is a thirty-six-year-old woman. After *Volksschule* she had acquired a nursing qualification and, having escaped from East Germany, she lived for years without any work or fixed abode. At eighteen she was put into a young people's home from which she escaped several times and lived for a while off men friends and on the profits from shady deals. All the reports from the home described her then as 'cheeky' and 'mendacious'. Before her marriage she had brought a child (the victim) into the world, and two years later she married (the offender). The marriage brought no stabilisation of her personality or way of life. Even shortly after the marriage she did not appear at home for days on end, had affairs with strangers, and was drunk most of the time. Eventually she was sentenced to one month's imprisonment for various offences against the drugs laws. She was having extra-marital relations at the time the incest was committed, and had left it to her husband to look after the daughter. The latter, who always cared for the family in an exemplary fashion, occasionally sought refuge and inner release in drink.

No less than twenty-two per cent of the women exerted – though with varying degrees of emphasis – a negative influence on the marriage and family life (see Table 12), and so contributed – mostly unwittingly – to the beginning of incestuous relations.

Finally, those cases are constantly to be encountered in which the reasons for the disorganisation are to be found in a polarisation of relationships within the family (ten per cent), which have become deeply and firmly entrenched long before the beginning of incestuous relationships. This peculiar psychosocial family constellation, sometimes at this early stage with an already incestuous colouring, is characterised by a close, exclusive tie between the child and one parent, mostly of the opposite sex, and the splitting of the interpersonal relations of parent and child into two rival groups. Feelings of rejection of the child brought into the marriage by the mother, and preference for the child born of the marriage, shown by one or other parent, and a constant meddling in the affairs of the family by the parents-in-law, are further causal factors in this situation.

Case 9: Subject: fifty-one years of age, married for the first time, comes from a well-ordered, comfortable family background, has hitherto not been before the courts and is well adjusted socially and in his work; financially he cares very well for his family; his monthly income is up to DM 2,000 and the living accommodation is more than adequate. The wife is somewhat younger and has a daughter from her first marriage. The victim is the fruit of the present union. Even at the start of the honeymoon there had been a serious disagreement between the couple, because the husband had openly voiced his strong dislike of his stepdaughter. In the early years of the marriage this was a constant source of tension and several violent, open scenes. The husband suspected his wife and his stepdaughter of 'plotting against him' and accused them of trying to lead 'an easy life' at his expense. Even when his own daughter was a very small child (later the incest victim) he had tried to alienate her from her mother and preferred her quite openly to her half-sister. Thus a situation of polarisation had been arrived at within the family long before the start of incest: on the one side the father and his own daughter, between whom a deep relationship of trust had developed, and on the other side the mother, who together with the daughter of her first marriage, was increasingly forced on to the defensive.

Mistrust, envy and jealousy had poisoned the family atmosphere long before the start of incest, and threatened the emotional stabilisation of the individual. The 'area of secrecy' here runs through the middle of the family and is not just the result of incest. The disruption of marital sexual relations is at this point sometimes only one of several possible reactions to the loss of social as well as emotional equilibrium within the family.

b) The married couple's sexual relationships before the start of incest

From the material presented earlier it is easy to understand that a disruption of the interpersonal situation can occasionally also overlap on to the couple's sexual relationships, or, conversely, disturbed sexual relationships may become a special motive behind marital tensions.

If one examines the statistics on heterosexual satisfaction within the framework of marriage (Table 13) it is worth noting that in forty-one per cent of cases – according to the concurring testimony of both marriage partners – *already before the start of any incest* there were no 'regular' sexual relations, i.e. in some cases there had been no physical contact for one to four years (six per cent), or (thirty-five per cent) sexual intercourse occurred only rarely (less than once a week). In these last-mentioned cases gaps of several weeks or even three months are not unusual. Completely similar results are shown by both French and German surveys (Gerchow, 1955: in thirty-two per cent of cases the men were in a state of 'sexual need' before committing incest; Szabo, 1958; in fifty per cent of cases the sexual relations of the married couple were more 'infrequent' than 'regular').

TABLE 13 Sexual relations of the married couple before the start of incest: heterosexual satisfactions per week (N = 54)*

	Extremely seldom (intervening gap of at least one year)	Seldom (less than once)	Seldom to regular (⟵⟶)	Regular (one to seven times)
abs.	3	19	5	27
%	6	35	9	50

*Concurring statements from both partners – in a further four cases there was no agreement, and in one case the man was living alone before the incest began. According to Kinsey and colleagues (1964, p. 518) American men aged between thirty and fifty have sexual relations on average 1·8 to 2·9 times a week.

Now, these figures so far show nothing, and it will have to be questioned whether one can even talk of 'disturbed' sexual relations as far as this not inconsiderable number of married couples is concerned (two-fifths of the sample).

In fact twenty-six per cent of the men (N = 14) stated that *'marital sexual intercourse before the start of incest was not "satisfying"'*, and they described their wives as 'frigid', 'cold' or 'not interested in sex'. In only one of these cases did marital intercourse take place 'regularly', in the remaining cases it occurred 'rarely' or 'very rarely' (see Table 13). The Kinsey group provides even higher percentage figures: twenty-eight to forty-six per cent of men were 'rather' to 'very unhappy' (Gebhard and colleagues 1965, p. 601). What were the causes? Almost a third (thirty-one per cent) of the wives behaved in a rejecting fashion towards their husbands. They either refused outright to have sexual relations, withdrew from their husbands and appeared not to be interested in sex, or they were very reluctant and made the excuse of being ill (seventeen per cent predominantly with abdominal complaints). In the first motive-group were often those wives who rejected their husbands because of their alcoholic excesses or violent behaviour. Admittedly there are other possible motives at work here, as, for example, frigidity, anorgasmia, etc. However this may be, an analysis of the material makes it quite clear that the restriction of marital sexual intercourse to an extent which departs from the norm ('extremely seldom', 'seldom': see Table 13) is plainly evidence of a much more general social and emotional disturbance in the relation between the two partners. Just how great a part can be played here by the fateful emotional and social estrangement caused by the results of war has been shown by surveys conducted amongst German P.O.W.'s who returned home from Russia and who then committed incest (Gerchow, 1953, 55). The completely normal marital and family situation may also have its internal system of relationship altered in a negative way by external influences or vicissitudes of fate.

After examining these factors in the family situation before the start of incest one will hardly be able to refrain from concluding that *incest is not the cause, but the symptom or result of a disturbed family order*. In the two following chapters we shall explore by means of the empirical results of surveys, the social, psychological and criminogenous results which grow out of such a disruption of marriage and the family.

6. The personality of female incest victims

A family with a disturbed internal constitution can fulfil its primary tasks of the socialising and personality-forming of the children only partially, or not at all (cf. 'Functions of the taboo' [p. 58]). Against the background of the previous chapter we have therefore to observe the consequences for the complete development of the young girl which arise from disorganisation of the family. In so doing we must take into account in each individual case the influence on the development of the personality exerted by the incest situation, and examine for any noticeable psychopathological forms of behaviour or for symptoms of disturbed personality, as well as establish the exact times of these manifestations. The lack of information about this subject in previous studies of incest will restrict us mainly to our own statistical evidence.

Prior remarks on puberty

We must remind ourselves once more that here (in our examination) we are dealing predominantly with girls who were, at the beginning of the incestuous relationship, on the threshold of puberty or already in the middle of this maturing period; moreover that the overwhelming majority (seventy-two per cent) were, at the time of the examination/legal enquiry, between twelve and twenty years of age, and that some were even adult (between twenty-one and twenty-eight). A few brief remarks on puberty therefore seem not to be out of place.

Today there no longer remains any doubt that puberty, a term generally used, together with 'youth' or 'adolescence', to refer to that period of life between childhood and adulthood, is (*a*) a *critical stage*, a 'normative crisis', i.e. a normal phase of increased conflicts (Erikson, 1966) and (*b*) represents for the young person a time when he is most easily hurt and endangered. This period is characterised by processes which stretch to include the first hidden changes of the endocrinal secretions (above all of the sex hormones), physical development (growth), the formation of the primary and secondary sexual distinguishing marks, the psychological rebuilding and reorientation of the personality, and the gradual taking over of an adult role. Psychologically the remoulding of the infantile sex life is also linked with the readiness of the child in puberty to transfer its reawakened erotic-sexual needs and wishes to its parents. In the normal course of events these tendencies are overcome and followed by the dissolution of parental authority, a process which introduces the extra-family choice of partner/friend (boy or girl), fiancé(e). During this period, when 'the most important, and also the most painful efforts' are needed (Freud, 1922, p. 89), the young person is thrown hither and thither between his defensive efforts at controlling his sexual drives, efforts called forth by his conscience and social taboos, and a massive breaking through of drives as a result of his physical maturing. The successive building up of sexual conduct, modes of behaviour, and practices, all take place in a short span of life, when the young person is still searching for a clear definition of self. A picture of self, and an 'identity' (Erikson, 1956), has still not been found. Social isolation and sexual laxity are but two extreme opposing possibilities to which a failure to deal with the sexual problems of this period of life can lead. Social and psychological, not to mention contemporary forces and influences can contribute to, or broaden, this danger zone. In the case of the young girl it is the frequently occurring, narcissistically coloured, *need for increased status*, linked with the 'enjoyment of her own erotic attractiveness' (Groffmann, 1962, p. 166) which can be a *danger to herself*, although this need not at all be a question of primarily sexual needs or wishes. Thus it happens that the young person has long seen the failings and the unconvincing attempts at concealing the facts in the moral system in our society, and for that very reason experiments with sex in a provocative way, but has to suffer the repercussions of failures should playful, unfettered intimacy turn into habitual promiscuity or develop into a neurosis. Whether and how far this stage of self-endangering is prematurely developed and strengthened in the girl by contemporary *acceleration* (by an earlier recognition of sexual maturity and an impetus to pubic growth) is difficult to judge in all but individual cases. It is nevertheless worthy of note that amongst young mothers below the age of sixteen there is a high number of girls of precocious development (Böhm and Böhm, 1956). In other German researches sixty per cent of girls up to the age of twenty had experience of pre-marital intercourse (Beer, 1960), and in a more recent survey of 155,800 girls in the Federal Republic nineteen per cent of the fourteen-year-olds, twenty-three per cent of the fifteen-year-olds, thirty-seven per cent of the sixteen-year-olds and fifty-two per cent of the seventeen-year-olds were already deflowered (Kepp, 1967). Moreover, the blurring of the dividing lines between the generations, by the initial level of 'adulthood', and at the same time by the 'youthfulness' in the style and fashion of clothes and make-up for young girls, have not gone without influence on the mutual effect of heterosexual attraction. The attractiveness of the female sex for the man has broadened to include young girls who had previously been rendered undesirable by clothes and make-up specific to their age, and who did not yet exert the 'charm' which today belongs to the commercial, and at the same time collective, attributes of behaviour and make-up of girls in puberty. If, however, the acceleration process and experience of attractiveness are linked to a desire to have the sexual rights of an adult, additionally stimulated by a need for increased status, a situation of temptation arises, the outcome of which depends upon various component factors (amongst the most important are previous disturbances of personality and family milieu). Sexual offences against girls in puberty must therefore always be viewed against the background of this specific phase-conditioned moment and 'epochal psychological' influences (Müller-Lückmann, 1963).

School performance and intelligence levels

Stereotyped images are more easily drawn than corrected. The traditional picture of the 'weak-witted' daughter who is abused by her father, or of the 'sexually unrestricted' because 'spiritually weak' girl who seduces her father, does not conform to reality. Admittedly there are cases embodying such features, but they are not the rule, and are not material for typical cases.

Levels of intelligence and capabilities are reflected in performance at school. Failure and bad reports do not, however, always indicate a low intelligence level, but they can be signs of an emotionally disturbed personality. About two-thirds of the girls in our enquiry had gone through school this far without having to repeat a year, but a third had under-achieved academically (see Table 14), i.e. they had stayed down for at least one year, or because of their failure they had had to change to a lower type of school, or they had not quite completed their schooling (left in seventh year). A half of the school failures were in no way less gifted than others, but their capacity to perform was hindered by emotional disturbances or the consequences of sickness (lengthy absences from school); in the case of the other half there was evidence of their being less gifted. The quotas of non-achievers in no way depart from the picture obtained on the basis of surveys in German *Volksschule* in the nineteen-fifties (roughly a third of school under-achievers: Fromberger, 1955).

TABLE 14 School performance of female incest victims (N = 70)

	School achievement inadequate	*adequate*	*School performance satisfactory*	*good*	*Not at school*	*No information*
abs.	22	16	18	9	3	2
%	31	23	26	13	4	3

These facts alone would seem to testify against the idea that less gifted or 'intellectually sub-normal' girls are especially numerous amongst female incest victims (Stelzner, 1924; Holder, 1949; Plant, 1934, 1960). Then how do matters stand regarding the intelligence levels of these girls and women?

Of the girls psychometrically examined *roughly three-quarters* (seventy-seven per cent) *were quite 'normal'*, i.e. they were classified as of 'average' (sixty per cent) or 'above average' intelligence (see Table 15). Almost a quarter (twenty-three per cent) returned verdicts of 'below average' so that only a *small group* (eight per cent) was unequivocally 'weak' (IQ from 73 to 79), and the remainder (fifteen per cent) were on the borderline between normal intelligence and the less-gifted (IQ 81 to 89). Three girls in this latter group returned 'low' intelligence quotients (IQ 86, 87, 89) only because they put on an act of bravado as a barrier during the period of the examination. As is shown in Table 15, the division of intelligence quotients amongst the girls we examined is quite close to the normal one for citizens of the German Federal Republic between the ages of six and sixty, only the 'highly gifted' (IQ above 127 to 130), and the very lowest group (IQ below 70) are missing in our picture.

TABLE 15 Intelligence levels of female incest victims between six and twenty-three: Intelligence quotients divided according to the Hamburg–Wechsler Intelligence Tests for children (= HAWIK) and adults (= HAWIE) (N = 47)

Intelligence according to IQ

Test	Extremely low	Very low	Low	Average	High	Very high	Extremely high
HAWIE	69	70–79	80–89	90–109	110–119	120–129	130
HAWIK	62	63–78	79–90	91–109	110–117	118–126	127
abs.	0	4	7	28	6	2	0
%	0	8·5	14·8	59·6	12·7	4·4	0
Normal standard	2·2	6·7	16·1	50·0	16·1	6·7	2·2

Based on a standardisation of HAWIE and HAWIK (Wechsler 1956, p. 52, and Priester 1958, p. 61).

What picture is there of the intelligence structure of these girls and women? Apparently the more practical kind of intelligence seems on average better developed in them than the theoretical (only the older [16 to 23] group of girls, however, presented any statistically significant difference). In this connection it is worth noting that there is a relatively low level of average knowledge and education, as well as a relatively low average performance in arithmetic compared with the other intelligence capabilities (the mean value difference between the values recorded and the standardisation norms is, however, throughout less than two points). It will have to be assumed that this state of affairs results from a low demand for general education on the part of the girls' milieu. From another angle it could also reflect the girls' own attitude of low intellectual interest.

If one takes into account, apart from the girls psychometrically examined (N = 47), those whom for various reasons it was impossible to measure for IQ (N = 5), but in whom under-intelligence can be excluded on other grounds (school reports, other research), and those in whose cases only school reports or testimonies were available, then the picture is as set out in Table 16.

TABLE 16 Distribution of intellectually 'normal' and 'sub-normal' female incest victims (N = 68)

	'Ordinary' IQ 86–121 at school 'satis.' to 'good'		*Extraordinary* IQ 73–84 at school 'weak'	
abs.	39	15	8	6
	54		14	
%	80		20	

For two of the girls examined in the sample there is no reliable evidence.

Viewed as a whole the intelligence level of this group is thus in no way characterised by below average talents or weakness (roughly twenty per cent), but by the predominant number of 'ordinary', normally intelligent girls and women (roughly eighty per cent). A comparison with the intelligence level of juvenile female victims of other sexual offences (predominantly non-incestuous offences) lends support to the assumption that there is a lower incidence of both mild and serious degrees of subnormal intelligence amongst female incest victims than amongst other groups mentioned above (Geisler, 1959:

forty-seven per cent of 'below average' intelligence; Nau, 1965: twenty-seven per cent 'under-intelligent', fourteen per cent 'subnormal'; Schönfelder, 1968: thirty-two per cent girls of 'below average' intelligence).

Symptoms of disturbed personality development

The forms in which personality development disturbances express themselves in the growing girl are as manifold as the factors which cause them. The symptoms of such disturbances may come to the notice of the world around, and can themselves precipitate difficulties in interpersonal relation to the environment, but they can also remain concealed from outsiders, and merely present a burden to the people concerned. In one case it may be a matter of mere physiological (functional) disturbances or difficulties without there being any recognisable physiological cause(s) (psychosomatic symptoms), in another it may be mere inner psychological difficulties and abnormalities in behaviour (*behavioural disturbances* and *neuroses* in the more narrow meaning), and in yet other cases it is more a matter of socially undesirable attitudes and forms of behaviour which can, under certain circumstances, come into conflict with the law (disturbances of behaviour of the 'in need of care and protection' type, juvenile delinquency). Not infrequently such symptoms appear in combinations or consecutively, and the causes are not always to be found merely in the family milieu. Inherited physical constitution, diagnosed or suspected brain damage, can equally cause symptoms of disturbances in personality development, stimulate and strengthen them and even – like the age of the individual – determine the form and mode of expression of the disturbance.

a) Psychosomatic symptoms

As Table 17 shows, twelve girls and women suffered eight different psychosomatic symptoms (twenty times) and by far the most frequent were *enuresis nocturna* and *diurna* (wetting oneself at night and in the day). In the majority of these cases ($N = 10$) several psychosomatic symptoms appeared simultaneously or alternately, or one was dealing with only *one* symptom amongst others, as for example *pavor nocturnus* (crying out in fear in one's sleep), somnambulism (sleep-walking), fear of suffocating, fear of death, or signs of need of care (lying, stealing, sexual laxity, etc.), isolation from social contacts, moods of depression of a psychogenous kind, etc. This catalogue of symptoms already conveys the impression that one is dealing with maladjusted girls whose personality development has been disturbed.

Was the incest situation a cause or a part cause of the psychosomatic symptoms? Generally not, for in the case of ten girls the symptoms had already appeared before the start of incestuous relations, and in only two cases were they in evidence afterwards (the chi-square of the variation in division is not significant). Whilst psychosomatic disturbances typical of childhood (enuresis, encopresis, obesity) were dominant before incest, only after the beginning of it were there two cases of functional disturbances such as heart trouble, and difficulties with breathing and sleeping. But even in these latter cases there is no discernible causal connection between the symptoms and incest, since both victims exhibited signs of a disturbed

TABLE 17 Psychosomatic symptoms of female incest victims: (N = 12)

Psychosomatic symptoms	Frequency of occurrence of symptoms
Enuresis nocturna (night bed-wetting)	9
Enuresis diurna (wetting in the day)	2
Encopresis (dirtying oneself)	2
Obesity	1
Serious difficulty in getting to sleep	1
Heart trouble	2
Attacks of breathlessness	2
Recurring pains in the body	1
Total amount of symptoms suffered	20

personality development even before the beginning of the sexual relations. Disturbed intrafamily relations in the majority of cases (N = 10), however, would indicate harm brought about by immediate environmental influences (milieu).

b) Symptoms of dissociality

When a sexual offence against a juvenile is made public, especially if it is an offence against a girl, public opinion and the reactions of those connected with her usually vary between extreme revulsion and sympathetic belittling of the seriousness of the offence. The role of the girl is 'identified accordingly as that either of an innocent victim or of a dissocial precocious seductress' (Schönfelder, 1968, p. 1). Though the question of latent or manifest sexual immorality in juveniles before incest seems to be of absolutely central significance for the forming of opinions on sexual offences, what we mean here by dissociality is much more, i.e. socially undesirable, or simply anti-social forms of behaviour and attitudes. Let us try to explain this by means of a catalogue of symptoms (see Table 18).

TABLE 18 Symptoms of dissociality and frequency with which subjects affected: number of girls affected = 17*

Nature of symptom	Frequency of occurrence
Frequent lying	7 (= 10%)
Truancy	3
Difficulties in upbringing	3
Running away from home	3
Away from home for days/weeks	3
In sexual danger (provocative behaviour)	3
Undesirable sexual relations	9 (= 13%)
Falsification of signatures	1
Embezzlement	1
(Repeated) theft of money	3
Total frequency of occasions	36

* Percentage figures relate to N = 69.

Seventeen girls and women (twenty-five per cent) showed in the pre-pubic period or in puberty, symptoms (ten different ones) of dissociality of a more or less serious degree (total affected instances: thirty-six, twelve girls were at times affected by more than one symptom). Amongst the symptoms of dissociality undesirable heterosexual relations were mostly to the fore – usually with one or more adult or juvenile males. This is not specific to female incest victims but – as has been known for some time – it is absolutely specific to the dissocial development of girl minors. (According to Gregor and Voigtlander (1918) about forty-six per cent, according to Tumlirz (1952) sixty-three per cent, and according to Specht (1967) sixty-one per cent of girls with anti-social behaviour were sexually dissocial, in male juvenile offences theft and other property offences were dominant.

In the majority of cases the rapidly worsening anti-social reactions could be traced back into the pre-pubic period. Four girls with such habitual forms of behaviour fell foul of the law because of repeated theft or embezzlement, two were put under care and protection for having undesirable sexual relations, loitering, and difficulties at school, and in one case the authorities ordered protective custody for the same reasons.

Case 11: A young woman almost twenty years of age, married; incest with natural father from fifteen to nineteen, child as a result. The first signs of dissociality appeared at age nine or ten. In the third year at school the girl was recorded as a 'very difficult child', frequently lying and performing badly (lack of attention and difficulty in concentrating). At school she was regarded as 'impertinent, truculent, aggressive, and lacking in willpower' and was said 'not to have fitted in with her classmates'. She was removed from this class for her behaviour. In a report at the time the class teacher showed signs of general discouragement, and the girl's father himself told the school authorities he was afraid the girl would 'slide back' again. At the time the girl was twelve/thirteen the complaints from school increased: she was alleged to have spread 'dirty stories' round the class. The school's opinion was that it was 'urgent' that she be put in a home. At about the same time she came to the notice of the police for several minor thefts of money, running away from home, and staying out all night. It was also at about this time that she began to take a noticeable interest in boys. The *Jugendamt* (youth office) recommended protective custody. After the beginning of the incest (at age fifteen) she had her first heterosexual relations with a juvenile, and began to frequent 'doubtful' drinking places. Despite the total disruption of her life after the birth of a child by her father – who no longer wanted the eighteen-year-old to share his house, so that she was forced to stay in various camps and homes for unmarried mothers – there was no sign of increased sexual dissociality. After the discovery of the incest a certain (at least outward) stability seemed to set in when the girl married.

From the point of view of the course of dissocial behaviour this is an average case, which looks no different from that of a girl not involved in incestuous relations. This girl had drawn attention to herself long before the incest began and the dissociality ran its course quite independently of the latter. Is this always the case? By no means. The following example demonstrates a process of growth of dissociality and the specific conditions of incest.

Case 10: Girl aged nineteen and a half years, with whom the forty-four-year-old stepfather had had, at the time of the main legal proceedings, incestuous relations for five years. With time there had developed – not without the initiative of the victim – a regular love relationship (which continued between the ages of eleven and seventeen). The girl, who had shown exceptional sexual curiosity at the age of eight, and who, as an eleven-year-old, had frequently hidden and watched her parents having intercourse was, at the age of thirteen and after the beginning of incest, reported for the first time at school for lying, spreading 'suggestive stories' and using foul language. Her behaviour was variously described as 'cheeky', and her approach to other people as 'brazen', 'lacking in respect' and 'erotically provocative'. In class she quickly became an outsider, but, through her 'extravagant' behaviour, her strong interest in boys and her ability to attract attention, she exercised an 'undesirable' influence on the more 'unstable' girls in the class (teacher: 'They flocked around her'). On these grounds, and at the instigation of the headmaster, she was removed from the school and sent to another. The girl's behaviour, as reported by the school, was subject to periods of restless depression, in which the class teacher heard her express on several occasions the wish to be sent to a children's home, without the former having any knowledge of the true background: 'She is always longing for the day when she can leave home. She hates her mother and doesn't want to have any contact with her again.' As time went by the school registered disturbances in academic performance. A thoroughly understanding guardian was unable to exert any influence on the fourteen-year-old. By that time the teachers already knew of the girl's 'disturbed emotional condition'. She was first entered on police records at the age of sixteen for 'loitering', and finally, later in the same year, she fell foul of the law as a result of several thefts of money. After this she attempted suicide with sleeping pills. As a motive for this she gave 'lack of love' on the part of her mother. At about the same time she had also taken up sexual relations with a young foreigner and had been intimate on several subsequent occasions with men, most of them older than herself.

The girl's family and home relationships were depriving in their effect. As the illegitimate and unwanted child of a mother still young, who had on earlier occasions been in a mental hospital, she had, up to the age of eight, grown up without a father and in unfavourable conditions, cared for mostly by her grandmother. Her mother showed her no love and was occasionally violent to her (kicking, biting and beating). Her stepfather, an unstable, weak and under-achieving personality, was the first one in her life to adopt a friendly and caring attitude towards her. She soon came to regard him as her 'guardian angel' against her harsh mother. This unstable woman's activities even caused the stepfather to seek the advice of his daughter's legal guardian. As a result of the seriously disrupted family environment – the mother did not attend to her duties in the home either – the girl's legitimate younger brother also became in need of care and protection. Truancy, running away and theft had already caused him to be put on probation in his first years at school.

A further detailed knowledge of the life history and personality make-up of this young girl would leave no doubt as to the influence of the *incest situation* on the process of moral collapse and on the failure of personality development connected with it. But – and there is equally little doubt of this – the early emotional neglect of the girl by her unfeeling and unloving mother and the sudden indulgence by her stepfather during the pre-pubic period, must have contributed in a fundamental way to the disturbance in personality development. The polarisation within the family which had already taken place before the start of incest was then brought to perfection by the incest situation, and the influence of the latter brought the girl's psychological stresses, caused by various factors, to a crisis.

Let us remember that eighty-eight per cent of the families examined by us showed signs of disorganisation before incest, fifty-seven per cent of the girls had often grown up for long periods alone with their mother, or later with a stepfather (forty-six per cent) or a stepmother (eleven per cent), and thirty per cent were born illegitimately, or outside the marriage. The number of girls in these statistics with anti-social forms of behaviour is at various times around a third (ten per cent illegitimate, seventeen per cent from families including a step-parent, all, that is twenty-five per cent, from disorganised families) and is thus in no way surprising. The influence of the incest situation as a causal agent of the signs of dissocial behaviour could not be statistically quantified (in the groups), for ten of the girls already suffered symptoms of moral collapse (about twenty in number) and in nine cases there were sixteen anti-social phenomena after the start of incest (two of the latter girls were anti-social even before the beginning of incest). Admittedly this does not mean that there is no case in which incest produces signs of moral collapse or encourages or reinforces such a process. But analysis of the material of these relatively disturbed girls and women shows that the decisive (pathogenetic) factors conditioning their faulty development could in the majority ($N = 13$) of cases be traced back to an early, conceivably unfavourable, environment which was of relatively long duration. Essentially it is distinguished by (*a*) the absence of a continuing, stable relationship with an adult who is the object of love, (*b*) the lack of a uniform, consistent educational attitude, and (*c*) the total absence of a mother, a lengthy break in the mother–child relationship before the age of four to six, or a mother–child relationship which is unsatisfying from the outset. As a result of constant changing between mostly contradictory systems of education and expectations in the surrounding world, the girls' orientation towards unambivalent and reliable social roles remains fragmentary (from institution to institution, from grandparents, foster-parents to the mother, from the family with a father to the family with a stepfather, and so forth). Both the following cases are examples of this.

Case 50: Sixteen-year-old illegitimate girl, spent the first five years of her life with her mother in the house of her maternal grandmother, from six to eight she was in a children's home, then she went back to her mother, who in the meantime had remarried. From the age of eight to nine she lived with her mother at the house of an uncle, since her parents had now separated. After that mother and daughter spent two years in a camp without the stepfather. At thirteen she was put in a home because of sexual delinquency, and when she was released two years later she returned to living with her mother and stepfather. Serious disturbances in the mother–child relationship (the mother rejected such a relationship) which were apparent from the beginning, constant change in the persons responsible for upbringing and education, and instability in relations with the surrounding world – these were the decisive peristaltic factors in a failure of personality development.

Case 43: These emotional deprivations and instability in relationships with the surrounding world are as nothing compared with those in the following case. Nineteen-year-old girl, born illegitimately to a promiscuous mother with a criminal record. The child had been removed from the mother's keeping: fostered till the age of twelve months, in a home from two to three, with her mother and a man later to become the stepfather ('uncle') from four to five. At the age of five she went to stay with an aunt, from seven to nine she was in a foster-home, from ten to eleven in a children's home, at eleven she went back to her mother and stepfather. As a result of sexual delinquency she spent her sixteenth year in a home; after this she returned once again to the mother and stepfather.

It is easy to guess how much suffering and tragedy must lie behind the dry lists of dates in such a brief sketch! The lack of security and love which these girls experience from early childhood, often accompanied by hostile threats from the world around them, make their frequently negative and fatalist attitude to relationships with other people and their lack of trust entirely understandable. A seventeen-year-old, who described herself as 'quarrelsome and argumentative', revealed her loss of confidence in herself and her tension-ridden relations with those around her in the remark: 'I'm not interested in what other people think about me. They'll only think the worst anyhow. But as they go on talking about me I know that I'm still good for something, because if they were to stop talking about me, that would be even worse!' She preferred to be seen in a negative light by other people rather than not at all. It is precisely in this type of girl that one encounters over and over again a primitive, purely opportunistic realism, characterised by a completely amoral attitude towards sex and other spheres of experience. Thus it is that one seventeen-year-old, who showed signs of anti-social behaviour before the start of incest, for years allowed herself to be paid for having sexual intercourse with her stepfather. Whilst others similarly took advantage of the situation to secure favours for themselves, such as being allowed to go out in the evening or to go to the cinema etc., one sixteen-year-old literally got financial credit from her own father! The lack of an older 'conscience' who might guide behaviour and provide social orientation, and the frequently associated infantile adherence to the pleasure principle (*Lustprinzip*), leads in most cases to constant collisions with the demands of reality. One young girl, sacked from various trainee positions for shirking, and who, in the early years of her life, had been seriously emotionally neglected by her mother, and later often ignored in favour of her half-brother, said, in her own description of herself: 'Mostly I don't do what I ought to, like working, for example; sometimes I just don't feel like going, so I just stay at home. I wasn't interested any more in the job I had started to learn. Because I'd rather have learnt something better, but then I would have had to go to school for a year and I didn't want to do that.' Not infrequently one can discern behind the indifferent, apparently emotionally cold behaviour of these girls moods of dysphoric resignation, which approximate to a feeling of helplessness and hopelessness ($N = 6$), and under certain circumstances can lead to attempted suicide ($N = 2$).

All these peculiarities are not limited to antisocial female incest victims, but belong to a very familiar and well-studied psychopathological picture of immorality of a neurotic and non-neurotic variety (Aichhorn, 1925; Zuliger, 1957; 1960; Bowlby, 1956; Künzel, 1965; Specht, 1967; and others).

c) Special neuroses and other behavioural disturbances

It will by now have become clear that the psychopathology of female incest victims is completely non-uniform, and does not in any way differ from the symptoms and noticeable signs of disturbed personality development in childhood and in adolescence – with perhaps one possible exception, about which we will be talking later. But in general the ensemble of psychopathological phenomena only increases, the more observation proceeds.

TABLE 19 Symptomatology of behavioural disturbances of various origins in female incest victims (according to case history)

Kind of symptoms and signs of disturbance	Frequency of occurrence	
Specific anxiety symptoms	7	5 patients
1. Fear of death	1	
2. Fear of suffocation	1	
3. Anxiety dreams with hallucinatory phenomena on waking	1	
4. Fear of going to sleep (phobia traits)	1	
5. Claustrophobia (special neurosis)	1	
6. Pavor nocturnus	2	
Suicidal tendencies	7	7 patients
7. Attempted suicide	4	
8. Thoughts of suicide	1	
9. Danger of suicide in states of emotional decompensation	2	
Disturbances in social contacts and performance	17	15 patients
10. Failures at work	3	
11. School failure (patients of normal intelligence)	7	
12. Isolation from social contacts	7	
Other		
13. Somnambulism (in one case with illusory perceptions)	2	2 patients
Total frequency of occurrence	33 i.e. 22 patients	

Note: Because some symptoms were suffered more than once the second column would appear to give a higher number of patients (29), but in reality this is only 22. The list of symptoms also contains those cases with psychosomatic disturbances and (sexual) delinquency.

The group of *behavioural disturbances with a more or less tangible neurotic structure and genesis* (development) is represented by twelve of the girls (about seventeen per cent) in the sample. The symptoms of these girls and women stretch from serious isolation from social contacts, through the whole edifice of anxiety symptoms (fear of suffocation, fear of death, claustrophobia, failures of normally intelligent patients at work and at school, and attempted suicide [see list of symptoms, Table 19]). Symptoms that could be diagnosed biographically show a particularly high frequency in this group (eleven different symptoms which occurred on seventeen occasions), not counting those disturbances which only showed up when a differentiated diagnosis was carried out (e.g. psychogenous depression, vague feelings of anxiety, sexual conflicts, hypochondriac fears, inferiority complexes, etc.). The disturbances in some of these girls are of special interest, because here, as in no other case, the psychological attempts at mastery involved in the incest experiences colour, and in the last analysis shape, the whole psychopathological picture. Here one is dealing with *special neuroses*, in fact with four *traumatic neuroses*. The often complicated connections between the formation of symptoms and incest can only be shown here in a very fragmentary form.

Those girls who were still at the adolescent stage (sixteen to twenty years) were either haunted by terrifying recurring dreams, plagued by obsessive brooding on the experiences of incest, or their condition had become one of physical and emotional collapse liable to be brought on by external or internal stimuli connected with the incestuous events (e.g. an imagined smell of alcohol, the sight of certain objects). One young girl who (after almost ten years of incest) suffered a serious emotional breakdown and almost a physical collapse, whilst performing an intelligence test which would not normally have roused any sexual associations, later showed an almost compulsive, constantly recurring need to talk about that *awful thing* (incest), yet at the same time she sought to stop herself from so doing. This peculiar ambivalence towards the 'compulsion' which serves the need for inner unburdening, this compulsion to talk about the incest (compulsion towards repetition), is one basic characteristic of traumatic neuroses: the need to unburden oneself of the painful tension-producing experiences, and, at the same time, the need for 'fear' which creates a defence against painful reliving of the experience. The symptoms in which this tendency was expressed in our four girls are different according to the individual. The following case illustrates this aspect of disturbances in the form of a recurring dream.

Case 9: The set of symptoms which the patient suffered first appeared some two to three years after the start of incest with her own father at the age of about sixteen. First of all there were anxiety dreams, in which an unknown man would appear, approach her bed and sometimes try to strangle her. The scene was almost always the same, with the same feeling of menace and anxiety which then led her to wake up. Occasionally she would wake up quite suddenly, jump out of bed and then suffer delusions, in which the father was seen as a threatening attacker. In the course of one such scene she ran out into the hall, yet still did not recognise her father who happened at that moment to be arriving at the front door. She only awoke from her somnambulism when her father calmed her. He later told her how she had attacked him. These anxiety dreams became less frequent as time went by and disappeared altogether after her father had been arrested. Some little time after the onset of the symptoms described above the girl developed a fear, bordering almost on phobia, of going to bed at night. After the father's arrest this disappeared also. On the other hand various indefinable fears came to the surface as soon as it was dark. At such moments she occasionally was subject to an almost compulsive, anxiety ridden fantasy that her father was about to come home from prison at any moment. An examination of the incestuous relations over several years between father and daughter brought to light the following fact, so highly informative for a study of the symptoms. At the age of thirteen the girl had visited her father at his place of work, as she had done on many previous occasions in the past. For some reason the father did not want to go back with his daughter to his family until the following day, so that both had to spend the night in the father's office flat. The girl then lay down in the evening on her father's couch, which again had no special significance, since she had on several previous occasions spent the night there. The father was still working, so that when he returned he found his daughter already half asleep. The girl could not remember exactly whether her father had had any clothes on when he came to her, but she could recall that when she awoke he was already completing coitus with her. The one thing that was stamped clearly in her mind about this initial scene of incest was that she had not resisted, as indeed she did not on any subsequent occasion. Neither had she understood at all what was being done to her. Only when she was sixteen did she come to appreciate the full gravity of everything that had happened. She suffered serious feelings of guilt, particularly towards her mother, with whom her relations had already for some time been very tense; she repeatedly tried to make her father understand that their relationship was 'a sin'. At about the same time the first nocturnal symptoms of anxiety appeared. It is worth noting in this connection that since early childhood, encouraged by the polarisation of relationships within the family, the girl had been bound to her father, trusting him implicitly and endowing him in her own mind with 'godlike' omnipotence ('I idolized him'). This unconditional trust would not allow her to think that he might do anything 'unjust' or 'wicked'. The conflict within her was therefore so much greater when she became fully aware of how a taboo had been broken and how impermissible their actions had been, and her internal defence mechanisms were on longer sufficient to mask what had happened, the 'sin'.

The connection between incest-trauma and the anxiety dream can hardly be said to have been demonstrated here, if one remembers that (*a*) the father appeared in the delusions and adopted the same threatening attitude as the unidentified man had done previously in the dream and (*b*) that the dreams ceased as soon as the father was arrested. The dreams date from the time when, unable any longer to suppress the pain aroused by a chronic traumatic experience (coitus caused the girl to feel disgust) in which she played a passive, tolerating role, the girl became fully aware of her 'sin' and the vicious circle of tolerating, feeling guilty, and having an ambivalent attitude towards the father, took its course. Also noteworthy in this connection are the phenomena of physical escape at times associated with the dreams: i.e. physical flight when in a somnambulous or somnolent state. In this one can see an active part of the (repressed) inner defences against the father's sexual desires, which indeed they externally never failed to accompany (since the girl was in fact in her turn strongly attached in incest to the father).

With this example we have tried to show what role incest can play in the pathogenic conflict of the formation of neurotic symptoms. Admittedly – and this should be emphasised here – 'trauma' is a relative concept, i.e. whether and to what extent an occurrence has a 'traumatic' effect differs according to individual cases, and is greatly dependent on the structure of the personality or neurotic predisposition (Ferenczi, 1934; Fenichel, 1960). In all four cases above conflicts were already present before the beginning of incest, centred around the relationship towards the parents, in two cases conditioned by strong wish-attachments with incestuous undertones on the part of the daughter towards the father, and in all cases by disturbed family relationships. They explain the manifold (psycho-) neurotic complications which arise in conjunction with the traumatic symptoms. Shyness in social contact to the extent of isolation, unstable moods, moods of depression with thoughts of suicide, disturbed sense of self-evaluation and mistrust, disturbed capabilities at work and hypochondriac fears, these are only a few of the very numerous neurotic symptoms which give at least a rough idea of the extent to which these girls were disturbed in the continuity of their personality and their adaptation to reality. The trait common to them all is the ambivalent guilt-laden attitude towards sex, and their own sexual role, expressed in the recurring questions of the girl whose dreams we have already depicted: 'Will I ever get married? Of course I shall never marry. How could I tell my husband about what happened?' Here the experience of incest has become a conflict-producing or sustaining agent in a set of sexual problems, which, situated between 'abhorrence' and 'attraction', arouses fears for the future and places the girl's own sense of identity in question.

In contrast to specific neuroses and non-specific neurotic developments one encounters a different situation when dealing with those behaviour disturbances which are not only reactions to environmental influences but also, or perhaps primarily, have an organic background. The majority ($N = 10$) of the fourteen less gifted girls showed behaviour disturbance signs (manifestations of depression, hypochondriac fears, isolation from social contacts, attempted suicides, etc.). Only nine girls were suspected of having brain damage, and only in one case was this clinically and neurologically demonstrated (epilepsy). The girls whose intelligence quotients were between seventy-three and eighty-four were all noticeably slow in their thought processes, lacking in critical faculties, and weak at arithmetic.

One patient had a congenital heart defect (in the auricle septum), and one girl suffered attacks caused possibly by damage to the brain organisms. Lack of talent and harm caused by milieu are closely interwoven in all cases, and stamp the whole psychopathological picture.

How do matters stand, then, with the personality disturbances with which we have dealt here, and the *connection in timing between manifestation of the symptoms and incest?* As we have seen, there is an unmistakable influence exerted by incestuous relations on the formation of symptoms in traumatic neuroses. Yet this is obviously not applicable to all the symptoms (dealt with in this section) of behavioural disturbances, since the totals show no statistically significant accumulation of signs of disturbance after the start of incest.

d) Manifestations of depression

As well as the relatively high percentage of incest victims with anti-social forms of behaviour (twenty-five per cent) another remarkable percentage figure provided by our survey is the relatively higher number of girls and women with depressive tendencies (twenty-eight per cent). The depressive emotional qualities of the nineteen girls concerned were characterised basically by moods of dysphoric suspicion, feeling oppressed, or conditions of complete helplessness and hopelessness, in some cases by the wish 'to give oneself up'. A third ($N = 6$) carried out attempts at suicide, and two other girls had thoughts of suicide. In most cases it was a question of *protracted psychogenic depression* (in the sense of Kielholz, 1965) brought about by chronically disrupted family relationships and/or the incest situation which often persisted for some years. Especially characteristic were the long-drawn-out extent of time and the depressive feelings of failure in those cases of previous disturbance of mother–child relationship (home, foster-homes, etc.) and an incest situation of lengthy duration (see p. 159).

Diagnostic classification of personality disturbances

The foregoing sections dealt with the symptomatology, i.e. the phenomena of personality disturbances in female incest victims. In doing so we worked on the basis of paradigmatic individual cases and also accepted in part the conditions for the appearance of, i.e. causes of, psychopathological phenomena. Diagnostic classification or co-ordination of the disturbances (from an aetiopathogenetic point of view) gives the picture presented in Table 20. According to this at least seventy per cent (N = 49) of all the girls and women were disturbed in their personality development, which means they had developed specific or non-specific neuroses (twenty-seven per cent), and probable neurotic disturbances (twenty-three per cent) or that it was a question of under-endowed girls (twenty per cent), with or without serious behavioural disturbances. A collation of the neurotic disturbances into a group can only be undertaken when (*a*) a neurotic conflict in the sense of the psychoanalytical treatment of neuroses has been proven beyond doubt, and (*b*) there is a relatively safe criterion for assuming that the conflict of incompatible drives plays a causal role in the disturbances we are dealing with. In only *thirty per cent of all cases were no psychopathological phenomena* of the kind described present or definable.

TABLE 20 Diagnostic classification of personality disturbance (from an aetiopathogenetic point of view) (N = 49)

	Specific neuroses: traumatic N phobia		Non-specific neurotic disturbances	Probable neurotic disturbances	Low talents with or without behavioural disturbances	
abs.	4	1	14	16	10	4
%	7		20	23	14	6

NB: Total sample N = 70.

Time and manifestation of the symptoms

Faced with the, in part, seriously disturbed family atmosphere in which the majority of these girls and women have grown up, one will not be surprised at the high percentage of disturbances in personality development. There is on the other hand also the difficult problem of the degree to which incestuous activities can be held to account for these disturbances. Without going into the question of the results of incest (see p. 207) at this point one must first come to some assertions about the time of appearance of the psychopathological phenomena.

If a psychopathological phenomenon were to appear only after the start of incest, then one could conceive of some connection with the incest, even though a temporal connection is not necessarily a causal one. Nevertheless such a connection is the kind of fact which might help in deciding whether the incest situation *could* have anything at all to do with disturbances in the development of personality.

TABLE 21 Time of manifestation of psychopathological phenomena (before or after start of incest): the distribution of frequency and results of the chi-square test (to check the difference in division)

Nature of symptoms	*Time of appearance*		*Total*	*Chi-square*
	before incest	after incest		
Psychosomatic symptoms	14	6	20	not significant
Delinquent symptoms	20	16	36	n.s.
Behavioural disturbances	17	22	39	n.s.
With depressive manifestations	(25)	(34)	(59)	n.s.
Total	51	44	95	n.s.
With depressive manifestations	59	56	115	n.s.

From Table 21 it will be seen that there are certain (frequency) differences between the manifestation of symptoms before and after incest, but they are (according to the theory of probabilities) only a result of chance. In other words: Amongst the female incest victims in our survey *the symptoms of disturbed personality development were no more frequent after the start of incest than before*, and the deviations from this expected equal division which *were* found could be explained by pure chance. What is the significance of this fact? It could mean that the negative influence of the incest situation on personality development in these girls and women is no greater than that of other environmental factors, independent of the incest. Whether this hypothesis is tenable or not we shall have a further chance to discover in the chapter 'The effects of incest'.

7. Conditions giving rise to incestuous relationships, and the course of these relationships

Psychiatric, psychological and legal experience have shown time and time again that incestuous relationships relatively seldom begin and end with one solitary sexual act (cf. p. 109). The social proximity of those concerned and the consequent absence of the anonymity and transitoriness of other human intercourse are indeed two essential factors which separate incest from many other forms of legally punishable sexuality – but they contribute little, however, to an understanding of the origins and development of the events themselves. Neither the identification of individual 'causal' moments and factors, which are often cited in a biased way to the detriment of the person committing incest, nor the limitation of psychological and psychiatric research to a restricted period of the incestuous relationship, can quite do justice to a scientific examination of the events. Behavioural patterns in human intercourse are based upon mutual relationships and forces which change with time. The behaviour of one or other of the incest partners at the start can be diametrically opposite to that in the further course of, or at the end of, the relationship.

Only a consideration of all the factors and all the events and their chronological classification can give us anything remotely like an adequate basis upon which to form opinions. We shall attempt that task in this chapter.

Predisposition

The possibility, or the danger, of two people within narrow social confines taking up an incestuous relationship with each other, seems to depend on a very varied set of preconditions which it is impossible even today to classify as specific to this form of deviant sexual behaviour. Apart from this, these preconditions, some of which in particular occur very frequently, explain neither the manifestation of such relationships nor their progress and course. Other factors and stages which have their basis equally in the personality and behaviour of the incest partners, in their relationship to the family world around them, and in circumstances conditioned by the individual situation, enter into play, induce the events which occur, and condition their course and termination.

Against the background of what we have presented above it will not seem strange that *the most prominent role amongst the predisposing* phenomena is played by *disturbed interpersonal relationships* in both incest partners (see Table 22). Disturbed contact before the act between the male partner and his wife (Tables 22 and 23), and a negative to openly hostile relationship on the part of the victim towards her mother (sixty-one per cent), belong to the essential characteristics of that disharmony which is symptomatic of family disorganisation (eighty-eight per cent). This situation, in which both incest partners frequently find themselves before the start of the relationship, can become the starting-point of a one-sided or mutual preparation for the crime, though its nature and extent are variable. A completely decisive role at this stage is played by the personality and behaviour of both partners.

TABLE 22   Phenomena predisposing towards incest (N = 65*)

Predisposing phenomena	abs.	%
Constitution of the family		
Signs of disorganisation before incest	57	88
Adult partners		
Socially and emotionally disturbed relationship with wife	56	86
Unsatisfying sexual partnership	34	52
Detectable psychopathological personality	35	54
Labile personality (violent, quick-tempered)	20	31
Reduced self-control as a result of heavy drinking	14	21
Incestuous and jealous attitude towards daughter/stepdaughter before start of incest	12	18
Hypersexuality/sexual passion	11	17
Victims		
Dependent on authority of father/stepfather	52	80
Unsatisfactory relationship with mother/stepmother	40	61
Uncritical attitude, not gifted, normal intelligence	19	29
Extreme sexual curiosity	18	28
Strong oedipal connection to father/stepfather	16	25
Low intelligence	13	20
Neglected	10	15
Socially isolated	9	14
Previous heterosexual experience (coitus)	8	12

* In a total of sixty-five father–daughter/stepfather–stepdaughter relationships all these phenomena and those listed in following tables were observable. The percentage figures which are lower or higher than those presented in earlier tables can be explained either by a lack of information in certain individual cases which are therefore not reflected here, or by a higher incidence of incestuous partnership relations (e.g. double incest). A sum total of 104 phenomena for the whole course of the incest was registered, including the predisposing phenomena.

Moreover, the emotional subjection of the daughter to the authority of the father (eighty per cent), connected closely with a disturbed family make-up (phi-correlation: ·40**), is obviously of primary dispositional significance. Interestingly enough it is rather the dissocially noticeable girls who are socially, but not emotionally, dependent on the father's authority (phi-correl.: —·32*). Their self-possessed and at times protesting attitude towards their fathers show quite clearly that not every social dependence is of necessity also an emotional one. When, however, both coincide in the daughter and/or there is a lack of an emotionally stable and trusting attitude towards the mother or other members of the family, then the likelihood of, or preparation for, active resistance to the father's sexual advances is limited and weakened.

There are admittedly other factors or groups of factors disposing towards incest such as, for example, limited intelligence (twenty per cent), allied to an uncritical attitude, previous heterosexual experience (twelve per cent), and an uncritical attitude on the part of victims of normal intelligence, but with below average talents (twenty-nine per cent). In individual cases they can carry a great deal of weight, but they do not characterise the whole group of victims.

There is a similar picture with the *predisposition of the adult partner*, although here in at least half the cases (fifty-four per cent) a large role is certainly played by groups of psychopathological factors (see Tables 22 and 23).

Unstable personality (thirty-one per cent), closely connected with a lack of self-control as a result of heavy drinking (twenty-one per cent), sexual passion (seventeen per cent) and, more rarely, limited intelligence (nine per cent), sexual perversions (eight per cent) or disturbances of potency (five per cent), are some of the essential traits of abnormal personalities, which, given the appropriate conditions, can favour the collapse of the barrier to incest. Yet what they still do not explain is the process of drifting into an incestuous relationship. After all is said and done, about fifty per cent of these men are socially and psychopathologically quite normal. Yet even in this group the majority live in a disharmonious family situation. And very often it is just this situation which prepares the ground for an attempt, which is at first unilateral, but with the course of time mutual on

TABLE 23 Predispositional groups of factors (correlations) in victims and adults (N = 65)

Connection of factors	Phi-correlation
Victims	
Uncritical attitude with normal intelligence and less than average gifted/less than average gifted	·69****
Unsatisfying negative relationship with mother/sexual curiosity	·42***
Sexual curiosity/neglected before incest	·40**
Disturbed family relations/emotional dependence on authority	·40**
Oedipal connection to father/negative relationship with mother	·38**
Negative relation with mother/neglect before incest	·34*
Emotional dependence on authority/neglect	−·32*
Adults	
Psychopathological/unstable personality	·55****
Unstable/lack of self-control (alcohol)	·54***
Psychopathological/lack of self-control	·49***
Psychopathological/sexual passion	·34*
Unstable/jealous of daughter	·54***
Unsatisfactory emotional relationship with wife/unsatisfactory sexual relationship with wife	·33*

*Significance level of phi-correlations: **** = 1 per 1000; *** = 1%; ** = 2%; * = 5%.

the part of father and daughter, to overcome the family crisis or to escape into an incestuous relationship (cf. Gerchow, 1965). Such a point of departure may be confirmed or strengthened by the situation or behaviour of the daughter. Strong oedipal ties to the father (twenty-five per cent), closely connected with an unsatisfying emotional relationship with the mother/stepmother, sexual curiosity (twenty-eight per cent), allied with symptoms of neglect (fifteen per cent), social isolation (fourteen per cent) or the taking over of the running of the household while the mother is ill for some considerable period (nine per cent) may be of just as much consequence as the father's jealous and incestuous behaviour (eighteen per cent). It is then frequently only really internal or external, often quite casual, factors and moments which create a situation of temptation and lead to the contravention of the taboo. We shall shortly proceed to examine the exceptions to this rule.

Factors instigating or favouring incest

There are various possibilities which, given the required preconditions (= predisposition) and/or an emotional starting-point, can set an incestuous relationship going or lead to a breaking of the taboo (see Table 24). It should be said *en passant* that *rape*, i.e. the most abrupt, in any case most aggressive, action, connected with violence, is amongst *the more rare occurrences* (six per cent) – a fact which has been re-emphasised recently by American research works (Gebhard and colleagues 1965, p. 266). Also the *direct effects and role of alcohol* have doubtless been over-emphasised. Thirteen of the adults (twenty per cent) had indeed drunk alcohol before the first incestuous act, but only two (three per cent) committed the act in a drunken stupor (and were legally incapable of responsible judgment), and four were of diminished responsibility (six per cent). Completely similar results were reached by the American Kinsey Institute research group (Gebhard and colleagues, 1965, pp. 223, 244, 266: twenty to thirty-one per cent were under the influence of alcohol, but only eight per cent were completely incapable of responsible judgement or were of reduced responsibility). On the other hand, however, one must concede that alcohol may very well *indirectly* favour incestuous activities, namely when its influence reduces self-control. Precisely this latter fact can naturally much more easily be the case with those whose sense of control is already prejudicially affected by too much drink.

Since the pioneer work done on incest, researchers have never tired of raising the question of *lack of space in living conditions* (Marcuse, 1908, 1915; von Hentig, 1925; Riemer, 1936; Nürnberger, 1955). It may certainly play a great role in times of economic depression and general lack of living space, but it is in no way of causal significance (Plaut, 1960).

TABLE 24 Factors instigating and favouring (the beginning of) incest (N = 65)

Instigatory and favourable factors	abs.	%
Adult's behaviour		
The victim's biological maturity as 'instigatory function' (breasts, menarch)	51	78
Imbibing of alcohol	13	20
Rape	4	6
Victim's behaviour		
Unequivocal initiative (provocation)	4	6
Behaviour of adult and victim		
Both partners love each other	5	8
Situationally conditioned factors		
Wife at work while husband is at home	22	34
Wife ill at home or in hospital	17	26
Wife away from home a great deal for some other reason	3	5
Husband at home a lot, because ill or out of work	7	11
Adult and victim sleep in same place	12	18
Adult visits his daughter or they go on holiday together	3	5

In eighteen per cent of the cases offender and victim did indeed share the same sleeping place at the start of the incest, but in only one case (one per cent) was there an urgent situation of need where both were forced to sleep in the same bed, and even in this case other sleeping arrangements could conceivably have been made. (Weinberg [1963] found two such cases amongst 159 examined in the USA.) Of ten males who had slept in one bed with their victim for a time shortly before the incest, nine had introduced this sleeping arrangement without any compelling reason. Nevertheless living conditions can, in individual cases, be a factor favouring incest, but hardly a causal factor. Not causal for the reason that, if this were the case, one would expect a higher incidence of incest in refugee camps in post-war Germany than amongst the native population, and this was in fact not the case (Gerchow, 1955).

A far greater role amongst the factors favouring incest is played by certain stages peculiar to the particular situation which are brought about by more or less chance circumstances. A wife who is seriously ill, confined to bed for a lengthy period, or perhaps even has to go to hospital, a mother who is having a baby (twenty-six per cent), the fact that the couple go to work at different times (thirty-four per cent) or a father who is at home a lot because of either unemployment, sickness, or being an invalid (eleven per cent) – all these are opportunities which, under certain conditions, may give rise to situations of temptation. In almost seventy per cent of the cases ($N = 45$) at the beginning of incest there was discernible in our examination this temptation-situation and other combinations (separation and divorce or the death of the wife seemed apparently in the American material examined by Weinberg (forty per cent) and by Gebhard and his colleagues (four to twenty-eight per cent) to have a greater significance).

Are these more or less chance conditioned circumstances, which, given a certain predisposition, can lead to situations of temptation, already sufficient stimulus to incestuous events? In a few cases, yes; in the majority, no. It is certainly the case that the age of the victim, more precisely the *biological maturity of the daughter*, is, as a rule, of great significance for the father/stepfather (cf. pp. 105 ff.). In seventy-eight per cent of cases the man's behaviour, the first breaking of the incest taboo, was influenced by the victim's biological maturity, that is the developing or already developed female body (rounding of the hips, breasts) achieved a sexual value and became a *stimulant* for the man. The English human geneticist Tanner (1962) believes that the secondary sexual distinguishing marks, especially the female breasts, possess a 'triggering-off function' for the human drive towards mating. As far as the male's incestuous behaviour is concerned the analogy from the area of experiment into (animal) behaviour can be postulated at least as far as (*a*) the age of the victim at the start of incest (>10) and her biological maturity are very closely connected (phi-correlation $\cdot 82****$) and, moreover, (*b*) that there is just as close a connection between the age of the victim at the start of incest (>10) and statements by both incest partners to the effect that the male's interest in his victim set in with the latter's coming to maturity (phi-correlation 78****).

Case 45: A man forty-one years old at the beginning of incest, his marriage had been full of tension for some years and he had no satisfactory sexual relationship with his wife. He began sexual activities with his daughter a year after her menarch: 'She had really always been quite reserved and always dressed and undressed alone. I only ever saw her dressed, all the same I could see that she was already quite well developed!'

Case 18: A girl who was fourteen at the beginning of an incestuous relationship lasting over three years with her natural father, who was fully forty, declared that her emotional relationship with her father had been very good until she had her first period (at thirteen). 'Things changed when I was something like fourteen and I began to develop round the breasts. He kept looking at me for long periods, wouldn't let me go anywhere, and said that I was always hanging about. There were always rows and arguments at home, ever since I was fourteen, and all because my father was jealous.'

Case 57: Subject was forty-three years old at the start of the incest, which was with his own daughter and which went on for two years. Under various pretexts he came to an agreement with his wife about sleeping which was different from the normal one, and enabled him to share his bed with his daughter: 'My daughter, who was then fourteen, had just previously had her first period and was already quite a young woman. The shape of her body excited me.' About six months after the conscious introduction of this sleeping arrangement which provided opportunities for physical contacts between the two incest partners (stroking, manipulation of the genitals) coitus first occurred.

Only under these conditions does the absence of anonymity and transience in the interpersonal contacts, the daily encounter between both incest partners within narrow social confines, gain in significance. The temptation accumulates in the more or less casually created living situation where favourable opportunities arise, or under the influence of alcohol, and a series of events is set in motion the predisposing factors to which have been described. That the personality and behaviour of the victim play a role in this too is beyond any doubt. The question is: *what* role do they play? The stereotyped views about this vary between seeing the girl as a sexually precocious 'seductress', and as an innocent 'victim'. Neither view corresponds to reality. Amongst our cases there were only four (six per cent) in which the unequivocally *sexually provoking behaviour of the victim* in the initial situation gave rise to the incestuous activities. Two of these girls in puberty had fallen in love with the adult (stepfather) before the beginning of the incest. In five cases (eight per cent) both partners were in love with each other, but only two girls provoked the contravention of the incest barrier in an unequivocal way, i.e. sexual interest and provocations at this point coincided. The behaviour of these girls was in no way different from that of their contemporaries who were already fully aware of their womanhood, and in the later stages of puberty sought tenderness and satisfaction of sexual needs outside the family, in doing so they were experimenting with the means at their disposal and waiting for a male response (see 'Introductory remarks on puberty' [pp. 146 ff.]). On the other hand, the number of girls who, already at the first breaking of the taboo, showed *active resistance* (including violent means) is very small (three). Yet even this is not surprising if one takes into account the fact that the young girl in an incest situation is subject to a completely different set of conditions regarding defence, tolerance and participation from the child or maturing girl who meets a completely unrelated adult aggressor or a transient, perhaps even unknown sexual partner. Emotional dependence on the authority of the father/stepfather and shaken confidence in the mother are the two most basic independent phenomena (phi-correlation: $-\cdot 08$), which may explain the girls' *overwhelmingly passive and tolerant attitude* at the outset in the majority of cases. Surprise, fear, a failure to grasp what is happening, bewilderment, a mixture of fear and sexual curiosity, revulsion, disgust and escape into simulated sleep from a feeling of guilt, or sexually satisfying surrender with an orgasm – these quite different qualities of experience illustrate only partially what the possible kinds of feeling were in the initial stages of incest, as far as the girls we examined have reported them in retrospect. As in normal heterosexual behaviour in our culture, at first in incestuous contacts the *non-violent initiative of the man* is dominant – which has nothing to do with the punishable nature of these activities.

Conditions giving rise to incestuous relationships 179

The following examples which are accented in various directions should throw some light on what has just been said:

Case 44: Subject: a thirty-four-year-old man, regarded as completely beyond reproach in his job, a model in caring for his family, drank occasionally because of serious disharmony in his marriage, and had recently been drinking more than he could take. The cause of the family disunity was the wife, an earlier delinquent subject, several times before the courts, who led a promiscuous life, and with whom, unfortunately, the man was childishly infatuated. The couple's sex life had also been disturbed for some time before the incest began. During the course of the incest the victim's mother was having an extra-marital relationship, and it was left to the husband to look after the thirteen-year-old stepdaughter. When the man once again, as so often, returned home to find his wife not there, he took to drink as a means of escape. He drank for several days and one night raped his stepdaughter several times, although she put up strong resistance. The man, who confessed to the deed, was possibly, according to psychiatric opinion and the judgment of the court (under para. 51, 1 German Penal Code), in a state of alcoholic stupor and, therefore (under para. 330a of the German Penal Code), incapable of responsible judgment.

Here breakdown of marriage and the direct influence of alcohol on a psychopathologically unexceptional personality – the man was not a drinker – are well to the fore. The following represents a completely different relationship.

Case 43: At the time of the incest the subject was a thirty-four-year-old father of a family. Before marrying he had appeared in court on more than ten occasions, since then he had been in no further trouble and was socially well integrated. He provided sufficient means for his family, but his marriage to an easily excitable woman, who was constantly ill, had been an unhappy one from the start. For years sexual intercourse had occurred between the married couple only rarely. The stepdaughter, born outside wedlock, had had a disturbed and chequered childhood and in puberty showed signs of sexually lax behaviour, and was for a short while in a children's home (see p. 159). The girl's relations with her mother were, because of the neglect in early childhood, ambivalent and emotionally brittle. Contact with the stepfather was at first not particularly good since he tried to restrict her and she on her side did not want to recognise his authority. This situation was drastically changed one evening – the mother was in hospital and the daughter was running the house – when the sixteen-year-old and her step-father began a conversation about the hard childhood they had both had. This brought them closer together. Victim: 'It was then that I realised I liked my stepfather and not just as a daughter. I didn't resist his caresses because I wanted him. I thought of my mother but then I also remembered that my parents had not been very happy together for some time. Then my thoughts got muddled.'

One need add nothing to this human situation, immediately understandable, and which broadened later to become a real love tragedy. The factors predisposing towards a breaking of the taboo can be seen clearly in both partners, the more chance situational conditions favoured the revelation of a mutual attraction which had long lain hidden behind the façade of strict behaviour (the stepfather) and obstructive conduct (the daughter).

Case 22: Subject: the father of a family, in his fifties at the time of the incest. This was his first marriage and had lasted twenty years. In the years just before the incest the husband had also had sexual problems because of a disease of the lower part of his wife's body (so that on most occasions she refused him conjugal intercourse). The externally intact family relationship is concealed by the now chronic intrafamily tensions, and characterised by a polarisation of relationships into father–daughter/mother–son. Whilst there had been since early childhood a massive oedipal connection between the daughter and her despotic, nagging and obstinate father, there had never been a true emotional relationship with the mother, and the emotionally more spontaneous son had developed a tender affection for his childishly helpless and emotionally restricted mother. The long-standing incestuous colouring to the atmosphere in the family was reflected in its sleeping habits. Whilst the family was still living in bad accommodation father and mother, son and daughter slept in the same bed. This situation, which continued until the early years of the daughter's schooling, in no way led to incest. When living conditions were better the arrangement was repeated on certain days, even when the children were older. Even in puberty the daughter was often heard to say that she wanted to marry her father one day. She enjoyed his caresses – treatment she had never received from her mother. This situation, which precluded marital communication and affection between parents and children of the same sex, broke down the incest barrier between father and daughter, which had up till then been upheld in circumstances of far more 'favourable opportunities', only two years after the victim's menarch.

In this case the normal interpersonal contacts one would expect in an intact family have also been disturbed. The daughter transfers her emotional needs, unsatisfied by her mother, exclusively to her father whose response paves the way for a mutual attachment with incestuous undertones, even before it comes to a breaking of the taboo. The crucial deciding factor in this is, however, chronic disharmony in the marital partnership, which first made possible an escape route which entailed such psychological consequences as it went along, and brought it – under the influence of the daughter's biological maturity, her physical 'attraction' at a moment of favourable opportunity – to its 'goal'. This example, which could be backed up with other cases, is quite representative of those patterns of incest, which develop from a primary condition of (often mutual) 'paving of the way'. In this – as our last example showed – the affectively strengthened contact between father and daughter must not be taken to presuppose the later crime, but the progressive nature of a relationship which becomes more sexual is undetectable given the conditions in the family which we have outlined – the more or less gradual growing into a situation of sexual intimacy which is admittedly also dependent upon the personality factors of both incest partners, especially those of the father.

Factors sustaining incest

The question is always being posed as to how it is possible that an incestuous relationship between father and daughter can be maintained for so long and so extensively without conflict (cf. Gerchow, 1965). There is no patent answer which might supply reasons for this course of events, so dramatic and, in the end, so humanly tragic.

TABLE 25 The most common factors helping to sustain incestuous relationships (N = 65)

Factors sustaining incest	abs.	%
Victims		
Feelings of shame/guilt towards mother/stepmother	45	69
Fear of men	39	60

182 Incest

Factors sustaining incest Victims (cont.)	abs.	%
Passive behaviour (no sign of resistance)	37	57
Lack of knowledge about own rights	32	49
General feelings of shame	26	40
Fear of judicial punishment or being taken to a home	25	38
Fear of family breaking up	20	31
Fear of loss of father/stepfather	15	23
Encouraging and provoking behaviour	15	23
Sexual motives	14	21
Silence because of material advantages	12	18
Silence out of gratitude to man if latter is caring and protective	11	17
Apathy, indifference	10	15
Emotional attraction to partner	9	14
Belief that incest is father's right	6	9
Confession disbelieved by mother, thus disillusioned	5	8
Men		
Disturbed emotional relationship with wife	52	80
Warning child to say nothing	50	77
Disturbed sex life with wife	32	49
Threats and intimidation towards victim	30	46
Man at home while wife at work	30	46
Authoritarian tyrant in family	30	46
Caring and protective attitude to victim	24	37
Payments in money and kind, and other gifts	22	34
Victim falsely informed (possibility of prison, etc.)	15	23
Development of alcoholism	14	21
Favourable opportunity through being unemployed	13	20
Social isolation of victim (induced by man)	13	20
Emotionally coloured attraction to partner	12	18
'Magic' rituals	5	8
Development of a perversion	4	6
Use of force	1	1
Wife and mother		
Rejection or refusal of marital intercourse	17	26
Neglect on part of wife	12	18
Illness or death	11	17
Toleration of incestuous relationship (knowing)	8	12
Sexual promiscuity	7	11
Rejection of daughter's confessions	6	9
Collusion	3	5

Conditions giving rise to incestuous relationships 183

The percentages are reckoned with N = 65; higher or lower percentage figures for individual factors (as against earlier figures) are a result of changes in behavioural patterns or double counting as, for example, in the case of double incest (e.g. one man and two victims), or of the deletion of six cases (which were isolated instances).

The course of the incest in each particular case is determined by a series or chain of interactions in which not only the incest partners but also other members of the family and, in some circumstances, people outside the family circle, are indirectly involved. If one wishes to sum up the most important factors and stages contributing to the continuation of incestuous relationships, then one must take this matter into account.

Table 25 contains a survey of the most common factors sustaining incest. Six (nine per cent) of the sixty-five cases subjected to analysis represented isolated acts (see notes to Table 12).

a) Adult partners

Amongst the forms of behaviour of those fathers and stepfathers who attempt to maintain incestuous relationships, an absolutely essential role is played by exhorting the child to say nothing (seventy-seven per cent), verbal threats and intimidation (forty-six per cent), an authoritarian, 'family tyrant' type of behaviour (forty-six per cent), and giving false information to the victim (twenty-three per cent). These four kinds of behaviour are more or less closely linked one with another.

It is above all the authoritarian, 'family tyrant' type of father who has an especially marked tendency to threaten his daughter or stepdaughter with children's home or prison or to intimidate her physically (phi-correl. ·72****). It is precisely this group of adults which uses to an extraordinary degree the method of false information (home, prison) to intimidate (phi-correl. ·45***), and this points to a close link with the violent, easily angered type of adult (phi-correl. ·59****) and with those fathers/stepfathers who already before the start of the relationship had adopted a jealous, incestuous attitude towards their daugher (phi-correl. ·35*). Adults who pleaded with or demanded of their victims that they remain silent about the incestuous events also, in fact, issued threats, behaved in an authoritarian and tyrannical way and were psychopathological cases. The connections between the first-named most frequent forms of behaviour and the three last-named factors are, however, not nearly so developed (phi-correl. between ·33* and ·35*) as are those between the last-named factors and the authoritarian, 'family tyrant' group of adults.

A further, quite separate, form of behaviour which could criminologically be classed as one of the actions 'after the event', consists of financial or material gifts or other favours (34 per cent) shown by the adult to the victim. They play a greater role in the further course of a relationship than at its beginning, and not infrequently in such cases the adult's behaviour becomes a positively evaluated motive of the victim towards the continuation of the sexual relationship (cf. (b) Victims). Another behavioural trait is given concrete form in the tendency of some adults to isolate their victims socially (twenty per cent), that is to restrict their extra-family, interpersonal contacts. Constant control, spying, groundless accusations and suspicions of a sexual nature belong to the accompanying symptoms of this basic attitude, which is coupled to a great degree with incestuous and jealous behavioural symptoms before and during the period of the relationship (phi-correl. ·52*** and ·57****). Also notable in this respect is the close connection with disturbances in the adult's marital sex relations during the period of incest (phi-correl. ·46***).

The motives for incest in partly unilateral, partly mutual partnerships of emotional involvement (eighteen per cent) are of quite a different kind. They are closely connected with a caring and protective attitude on the part of the adult towards the victim (phi-correl. ·54***). Precisely the latter attitude, which to a great extent precludes authoritarian, tyrannical or brutal and quick-tempered forms of behaviour (phi-correl. −·52*** and −·37*) and threats (phi-correl. −·41**) shows that it is not always only the adult's fear-instilling pressures which contribute to the maintenance of incestuous relationships (see below b) Victims).

In contrast to all these factors contributing to the maintenance of incest the use of force (one per cent) and perverted or diseased developments in the adult (six per cent), in Giese's sense of the terms (1962), are relatively meaningless as a group characteristic (cf. 'Style and forms of perversion' [p. 153 f.]).

On the other hand situations conditioned by the moment should not be underestimated, as for example the fact that the marriage partners work during different periods of the day (forty-six per cent), or unemployment or illness and being an invalid (twenty per cent), sickness or death of the wife (seventeen per cent) as a cause of 'favourable opportunities', and also, in the case of the wife's illness, of a situation of enforced sexual abstinence for the male (phi-correl. ·38*). Psychologically it is completely understandable that some of these forms of behaviour – like the maintenance of the incestuous relationship itself – can receive considerable reinforcement and strengthening of motivation from the usually chronic disruption in the married couple's emotional relations (eighty per cent) and the insufficient marital sexual partnership frequently (forty-nine per cent) allied to this (phi-correl. ·49***).

We have already discussed the fact that the rejecting behaviour of the wife, her refusal of marital sexual intercourse (twenty-six per cent), signs of neglect (eighteen per cent) and sexual promiscuity (twelve per cent) play a quite important role (highest correlation between disturbed sexual partnership with wife and rejection and refusal of marital intercourse by the wife: phi-correl. ·58****).

The indirect amount of influence of the wife and mother on the progress of the incest only achieves any special emphasis, however, when, from whatever motives, she tolerates the incestuous relationship (twelve per cent), becomes an active co-participant (five per cent; in Gebhard and collaborators (1965) three per cent), or rejects the daughter's confessions of incest as 'incredible' (nine per cent).

b) Victims

What forms of behaviour or attitudes does the victim show, then, in the further course of the incest, and what motives lie behind them? Some remarks should be made *en passant* about this question.

In so far as we are dealing here with specifically sexual questions the object of our enquiry must at times be removed or withdrawn from more refined methodological concepts. Not merely because the under-age female victim is in a situation of psychological stress after the discovery of a sexual offence (Müller-Lückmann, 1965), but simply because in certain circumstances tact towards another person should be more important than forensic or scientific interests. These considerations, as well as experience of reappraisals, rationalisations or backward projection by girls who are involved in sexual offences, throw a certain doubtful light on the findings below, in so far as they pertain to sexual matters (e.g. the question of orgasms).

TABLE 26 Forms of behaviour of female incest victims in the further course of incestuous relations (N = 65)

	Passive, tolerating	Encouraging, provoking	Other kinds of behaviour	Unclear kind of behaviour	Isolated act
abs.	37	15	4	3	6
%	57	23	6	5	9

Of the forms of behaviour of the female incest partners which have an extensive influence on the further course of incestuous events, two can be clearly distinguished: the passive, tolerating attitude (fifty-seven per cent), and that of encouragement and provocation (twenty-three per cent). They are, with a high degree of probability, mutually exclusive (phi-correl. −·78****). The percentile increase in encouraging and provocative forms of behaviour and the decrease in passive tolerating attitudes indicate that in the course of time changes take place in the girl's views, depending both upon the behaviour of the male partner at the given moment, and on the personality of the girl herself, and upon the effects of emotional and sexual interactions. The motives which – dependent upon the behaviour of the male – play a part in this are various and are best understood if presented graphically (Fig. 10).

Let us remind ourselves that many adults exhort their victim to remain silent, almost half issue threats and behave in an authoritarian fashion, while some seek to intimidate by using false information, 'You'll be put in a home', etc. Thus,

Conditions giving rise to incestuous relationships

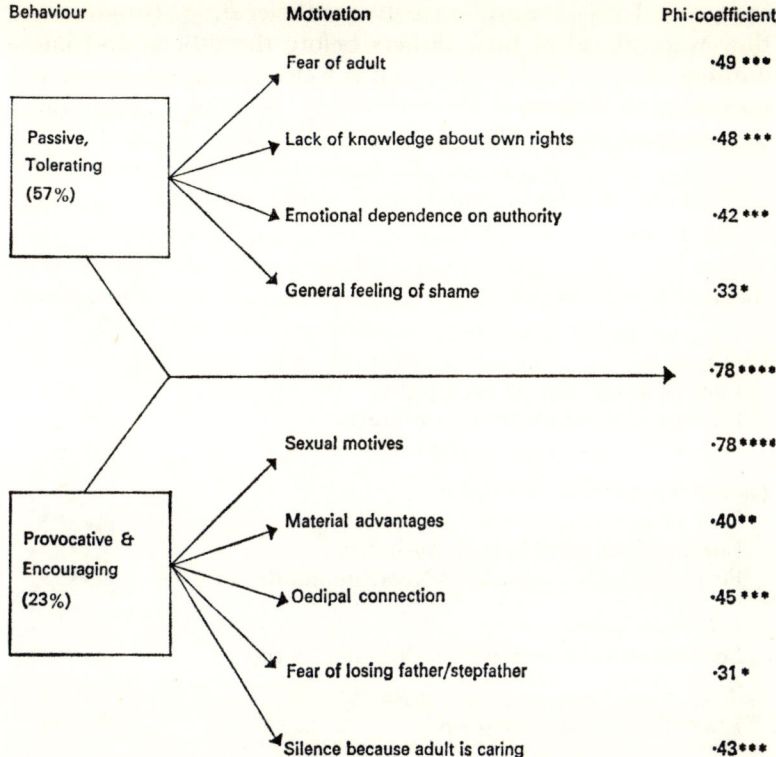

Figure 10. Behavioural patterns and motivations of female incest victims in further course of relationships (correlations)

for many girls, fear of the father/stepfather, closely linked to a lack of knowledge of their own rights, which, in its turn, is connected with the fear of being put in a home, or even in prison, is the decisive factor in motivation to silence, and the passive acceptance of the repeated sexual activities (see Table 27). Many of these girls feel that they share the guilt – only very few believe that the father has some kind of 'natural' right – but the trusting withdrawal to the mother is frequently cut off by a negative relationship with her, either as a result of guilt feelings or – more rarely – as a result of disillusionment from having a 'confession' rejected. On the other hand it can hardly be chance, either, that it is precisely the girls who were emotionally dependent upon their fathers' authority who tend to a great degree towards a passive and tolerating attitude, since they were afraid of their fathers before the others, and knew nothing of their rights of sexual self-determination, or of the possibility of defending themselves against abuses of authority (correlations, see Table 27).

TABLE 27 Motival connections in female incest victims (inter-correlations)

Nature of motival connections	Phi-coefficients
Fear of adult	
Lack of knowledge of own rights	·43***
Emotional dependence on authority	·38**
Fear of loss of father/stepfather	−·37**
Lack of knowledge of own rights	
Fear of home, prison, etc.	·42***
Emotional dependence on authority	·34*
Feelings of guilt towards mother/stepmother	·32*
Fear of home, prison	
Feelings of guilt towards mother/stepmother	·32*
Feelings of guilt towards mother/stepmother	
Fear of family breaking up	·44***

At this point general feelings of shame also come into play and make any revelations to a third person all the more difficult. It is also worth noting that fear of the father and the worry of losing him if the secret is revealed are, with a high degree of probability, mutually exclusive. On the other hand feelings of guilt and shame towards the mother and fear of the family breaking up if the secret is revealed are also closely connected (phi-correl. ·44***). This may be called a motival constellation, a complete bundle of interwoven stimuli which – in correspondence with the adult's behaviour – explain the passive, tolerating attitude of many of these girls. Admittedly, in discussing this attitude one has always to reckon with a passive sexualisation of the victim, even if it unambiguously excludes recognisably sexual motives with high probability with sexual motives (phi-correl.−·45***).

Case 57: In the case already mentioned above (see p. 157) a point was reached in the further course of the father–daughter relationship, which lasted two years, where, as well as coitus two or three times weekly, fellatio, cunnilingus and anal intercourse also took place. The passive sexualisation of the girl became clearer and clearer. The father exhorted his daughter to say nothing, and threatened her, saying that she would be put in a corrective home and he would go to prison if what they were doing became known. In order to bind her even more firmly to him he made her presents of clothes, sealed a pact of 'blood-brotherhood' with her, and carried out all kinds of magic rituals. For her part the daughter was jealous whenever the man slept with his wife. After the relationship had been discovered she explained that she had been afraid of being sent to a home, a threat which her father had kept before her all the time. In fact she continued to visit her father voluntarily for some time after the latter had found himself somewhere else to live.

Case 1: A violent and quick-tempered drinker, already before the courts on more than one occasion. Even before the incest began he had been used to keeping a jealous watch over his nineteen-year-old stepdaughter, beating his wife and children, and tyrannising the whole family. He maintained, by the use of constant threats, his incestuous relations ('thigh-pressing', etc.) over the course of two years. The girl who, even as a child, had been hemmed in and socially isolated by her stepfather, had become a mistrusting loner. The girl had never regarded her mother as a maternal or protective person, but only as a helpless creature, herself in need of protection, and also as just another of the stepfather's victims! Alleging that he was seriously ill and needed help at night, the latter forced his stepdaughter to share his bed for a year. On the question of why she had remained silent the victim said later with an air of resignation, 'Who could I have told? I didn't want to say anything to my mother, because she couldn't have done anything about my stepfather either'. In this state of total external as well as internal isolation she had accepted without resisting the 'fate' that was forced upon her by a tyrannical, unstable father figure by whom she had felt herself controlled since early childhood.

Of quite a different nature are the motives connected with encouraging and provocative forms of behaviour. Sexual satisfaction, closely linked with silence for the sake of material advantages, or other favours, on the one hand, and the experience of a caring-protective father/stepfather on the other, closely linked with a vague fear of losing the latter, should the incest be revealed – these are basic motives corresponding to a large extent to this behavioural type (for correlations see Fig. 10). It is here that we come across the genuine love-affair, the emotionally coloured partnership, as well as sexual experiment accompanied by mere fondness, or the predominantly sex-based contact without emotional ties (see p. 205). In a whole series of these cases the victim's progressive sexualisation, i.e. the change with the course of time from an initial passive attitude to one of active participation or sexual provocation, is unmistakably evident, and some of the girls even reported sexual satisfaction and orgasms. That sexual motives in this latter sense do not necessarily include provocative behaviour, and that a strong emotional tie on the girl's side will mask both sexual motives and provocative behaviour, is illustrated by four cases (other forms of behaviour, six per cent). Thus there are, notwithstanding, *almost thirty per cent ($N = 19$) of the girls whose attitudes and behaviour did not at first in any way give the adult the impression that they were against incest.* T. Schönfelder (1968) found thirty-seven per cent actively participating victims in a predominantly non-incestuous group, while Geisler (1959) found twenty-six per cent willing among female incest victims and Gebhard and collaborators (1965) found that, of incest victims of eleven years and under, the proportion of willing participants was forty-three per cent, according to the offender, and forty-six per cent, according to the court. For twelve- to fifteen-year-olds the proportion of willing victims was sixty-eight per cent according to the offenders, and twenty-three per cent according to the courts.

It is worthy of note that encouraging and provocative forms of behaviour and sexual motives, as well as the fear of losing the father/stepfather if the secret is revealed, show a close relationship with oedipal connections (see Fig. 10 and Table 28). The fact that no statistically relevant connection is demonstrable with relationship (father) or step-relationship (step-father), and that all the correlations are in the region of nil, indicates that this question of oedipal relations is just as true of father–daughter as it is of stepfather–stepdaughter incest. In this respect it is interesting that encouraging and provocative behaviour on the girl's part does not indeed exclude the possibility of feelings of guilt developing towards the mother, although a significant positive connection is not verifiable (phi-correl. ·13 est.). Also the lack of social critical faculties in cases of normal intelligence and below average talents seems, with these actively participating girls – as in incestuous relations generally – to play an insignificant sustaining role (phi-correl. ·13 est., in passive, tolerating cases: —·19 est.).

TABLE 28 Motival connections in female incest victims (intercorrelations)

Nature of motival connection	Phi-coefficients
Sexual motives	
Oedipal connection	·31*
Material advantage	·33*
(Sexual curiosity before incest)	(·60****)
Oedipal connection	
Fear of losing father/stepfather	·45***
Silence because adult protective	
Fear of losing father/stepfather	·53***
Fear of family breaking up	·41***
Oedipal connection	·50***
Negative relationship with mother	·36**
(Sexual curiosity before incest)	(·36**)
Fear of losing father/stepfather	
Afraid of home, prison, etc.	·32*

The following examples will throw additional light on the materials just presented.

Case 59: Eighteen-month-long incest between sixteen-year-old stepdaughter and stepfather in his forties. The relationship developed against the background of an unhappy marriage, and from a typical primary stage in which the stepfather talked to the girl a great deal about his broken marriage. He felt attracted to the young girl, and even spoke of divorcing his wife and marrying her. When the barrier to incest was broken down, which happened with the complete acquiescence of the young girl, an intense love affair at first developed between the two. Coitus occurred on average once a week, sometimes at the stepfather's initiative, sometimes at that of the stepdaughter. The girl stated that she reached orgasms during the coitus, and that the sexual relationship with her stepfather had above all become a 'habit' for her. The fact that the married couple worked at different times of the day provided ample favourable opportunities for continuing the incestuous relationship. When, out of jealousy, the stepfather tried increasingly to isolate the girl socially, spied on her and threatened her, the child became frightened of being sent to a home. Despite this social hemming in by the stepfather, and her increasingly ambivalent attitude, the girl went on provoking her stepfather in an unmistakably sexual manner, and played a major part in the continuation of the relationship.

Case 10: Five-year incest between stepfather and stepdaughter which, after an almost two-year primary stage (kissing, petting), broadened into a highly intense, emotionally coloured partnership, and represented a common attempt on the part of both partners to overcome an apparently negative attitude to the highly abnormal wife and mother. One to two years after the start of incest there was at times almost daily coitus. Victim: 'I felt as though I was married!' The stepfather was for most of the time unemployed and thus there were constant 'favourable opportunities'. The girl, who was already, in puberty, fully developed, would occasionally run around the house in transparent 'shorties' and excite her stepfather. On the question of resistance the girl later declared that her stepfather had always had such a 'coaxing and bewitching' way with him, had never 'used force', and neither had she resisted in any way. She neither feared him, nor was she afraid of being put in a home. Any kind of fear-instilling pressures on the man's part as incest-sustaining motives are here absent.

Factors bringing about the end of incestuous relationships

It is perhaps one of the most characteristic features of cases of incest of long duration that the initiative which is primarily developed in the male adult gradually slips from his hands as the victim grows older. The French incest expert Szabo (1958) established that younger daughters tend towards passive behaviour whereas older ones seek to a greater degree to resist. This is not, however, principally a function of the girl's age, but simply of the fact that the girl growing older in the course of an incestuous relationship has experiences and gains insights which have to do partly with the situation of incest and partly with the psychological and social stage of development she has reached in the meantime. From this there often result sudden or gradual changes in attitude which precondition the girl's behaviour, which mark a decisive turning point in the relationship with the adult, and in most cases – against the resistance and actions of the adult – bring the events to an end. In this situation the adult, whose influence on the girl is frequently threatening to wane at this point, often himself contributes through his own behaviour to the discovery or break-up of the relationship. He rarely (six per cent) gives the girl up voluntarily, however, and confessions for reasons of bad conscience or on other grounds are a forensic rarity (one per cent).

Those forms of behaviour on the part of the adult which most frequently contribute in essence to the ending of incestuous relationships include *jealousy* (forty per cent), with all its attendant symptoms, creating an air of heightened tension (surveillance of daughter, groundless suspicions, accusations, etc.). It is to be observed more often in those fathers/stepfathers who already showed such tendencies before the beginning of incest (phi-correl. ·58****), who sought to isolate their partner socially during the incest (phi-correl. ·57****) and whose reactions were extremely unstable (phi-correl. ·41**).

The male adult's jealousy is frequently, if not always – eighteen per cent were already jealous without grounds on many occasions before the start of incest – a sign that something has changed in the attitude and/or the manner of behaviour of the victim. Yet it is precisely the girl's change in attitude that worries the adult, annoys him, and not infrequently drives him to incautious acts which can come to the notice of the surrounding members of the family or the broader social world.

What then are the *basic motivations to such changes in attitude on the part of the victim*? The increasing tension between the incest partners which could be observed in fifty-four per cent of cases, is, on the victim's side, caused to a great extent by the growing extra-familial social orientation associated with her age, i.e. through learning, her work, and the search for a partner (engagement, marriage), and more by the associated coming to awareness of her own rights, as well as by conflicts of conscience, and finally by a growing passive resistance to the adult, i.e. by avoiding action, or even (more rarely) withdrawal from the family (schematic representation and correlations, see Fig. 11). Individual variations apart, the model case below illustrates the interaction of the incest partners in this final stage of the relationship.

Case 9: Six-year father–daughter incest which developed against a background of intrafamily polarisation and an unhappy marriage

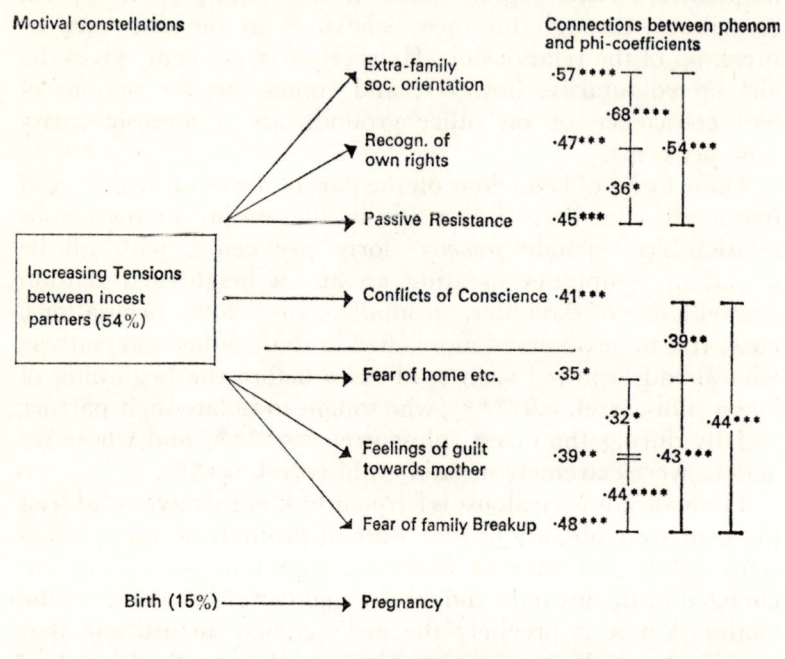

Figure 11. Schematic representation of the basic motival constellations in victims contributing to the ending of incestuous relationships. (Frequency and correlations.) N = 65.

Notes: phi-correlation coefficients: 1. division of correlations between factors printed in heavy type and those in normal type; 2, 3 and 4, division of correlations between the factors in normal type.

and out of the primary stage of a crypto-incestuous attachment (see pp. 143, 162 ff.). The close confidence shared by father and daughter began to worsen appreciably two or three years after the beginning of incest, when the father began to prevent the daughter from having contact with people of her own age after school. He began increasingly, as the affair continued, to accuse her, without grounds, of 'hanging around', and he kept constant watch over her. Up till then he had never threatened his daughter, but had told her that she was not allowed to marry until she was thirty. When the young girl gained extra-family contacts through her work and was occasionally asked out by girl friends or boy friends, there were violent scenes at home between her and her father. He threatened her, and for a little while longer she submitted quite passively, because she was afraid 'that something might happen' if she showed any resistance. In ignorance of her rights, and in the belief that she herself had committed a sin, she stayed silent, hoping 'that things would clear up and there wouldn't be a scandal'. Eventually she developed serious feelings of guilt towards her mother. When she became fully aware of the gravity of what had happened she tried to avoid her father by keeping out of his way. The constant arguments between father and daughter, as well as her first 'disrespectful' remarks, came to the attention of the rest of the family, and they became suspicious. Only when the young person met a boy out walking one day and was rather late coming home was there such an open bitter row between the incest partners that it resulted next day in the flight of the daughter to relatives, and her eventual confession to a third person.

Yet a similar constellation does not always bring about the end of an incestuous relationship. Compared with the frequency of passive resistance (forty-eight per cent), the cases in which the victims *take action to resist* (physical action sometimes) are relatively few and far between (seventeen per cent, of which five per cent occurred during single acts). Nevertheless this whole question shows that the girls' tendency to resistance in general – in whatever form – grows with time, i.e. with increasing age, and the experience gleaned from the incest situation (sixty per cent). A tragic, but in some circumstances conflict-free, end to the incest can sometimes be brought about by *pregnancy* (twenty per cent) or the *birth* of a child (fifteen per cent) as a result of such affairs, without any inner reorientation taking place on the girl's part (cf. 'Victims' [p. 210 f.]). In two cases (three per cent) there were attempts at suicide which led to a disclosure by the victim.

It will perhaps surprise the reader to learn that in only seventeen per cent of the cases did *tensions* or *disagreements*, caused by the incest, between mother and daughter contribute to a breaking-off of incestuous contacts, whilst *family strife not brought about by the incest* often led to the discovery of the latter (twenty-eight per cent). In only six per cent of the cases did the wife and mother surprise the two partners in incest, and in eight per cent the affair was discovered by someone else.

To whom do the victims reveal their secret? Forty-two per cent of the girls spoke belatedly of the incest to their mother, and seldom spontaneously, twenty-three per cent to relatives (brothers, sisters, uncles, aunts, etc.) and twenty-six per cent to non-related persons (friends, fiancé, etc.). The victim's revelations are, however, only in the rarest of cases instrumental in ending the incest; they are mostly merely a cause or release mechanism of final denunciation (in eight per cent of the cases the victims themselves denounced the incest).

8. Incest and abnormal sexual behaviour

It is beyond question that incestuous sexual contacts are deviant ways of behaviour, in so far as they go against the sexual taboo of the family, and contravene the prevailing norms and expectations in our society. But this is not only true of legally defined incest, and it is surprising that law-makers, who normally place so much value on a 'healthy popular outlook', shy away from it at this point. But the question which interests us here is whether, and to what degree, 'abnormal' sexual behaviour, in the sense of the above definition, is also pathological in the clinical sense.

Recent socio-psychological surveys 'On the question of prejudice towards sexually deviant groups' have shown that the human world around the groups tends to condemn sexual deviations as 'sick' or 'instinctive' (Schmidt and Sigusch, 1967). That people who commit incest are in no way as 'instinctive' as some scientists formerly assumed – and as is still widely believed amongst the public today – we have managed to show by means of empirical surveys. H. Giese (1962a, 1962b, 1967) and other sexologists (von Gebsattel, 1954, and others) have continually stressed the fact that an abnormal sexual attitude is not necessarily psychopathological. The widely held view that the greater the sin against the taboo the more 'sick' the behaviour is not scientifically justified – which has nothing to do with the fact that such a contravention of the taboo may in individual cases contain a psychopathological phenomenon or symptom.

Our earlier expositions have already shown us that incestuous contacts are not uniform from the point of view of sexual behaviour and personal relationships. This impression will be even more strongly confirmed by what follows.

Incest and paedophilia

By paedophilia is generally meant sexual contacts by adults with children and juveniles. This definition is precise at least as far as the age of the object of the instinctual drive is concerned (under-age sexual partners). It becomes questionable, though, as soon as it is applied to a normal psychological partnership between an adult and a biologically fully mature juvenile. Quite apart from the problem of the contested legal age of protection for juveniles (Jäger, 1957; Hochheimer, 1963; and others) it seems that a simple distinction between homosexual and heterosexual paedophilia is just as unrewarding as a threefold division, according to the age of the adult partner or committer, into early, mature, and late paedophilia (Hadden-Brock, 1965). The criteria for the diagnosis of paedophilia postulated by Giese (1965) beg the question of whether incest is also merely a variant of paedophilia or whether it should, in the final analysis, be considered quite separately.

With paedophiliac activities – according to Giese – the primary attraction is the physical immaturity of the partner, and – in contrast to normal heterosexual and average homosexual behaviour – only secondarily the latter's sex. Only the child and juvenile partner in whom the secondary sexual distinguishing marks are not yet developed (breasts, hair on the chin, etc.) are of adequate sexual attraction to the paedophile. And the latter attractions decrease with the progressive maturing of the juvenile's body. 'Sexual activities with partners who have passed the given age of maturity as a rule no longer represent true paedophiliac activities, even less so when it is a question of a casual relationship' (Giese, 1965, p. 25). And one further criterion is significant in this respect, namely the fact that the paedophiliac personality 'very frequently, perhaps as a rule' has a 'principally bisexual' aspect (Giese 1965, p. 26).

We have seen that in the majority of cases of incest it is precisely the maturity of the daughter's developing, or already developed, body which is a sexual temptation for the father or stepfather. Apart from this the relatively long period of time over which the incest is usually spread, and the male's attempts to 'hold' his victim for as long as possible, indicate little decrease in sexual attraction by the juvenile's developing female body. In fact, in contrast to paedophiliac activities, there is often an increase in the sexual intensity in the contacts between the incest partners. The physical and mental differences in maturity between the father and the daughter even themselves out as the relationship goes along, while they remain constant in paedophilia precisely because of the age limitation of the junior sexual partner. If, in paedophilia, the decrease in the difference in physical maturity leads to a break in the sexual relationship, in incest it increases the sexual attraction for the adult partner. There is one further (differential diagnostic) sign which would indicate a difference between paedophilia and incest: the 'basic bisexuality' in sexual sensitivity in paedophiliac personalities (Giese, 1965) is opposed by the exaggeratedly heterosexual orientation of most incest cases (Gebhard and collaborators, 1965). The American research group at the Kinsey Institute established that those who commit incest – compared with other sexually delinquent groups, a group of people arrested for other offences, and a control group of men not previously before the courts – develop homosexual contacts infrequently, after marriage not at all, and moreover have difficulty in reacting on a homosexual level of consciousness. As far as incest cases are concerned, there is a preference for the opposite sex, especially for those in their 'first bloom', as well as for those already physically mature examples of the opposite sex – just as in non-paedophile homosexuals, who are first and foremost concerned with their own sex and only secondarily with their partner's age (see Giese, 1962a). Thus incest *cannot* – at least from a sexological point of view – *be counted as a facet of paedophilia*. Such a distinction has not, as far as we know, so far been made in the writing on the subject.

Has incest then no relationship to paedophilia? There can be no doubt that there is an *incestuous form of paedophilia*, but this represents a relatively small group. It occurs mostly amongst fathers and stepfathers who commit offences against their still small children, mostly of both sexes (in our material two men and five incestuous relationships) and who, according to American research, were also previously receptive on the homosexual plane (Gebhard and collaborators 1965, pp. 219–20); in further cases one is dealing with late or senile paedophilia among grandfathers who not only concentrate their mostly masturbatory contacts on their grandchildren, but also involve other children (in our material three men and four incestuous relationships), and finally in extremely rare cases with highly abnormal mothers (one of our cases: a sexually inhibited, apparently congenitally weak-minded woman, twenty-eight, married, who committed fellatio on her three-year-old son and forced him to masturbate in her presence). These instances – however different they may be aetiologically – belong *primarily to paedophilia*, and only secondarily to incest. They are – as always with true paedophilia, in their 'basic bisexual' aspect – not always immediately recognisable, if, apart from heterosexual–paedophiliac offences, there is evidence already of like offences of a homosexual nature (Giese, 1965). It is therefore extremely likely that apart from the paedophiliac cases mentioned here (six men/women) there are some others concealed amongst those where non-coital contacts on the part of the male with under-age girls were concerned (cf. p. 105 f.). In the whole of our material (comprising sixty-seven males and females) only about *nine per cent could be definitely described as paedophiliacs* ($N = 6$). The following case illustrates a variant of true paedophilia.

Case 21a: At the beginning of the incest the male subject was fifty-four, violent and quick-tempered, an alcoholic, before the courts on more than ten occasions, predominantly for property offences, work-shy, and married three times. The marriage had not been harmonious from the start and had been absolutely destroyed in later years by the subject's heavy drinking. The intrafamily situation was marked by the formation of various polarised relationships: the father was very fond of both his own sons, while he disliked his stepdaughter and was openly prejudiced against her. This led to considerable tension and rivalry in the fight for the parents' favour. They, for their part, were always having violent scenes. The subject's extra-family contacts were minimal, so that he could be said to exist in a state of social isolation. His stepdaughter, who grew up mostly in children's homes, was beyond parental control at the age of fourteen, and had two illegitimate children by two different fathers. The close relationship between the father and sons then grew to include homosexual contacts with the nine- to ten-year-old son, including mutual masturbation. The boy, who was of average intelligence, said nothing for fear of the father and his threats. In the course of time the subject then tried to start sexual contacts with this boy's younger brother. At the same time he made immature sexual approaches to his stepdaughter, though not seriously, since she decisively rejected her stepfather's advances. These multiple incestuous relations were only revealed when the subject approached a six-year-old girl and tried to masturbate her while she was asleep. The whole of the man's life-history indicated a strong paedophile tendency which had also caused the collapse of his various marriages.

Incest and psychoses

Even in quite recent times various experts have quoted isolated cases of psychotic persons committing incest (Wahl, 1960; Kahn, 1965; and others). We have already recorded the fact above that there is only a very limited percentage of mentally ill subjects to be found amongst those who commit incest (cf. p. 131). It is worth noting that such men or women only slip into incest at times of illnesses which are accompanied by *heightened activity* (manic, hypomanic phases, schizophrenic episodes). Whether and to what extent in such cases the incestuous activity is one of many symptoms accompanying a pathological process or is a biographically explicable tendency, which manifests itself under certain conditions of illness, can only be answered for individual cases, and then probably not in every case. However one may answer this question, the decisive point here is the connection between incestuous activity and genuine illness. The only such case in our material should make this clear.

Case 78: Subject is a twenty-six-year-old man of average intelligence and married for several years. In his occupation he was at first regarded as hard-working and reliable. About three years before the start of incest he became increasingly abnormal and began giving 'wild' tirades at his place of work, he was irritable and had fits of excitement which were associated with acts of violence. Because of this he was sent to a clinic where a hallucinatory endogenous psychosis of the manic-depressive kind was diagnosed. His condition varied between subdepression and hypomania during which he voiced ideas for political and religious salvation, and the betterment of the world. Some time after his stay in the clinic he made a serious attempt at suicide. He began to change his job frequently, and had more frequently recurring fits of nervous excitement so that finally he had again to have psychiatric treatment. In the last six months before the beginning of incest he began to drink large quantities of alcohol and began to go sexually astray with other women. One evening he rushed at his elderly mother and masturbated her. About this event, he declared that it was surely 'natural' for every mother to wait for the day when her son, whom she had once carried in her own body, returned to her. By 'returning to his mother's body' the man had meant that she was only waiting for him to satisfy her sexually.

Style and forms of perversion

The negative evaluation of people who contravene a specialised sexual taboo in society is based on a generalisation. They are written off as 'disgusting,' 'sick' and not infrequently as 'perverted'. Particularly strong condemnation is incurred by offenders contravening the laws governing the inviolability of children and juveniles (Schmidt and Sigusch, 1967). Sociological research in the USA has shown that mother-son and father-daughter incest call forth the strongest negative reactions in society, whilst brother-sister incest is still, at some distance, the most tolerated (Weinberg, 1963). Even if in Germany there is still no evidence from socio-psychological researches into the surrounding world's attitudes towards, and opinions on, incest, it can safely be assumed that the contravention of such a strong taboo can produce negative reactions as strong as those Schmidt and Sigusch have indicated empirically for other sexually deviant groups.

The Swedish specialist on incest, Sonden, has already emphasised in 1936 that *incest very seldom has anything to do with perverse sexual behaviour*, and Schwab (1938) gave a figure for perversions of three per cent. If one takes Giese's (1962a) concept of perversion, and the criteria given by him, of which uncontrollable manias are the most important, then the number of perversions in our material is eight per cent (N = 6). This relatively high percentage is composed of two incestuous paedophiliac stepfathers, a paedophiliac mother and three incestuous–heterosexual fathers and stepfathers. The three sexologically interesting cases are the hetero-homosexual triads (three-sided intercourse), in two cases of which the male subjects' wives were also active participants. Fig. 12 contains three sexual constellations, of which the essentially perverse main symptoms (according to Giese) should be obvious from the example of the following case (Type A).

Case 52: The man and wife before the court were in their forties and for both of them this was their second marriage. They had not been before the courts before and although their social and professional development was completely unremarkable, financially they had looked after both their children very well. The family's living conditions were also sufficient and well ordered. But a look at their personalities and compatibility raises a few questions. The husband was an extremely unstable man and prone to violence. Despite his good performance at work, he was condemned by his superiors and his colleagues as 'arrogant' and 'obstinate', and was avoided by them. Towards the wife and stepdaughter he was despotic and tyrannical. His wife, on the other hand, was an intellectually unremarkable woman with a very serious inferiority complex which became especially strong in this second marriage. From the time of the wedding and for a considerable period afterwards sexual relations between the two partners were completely regular and normal. But the husband gradually developed a different form of sexual behaviour and two practices came continually to the fore: watching his wife masturbating at his request with various objects, and listening to reports of various 'sexual experi-

Incest and abnormal sexual behaviour 203

The hetero-homosexual triads

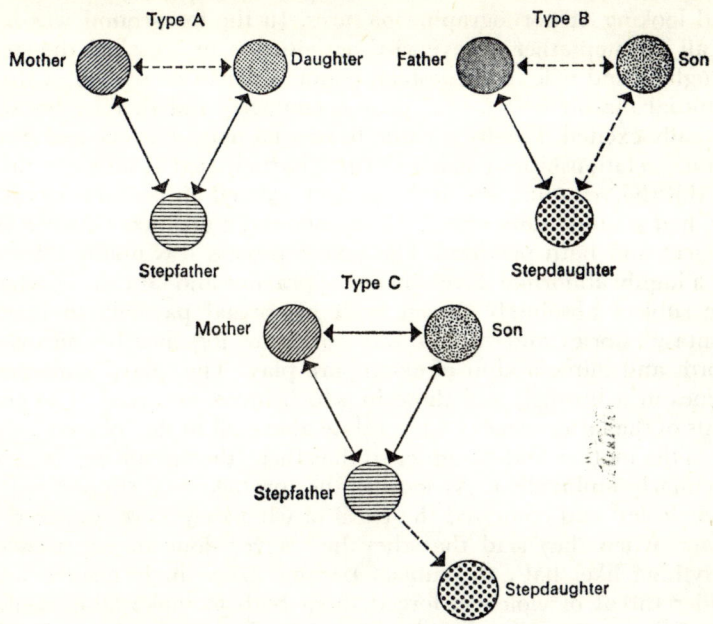

Figure 12. Schematic depiction of hetero-homosexual triads.
Notes: ⟨----⟩ = mutual sexual contact (masturbation, oral–genital contacts); ⟨——⟩ = coitus (heterosexual); ----⟩ unilateral sexual contact (masturbation, etc.).

ences' of a lesbian character, which his wife had to invent and relate to him. The act of coitus was then added to these 'fantasy' stories, and 'voyeurist' activities. Even if these practices could not in any sexological way be regarded as perverse in the real sense, the further course of events revealed what tendencies they concealed and what role they were to play in the development of the perversion.

The subject, who behaved towards his stepdaughter at the age of puberty with tenderness and care as well as strictness, developed an increasing sexual desire for her. Eventually he slipped into incest with her and extended the same sexual practices he employed on his wife to his stepdaughter as well. At this stage admittedly they did not get as far as coitus. At the same time he demanded of his wife, who had for some time been completely subservient to him in sexual matters, that she win over the daughter for a triad-relationship. In doing this the subject tried to persuade his wife that she had really had lesbian relations with her daughter before. The sexual contacts which now followed, developing between mother, daughter and stepfather, were accompanied frequently by drinking and looking at pornographic pictures. In the foreground was first of all the stepfather's 'voyeurist' activities as he watched the stepdaughter and wife in the lesbian contacts which he wished of them (mutual masturbation, oral–genital contacts) and thereby became sexually excited. Finally it came to mutual masturbatory and oral–genital relationships in which all three participated at the same time. In this the 'sex talk', which the subject ordered his partners to carry on, had a stimulatory effect. There followed coital acts between the subject and both partners. The sexual process was finally effected by a highly abnormal development of practice and fantasy, in which the subject absolutely forced both his sexual partners to invent 'fantasy' stories and in this way to create together by means of words and mime a kind of extempore play. The 'plays' concerned scenes in a brothel, and those in which incest occurred. The contents of the latter scenes had to relate above all to the 'players', that is, to the mother and daughter so that their 'theatricalising' became peculiarly ambivalent. As soon as the 'protagonists' slipped out of their 'roles' and contested the truth of what they were supposed to enact, when they said that they had never done or experienced 'anything like that', the subject became exceedingly excited and, under threat of violence, forced them both to make false 'confessions'. It is especially clear here how the fantasy developed by the subject and projected as it were to the outside, which had, as a 'fantastic story', to be 'acted' by others, served as a 'crutch' for a deficient sexual function. This attempt to introduce the sexual process, in fact to make it possible at all, is doomed to failure, above all when the discrepancy between fantasy and reality takes on for the pervert subject an unbearable and frustrating aspect, produced by the 'actresses forgetting their roles'. In this particular case, which apart from the other practices, finally led to excrementophilia, one can point to all the main symptoms of a real perversion mentioned by Giese (1962a) (decrease in sensitivity, increasing frequency and decreasing sexual satisfaction, construction of fantasies, abnormal practices, craftiness, warped receptivity and periodicity of stress and anxiety). The anonymity of the partner alone seems to be missing, since it is indeed a case of incest. Yet it is only apparently missing. Through the compulsion he exercises on his partners to 'theatricalise' the subject creates for himself – not, to be sure, knowingly or intentionally – an artificial social distance, a pseudo-anonymity which attains a great degree of illusory apersonality, especially in the 'brothel scene'. That this development led, shortly before his arrest, to the subject's complete promiscuity (an attempt to start up such relationships with other women as well) was – quite within the meaning of Giese's criteria for perversion – merely a logical outcome of the perverse aberration.

We have presented this case of a perverse development in slightly more detail, since it illustrates, we believe, a sexologically fundamental difference from 'average incest'. Here we are dealing not with incestuous, and thus abnormal, sexual behaviour, but with pathological sexual behaviour in the clinical sense which also contravenes a sexual taboo and a legal norm still strong in our society. It is perversion, and the destructive element peculiar to it (Bürger-Prinz, 1954; Giese, 1962a), which gives incestuous behaviour a pathological appearance.

Emotional partnership and 'free' relationship

Sexually deviant or abnormal behaviour still does not embody asociality from a sociological point of view, and abnormal sex behaviour in the sense of contravention of norms is still not identical with the pathological phenomenon of perversion (Giese, 1962a, 1962b). That sexually deviant behaviour 'brings about the desired social effect only indirectly' (Giese, 1962b, p. 186) and can quite easily be approximated to the norm, is shown by those, not quite so rare, impressive cases of incest which are characterised by an *emotionally loaded partnership*. The psychiatrist Gerchow describes a case history of such a relationship – an incestuous relationship of some years' standing between half-brother and half-sister – with the words: 'They both lived and live together as a model married couple. In this sociological sphere I have seldom seen a more stable or loving marital situation whose focal point and content is the care and upbringing of exceptionally well brought up children' (1965, p. 43). Especially tragic are those cases in which the brothers and sisters grow up apart, get to know each other later, and fall in love. In the USA amongst thirty-nine incest cases S. K. Weinberg (1963) found six such cases.

In general, however, one gets the impression that it is precisely brother–sister incest that represents a more or less emotionally charged transitional period of joyful sexual experimentation. As a rule this does not last and is resolved again free of conflict. This is backed up by the extremely short – compared with father–daughter incest – period of activity (according to Weinberg, 1963, p. 121: seventy-four per cent lasted less than one year, thirteen per cent more than three years).

It is no different with partner-orientated love relationships between stepfather and stepdaughter, to which the fact of relation by marriage gives the status of an offence. At the dissolution of the marriage, however, on which the marriage relationship is based, sexually deviant behaviour is no longer present, and there is no offence under the law, as long as the girl is not under fourteen–sixteen years of age (see § 173, section V, § 176, No. 3, and § 182, German Penal Code). From a sexological point of view, in this form of incest one can be dealing with a completely normal psychological partnership, depending on the kind of relationship between the people involved, a partnership which is essentially no different from an everyday one in which a middle-aged man falls in love with a sixteen- or seventeen-year-old girl, and she with him. That such a partnership is accompanied on the girl's side, not infrequently, with wish-fulfilment desires arising from the inadequacy of reality for her, and in some cases is forced by a narcissistically coloured need for a gain in status by subjecting the male partner to her youthful charms, is a completely different question. Such relationships may equally well be carried on from a sense of responsibility. The forensic reality of incest provides an increasing number of examples of this kind of 'false position within general order' (Giese), which has nothing destructive about it, if the family and marriage of the male partner were destroyed some years before the beginning of the incestuous relationship, and did not involve compulsion, threats, enticement or violence in the development of the partnership. The legal question of the age-limit, up to which the juvenile's sphere of sexual self-determination should and must be protected, is indeed regulated by the laws for the protection of juveniles, but scientifically the age-limit is still a debating point (cf. Jäger, 1957, pp. 53–4).

From these genuine, if chancy, partnerships must be distinguished the *free relationships* which, in incest – as in the everyday sphere – can take on the most varied forms. They stretch from the 'casual affair', through the relationship provoked by childish experimentation and curiosity about sex on the part of the victim herself, and the relationship dictated by the promiscuity of both incest partners, to those cases where the young girl is a simple sexual object for the male. We have produced examples for most of these forms.

What we have attempted to show is the *completely heterogeneous picture of incestuous relationships* which, although it carries the stamp of deviant or abnormal sexual behaviour, provides a spectrum stretching, from a sexological point of view, from the psychologically normal to the pathological.

9. The effects of incest

If relatively little space is devoted at the end of this book to the sociologically, psychologically and legally very interesting question of the effects of incestuous activities on the families and victims, then there are several reasons for this: 1) Scientific pronouncements pertinent to this theme presuppose research applicable to the subject, and to a certain extent this has been done, but in other respects there are still considerable gaps. This is especially true as far as possible after-effects on the victim are concerned. 2) Most scientific works on incestuous activities, as they are understood here, are based on legal and court-procedural material in which only a short period of the life of the family and the victim are dealt with (usually up to one or two years after the discovery of the offence). Previous attempts to explore, with adequate methods, the further life course of such families usually failed for ethical or technical reasons (Gerchow, 1965, p. 38). 3) Examinations of the mental effects on victims, which were carried out at some remove from the date of the offence, came up against extremely difficult diagnostic problems, because it then often proved practically impossible to establish a firm connection between later disturbances and the offence. On the other hand a very violent psychological reaction which arises indirectly from, or soon after, a sexual offence, need not of necessity lead to a lasting disturbance of the equilibrium of the personality. Here again there are prognostic difficulties if the victim of a sexual offence is examined soon after the event (Groffmann 1962). 4) In view of the very incomplete knowledge we have today one is hesitant about adopting a consciously responsible scientific attitude towards the question of the after-effects of incestuous activities.

The family

In complete opposition to the generally held attitudes and notions which are expressed in the motivation behind the law, most recent empirical surveys come to the conclusion that incest is not a cause but a symptom or result of a family whose inner order was as a rule already disturbed before the offence. This is obviously true also in those cases in which the contravention of the sexual taboo within the family meets the legal definition of incest (coitus). Sociologically there is **no** difference between the two offences separately defined and separately punished in law, but forensically the difference is perhaps only that the non-coital forms of contact in the primary stages of incest are retarded activities or are eventually seen to represent psychopathological behaviour (e.g. paedophilia).

But what in fact are the effects on the family, and, to be precise, the effects *during the incestuous relationship* and *after its discovery*?

It is today a well-tried and proven discovery of psychological and psychiatric research that the harmful effects on the family *brought about by the official discovery of the offence and punishment of it are more serious* than those which might arise during the course of incest (Gerchow, 1965). Since the beginning of this century writers on legal matters such as Mittermaier (1906), Hiller (1926) and Jäger (1957) have pointed to the same conclusion. The process of punishing and the act of condemning the man involved in incest not only bring about economic depression for the family over some period of time (forty-two per cent), but they also lead in many cases to a separation or to the arrest of both parents, which breaks up the unit (forty-four per cent) and – what is in most cases far worse – the sending of the victim to a children's home (thirty-six per cent) which makes the child feel that it is being punished. This is to say nothing of the often significant discrimination exercised by society (twenty-six per cent) which can break up the remainder of the family, and in some cases can lead to their being asked to leave their accommodation. What happens to families in which, after the discovery of incest, the wife applies for separation, but then, for whatever reasons, withdraws the application (around ten per cent), or decides unhesitatingly to keep the marriage going (forty-seven per cent), is known in only a few cases. They either remain completely free of conflict or the mother's decision leads to a crisis of confidence on the part of the daughter and, under certain circumstances where a close incestuous love relationship existed, to a jealous and hostile rivalry between mother and daughter. This latter situation is particularly sharply accented when the case concerns stepdaughter-incest resulting in the birth of a child ($N = 5$). There must be added to this the negative effects – often psychologically unassessable and unquantifiable – which arise for the wife and daughter from the police and legal investigations as well as from the psychological and psychiatric clarificatory examinations and from the trial itself. Already in 1915 H. Marcuse had pointed to the fact that the legal process, because of the '*psychological poisoning*' which it wrought, was a measure more likely to destroy the family than to protect it. An examination of the facts, however, might lead one to adhere none too closely to this argument.

Nevertheless there are, even during the period of the incest, direct or indirect effects on the constitution of the family. They centre essentially round the inevitably increasing tensions and disagreements which arise between the husband and wife (twenty-three per cent), as well as around the incest-conditioned tensions between mother and daughter (seventeen per cent). The latter arise most frequently where the victim has a loving or protective stepfather (phi-correl. 56***), or where the daughter is neglected and ethically indifferent (phi-correl. 49***). As a rule, however, there are no negative effects on the make-up of the family for a long time, and when there are they are only detectable shortly before the end of the incest. The reasons for this reside first in the fact that the intra-family situation in the majority of cases is already disturbed before the start of incestuous activities, the family atmosphere is unharmonious and tense so that the behaviour between man and daughter which eventually sharpens the general position is at first not at all noticed by the third parties, who are, as it were, used to rows, anger and tension. Second is the fact that, as we have seen, the 'secret world' of the incest partners within the family has existed for some time, however it may have arisen. When it is early broken through by the victim, it can happen that the mother does not believe her daughter's revelations (nine per cent) and/or nevertheless tolerates the sexual relations for some reason.

Above all there remains the question of the direct and indirect effects of the whole process on the victim.

Victims

Psychiatric work amongst young people offers constant proof of the fact that, among the direct physiological effects of sexual crime on very young girls, pregnancy is the most serious in human and social terms (Geisler, 1959; Wallis, 1965). The damage is less physical – young mothers have no higher rate of birth complications than adults – than psychological as a result of the grave nature of the offence and the discriminatory reactions of people around her which often heighten this.

In the group we examined, thirteen juvenile girls were made pregnant by their actual father (N = 7) or stepfather (N = 6), that is eighteen per cent of the whole group (taken as N = 70), and thirty-three per cent of the legally defined cases of incest. Ten girls between the age of fifteen and nineteen, i.e. fifteen per cent of the whole group, went through with their pregnancies. Finke and Zeugner (1934) as well as Plaut (1960) found, in groups which might be treated as comparable, completely similar percentages (thirteen or fifteen per cent). If one proceeds, however, from the basis of incest committed the risk of pregnancy is admittedly higher (my own researches: twenty-six per cent; Weinberg [1963] in the USA: twenty-one per cent; Schwab [1938] in Germany: twenty-eight per cent).

In three cases the fathers attempted abortions on their

daughters, and in two cases were successful. The pregnancy terminations were primitive and unscientific without the slightest precautions being taken against infection. In one case psychiatric grounds were produced for an *interruptio* and the termination was brought about by specialists.

At the time of giving birth the average age of the girls was 15·9 years, the youngest was fifteen and the oldest nineteen. The majority of fathers and stepfathers (N = 11) were at the time of procreation in their forties and fifties, the youngest was thirty-one and the oldest fifty-five.

How did these girls react to pregnancy and giving birth, and what was their attitude to the child? Of the thirteen girls nine experienced the pregnancy as a psychological burden. One seventeen-year-old was extremely indifferent towards what was happening, one girl was so childish still that her condition up to delivery meant nothing at all to her (isolated case), and yet another seventeen-year-old reacted to being pregnant by her stepfather with great joy. The psychological burden was less a result of the pregnancy itself than of the mainly negative reactions of her more immediate relatives and friends, and of the public at large. A critical part in this was played above all by the behaviour of the father or stepfather. Only six male incest partners pressed for or attempted abortions, and two of this group demanded of the girl that she name someone else as father of the child, or suspected that the pregnancy was the result of promiscuity. In five cases altogether there were, throughout, serious tensions between the incest partners and in two between mother and daughter. Two men carried on the sexual relations without any heed to the pregnancy. Six girls suffered serious situations of conflict as a result of the negative reaction of the world around them, and in three further cases there were close love relationships.

It is even more surprising that the *majority of the girls* (N = 8)

TABLE 29 Attitude of girls towards father/stepfather during pregnancy (N = 13)

Total	Positive	Negative	Ambivalent	Unknown
13	8	3	1	1

were positively inclined towards their partner, even during the pregnancy (this includes three close love relationships and one case of the daughter wishing for a pregnancy).

The following case illustrates this, as well as the individual reactions common to the girls.

Case 22: The subject who, in the course of an incestuous relationship of some duration with her own father, was made pregnant by him at the age of fourteen and a half, accepted her changed physical condition at first with a certain amount of resignation. She had not the slightest idea of what was happening to her. Her parents had never explained pregnancy and childbirth to her. Her own statements showed that she had absolutely no conception of the processes of childbirth. Until about the sixth month of pregnancy she was full of childish high spirits, although she was aware that her menstruation had ceased. Only in the seventh month, when she was told of her pregnancy by a doctor, did she begin to grasp that her father, whom up till now she had loved, and who moreover had never used violence against her, had done her a 'wrong'. She did not want the baby taken from her, although she had no notion of what was involved in bringing up a child. She continued going to school up until the last two months of pregnancy, but then asked to leave because she felt increasingly unsure of herself and hindered by her condition. She also feared that her classmates might discriminate against her. She was increasingly subject to fits of depression. At times she would cry helplessly, and say of her father who was in prison: 'But he's still my father, and he's always looked after us so well.' It was only with difficulty that she could give up her feelings of love for him, and she was continually trying to blur over what had happened, and her condition. Almost two years later when she was in a clinic as a result of a serious attempt at suicide, she explained in retrospect that sometimes during the last two months of pregnancy she had thought about her father's suggestions of an abortion, but had then decided to have the child since she would otherwise never have any proof against her father, who had denied the offence when arrested, and people would have been right in suspecting that the child was someone else's. She had, as well, been afraid of permanent damage to her health and was worried that an abortion might prevent her from having children later on. But these considerations had only arisen much later.

The story of this girl shows how first the gradual realisation of pregnancy and its resulting effects and then the father's reactions (suggested abortion) led to a serious spiritual crisis. In only one case was the process of realisation absent as a result of the victim's childish naïveté and lack of negative reactions from the people around her. The girl was spared a difficult emotional crisis, at least until delivery of the child. One other girl remained completely free of conflict, and we shall report her case shortly.

No less surprising are the young mothers' reactions at the birth of their children. Six of the ten girls adopted an absolutely positive attitude, did not want to be parted from their baby in any way, and tried to cope with their maternal duties as best they could. All the same, one of these girls (Case 22) made a serious attempt at suicide in a situation of social and emotional pressure, almost two years after the birth of her child. Two further juveniles gave up their children and had them put in a home and made available for adoption, and the very young mother, whose childish and artless pregnancy was mentioned above, did not want to see her baby at all. In the case of all

TABLE 30 Attitude of young mother to child (N = 10)

Total	Positive	Negative	Ambivalent	Unknown
10	6	2	1	1

six girls with a positive attitude it was not the child as such which was a cause of anxiety, but the conditions in which these girls were trying to fulfil their roles as mothers. Situations of emotional stress, often serious, also arose after the birth from the jealousy, envy and hatred of their own mother (especially in the cases of love relationships with the stepfather), and the negative reactions and actions of the male partner as well as discrimination from people around her. Emotional decompensation, psychogenic troubles, and bouts of depression so bad as to produce a short-circuit reaction on the part of the victim were effects of which, at the time of the enquiry, it was impossible to be anything like certain whether they were the initial symptoms of a deep-seated, far-reaching personality disturbance, or should be interpreted as only temporary phenomena. Just how free of complication and conflict an incestuous pregnancy resulting in a baby can be, if the family and surroundings are free of tension, is shown by the following case.

Case 60: The young girl concerned was made pregnant by her stepfather during an incestuous relationship completely free of conflict and tension. When her pregnancy was confirmed she told her mother, who then confronted the husband. He at once admitted the relationship and the 'family council' decided to keep the baby's origin secret. The man's wife forgave him, since he was in all other respects a good father to his family. She was of the opinion that it was quite likely that they could 'get this child through' as well. The daughter was glad about the pregnancy and the baby, since she had earlier been told by doctors that she would never have children, which had depressed her for some time. The stepfather paid his daughter regular maintenance, the relationship remained unclouded and the 'family peace' was preserved. It was only years later that the whole story came to light in the course of an adoption proceeding. In order to make possible the adoption of the child – the stepdaughter wanted to marry – the father, with the agreement of the whole family, put himself at the mercy of the law and was fortunate in finding a lenient judge.

Independently of the question of the psychological effects which might be brought about by pregnancy, attempted abortions and babies, the Swiss psychiatrist Friedemann (1965) reports several incest victims in whom such after-effects as frigidity, negligence, serious difficulties in learning and tendencies towards prostitution were evident. Other experts are convinced, on the basis of individual cases, that incestuous relations between parents and children 'already in themselves indicate grave psychological traumas' (Geisler, 1959, p. 85). Sloane and Karpinski (1942) found amongst five female victims of incest in the USA that there were later considerable disturbances of personality and tendencies to promiscuity. Only one young woman was well adjusted. In contrast to this Holder in Switzerland came to the conclusion that there were no grounds for thinking that 'girls involved suffered a premature awakening or heightening of sexual drive and an accompanying sexual degeneration and lapse into prostitution' (1949, p. 190). Dealing with 159 cases of father–daughter incest in the USA,

S. K. Weinberg (1963) came to similar results, and he thinks that a number of these girls later became well enough socially and sexually adjusted, although several turned to prostitution and others had to have psychiatric treatment. These few examples serve to show what varied pronouncements there may be on the effects on the victims of incestuous acts. Our own surveys have not helped to add anything to the question of after-effects (see the preface to this chapter).

There can, however, be no doubt that in some girls neurotic symptoms and other psychopathological phenomena appear after the start of the relationship; but our researches show that such symptoms occur no more frequently after the act of incest than before, when one is dealing with the development of a disturbed personality (cf. pp. 167 ff.). All the same, this says nothing about whether the symptoms which appear after the act may not eventually be more serious. On the basis of our experience we would tend to think this is the case, although no proof is at hand yet. If we disregard twelve of the fourteen less gifted girls where a judgment is difficult to make we achieve, through an analysis of the pathogenetic connections between incest and disturbance of personality, the results collated in Table 31:

TABLE 31 Pathogenetic connections between incestuous acts and disturbances of personality: frequency division and the results of a chi-squared test

Causal effect of incest	Heightening effect of incest	No connection	Chi-squared test
13	10	14	$p > 50\%$ n.s.

According to these figures in thirteen cases incestuous activity was completely decisive as the direct cause of the personality disturbance, in ten girls the set of symptoms as they existed before the act were possibly heightened by the act, and in fourteen cases there was *no traceable connection* between incestuous activity and psychopathological phenomena. If we take together the negative causal effect of incest and its influence on an already existing set of symptoms (N = 23) one would hardly be underestimating the psychological effects on the victims – without even taking into account the indirect, mostly transitory psychological reactions of these girls during the relationship itself (conflicts, fear of the father, feelings of guilt towards the mother, etc.).

10. Conclusion

This book arose out of the desire to inform, to destroy prejudices, to counteract the widely accepted caricatures and half-truths about abnormal sexual behaviour. In lieu of a summary the author would like to conclude with a few of the main points which have emerged.

1) From a historical and anthropological point of view the incest taboo emerges as a piece of cultural history. It has so far withstood all theoretical attempts to explain how it arose. There can be no doubt of the close connection between the taboo and man's attitudes towards religious cults and magic. In modern industrial society the incest taboo has indeed lost its socially vital significance, nevertheless it is an integrated part of the family structure and exercises important psychological and social effects on the development of the individual personality.

2) The variable nature of the legal treatment of incest reflects not only the uncertainty of official attitudes and postures towards the 'crime,' but also the dependence upon culture and epoch, and uncertainty about the punishable nature of, and the aim of guarding against, the 'crime'. The basic motivation of today's laws will withstand neither critical nor rational examination, nor empirical testing by the medical and behavioural sciences. They appear to be a kind of ingrained prejudice.

3) Incest is committed not only by highly abnormal personalities, but also at least equally as frequently by those whose

basic condition, both socially and psychopathologically, is in no way exceptional. The mentally or emotionally disturbed type is very little represented.

4) Families in which incest occurs are usually disturbed before it starts. To this extent incest is not the cause but one symptom of a disturbed family. The best defence against it therefore is an intact family order, and not special incriminations with massive threats of punishment. An intact family unit would strike at the very roots of incest, and at the same time afford a means of protecting the family unit.

5) Incestuous relations between father and daughter develop mostly against a background of disharmony or disorganisation in the family interrelationships, often a preliminary stage of one partner leaving, or of a mutual break-up. The beginning of such relationships is to a great extent dependent upon the biological maturity of the juvenile female partner. Whilst at the outset the 'initiative' of the male involved determines what happens, changes in behaviour take place in both partners over a longer period of time. As the female victim grows older and her extra-family social orientation grows, so the male partner finds, against his will, that the 'initiative' is increasingly slipping from his grasp.

6) Incestuous behaviour is only deviant or abnormal in so far as it goes against the sexual taboo of the family and injures the norms and expectations current in our society. Yet it is very seldom 'perverse' in the sexological sense. Incest cannot as a rule be considered paedophiliac, even though there may be cases of incestuous paedophilia. As far as partnership is concerned, that is from a personal and sexual point of view, incestuous relations cannot be forced into a pattern. They stretch from emotionally laden partnerships (close love relationships) to free relationships in which the victim is degraded to a mere sexual object.

7) The negative effects of incest on the family when it becomes known and is punished are often more serious than those which might arise while it is going on. Amongst the most serious psychological results on the victim is the burdensome situation brought about by pregnancy and the birth of a child, which

can be ascribed in the first place to the mostly negative reactions of the close family environment. The reactions of the victim go from attempted suicide and serious neurotic disturbances to neglect and promiscuous tendencies. The incest can also be completely free of conflict for the victim, though, and without obvious psychological after-effects. There is no verified information today, however, on the possible long-term effects on those involved.

Incest in English Law

Although, as A. S. Diamond has remarked, 'incest is one of the earliest crimes known to the law, along with murder by magic and a few sacral offences',[1] it is in fact one of the latest crimes to enter the English criminal law calendar, dating as it does from 1908. We shall trace the steps by which this crime emerged in England and Wales, being dealt with first exclusively by the ecclesiastical courts, until the decision to incorporate it in the domestic English criminal law was taken.

First, it should be noted that all societies have experienced the practice of incest and have developed prohibitions designed to control or prevent it.[2] We do not know what prompted the taboos and prohibitions which surrounded incest, whether it was the desire to preserve the unity of the family, to encourage mating outside the family circle, to protect the children of the family or to provide for the healthy psychosexual development of the child. What does seem clear is that it was universally condemned or thought reprehensible, and somehow the lofty sanctions of religious prohibition were attached to it as a means of discouraging this behaviour. As Diamond says, 'the practice of witchcraft, incest, bestiality, and adultery are considered to be offences against God, and to render a man unclean in a religious sense'.[3]

Trial was by ordeal before the priest, but the punishment was not always, as in the other grave offences, the death penalty. Pollock and Maitland say that sometimes these offences were punished in the ecclesiastical courts by whipping and other bodily penances; but often they were paid for with money.[4]

The records show that the English ecclesiastical courts were quite active in the period 1475–1640. From the time of the

[1] A. S. Diamond, *The Evolution of Law and Order*, 1951, p. 21.
[2] Clelland S. Ford, 'Sex Offences: An Anthropological Perspective', in *Law and Contemporary Problems*, Spring 1960, Vol. XXV, No. 2, pp. 225 *et seq.*
[3] *Op. cit.* pp. 188–9.
[4] Pollock and Maitland, *The History of English Law Before the Time of Edward I*, Vol. II, 2nd ed. 1968, p. 544.

Act of Elizabeth of 1558 there was a shared jurisdiction with the Crown, which exercised jurisdiction through the Court of High Commission concurrently with the Church courts. The smaller ecclesiastical courts continued to exercise a jurisdiction to police all sorts of immoral practices until 1640. The Court of High Commission was for persons of high rank, and the punishments were 'infinitely more serious'.[5] The Court of High Commission was abolished in 1640, the statute of Elizabeth was repealed and with it went all the jurisdiction of the ecclesiastical courts in these matters, including that of the minor ecclesiastical courts.[6] The Restoration saw the repeal of the statute of 1640, and in 1661 the jurisdiction of the ecclesiastical courts was restored, with the exception of the Court of High Commission. The Church courts continued to exercise their jurisdiction over moral offences throughout the eighteenth and nineteenth centuries, though gradually many of these matters were left to be dealt with by the ordinary civil courts, being made felonies by statute. By the time when Stephen wrote, in 1883, incest remained 'the only form of immorality which in the case of the laity is still punished by ecclesiastical courts on the general ground of its sinfulness'.[7]

In the late nineteenth century, however, it seems that cases of incest were not infrequently prosecuted as rape or (in the case of offences against girls under sixteen) unlawful sexual intercourse. However it gradually came to be realised that some separate provision should be made in the criminal law, and between 1893 and 1908 several unsuccessful attempts were made to establish a criminal offence of incest. There was at first considerable resistance to the idea of advertising such behaviour by criminal prosecution. The Lord Chancellor in 1899 and 1900 appears to have prevented any progress being made and the Home Office deferred to his view that such conduct was too rare to require legislation.

The Abortive Bill of 1903

In March 1903 the Member of Parliament for Essex, Epping, Colonel Lockwood, moved the Second Reading of his Incest

---
[5] Sir J. F. Stephen, *A History of the Criminal Law of England*, 1883, Vol. II, p. 422.
[6] *Ibid*. p. 428.   [7] *Ibid*. pp. 429–30.

Bill, designed to make the commission of incest an offence against the criminal law. He said he had been induced to introduce this measure 'by the number of such crimes being committed in the rural districts of England'.[8] He thought such conduct should be severely punished. The Bill passed all its stages in the House of Commons, but when it reached the Lords, the Lord Chancellor, the Earl of Halsbury, advised the House against adopting the measure. He believed that legislation of this character 'is calculated to do an infinite amount of mischief'.[9] One result would be more press publicity for this type of conduct and a tendency to multiply cases, 'and these are cases which it is inadvisable to drag into the light of day'. He thought that if the law which had prevailed for some centuries on the subject was to be altered, some greater case should have been made.

The Earl of Donoughmore, opening the Second Reading debate, said it was an undoubted fact that this offence was committed. Cases very often occurred both in large towns and in rural districts, and his enquiries had confirmed this. He appealed to the example of the United States, where many States recognised incest as a criminal offence, and particularly to the example of Scotland, where the offence had been punishable as a crime for many years. He thought the passing of the measure would be a most salutary preventive.[10]

Lord Davey agreed with the doubts expressed by the Earl of Halsbury concerning the wisdom of this measure. He thought that 'to ventilate a subject of this kind by means of prosecutions is likely to do a great deal more harm than good'.[11] There was no evidence that incestuous behaviour was becoming more common, or that it was necessary for any reasons to legislate against it. The Bill was by leave of the House withdrawn.

The Punishment of Incest Act, 1908

A second attempt to introduce legislation to make incest a criminal offence succeeded in 1908, largely because the Home

[8] Hansard, House of Commons, Vol. 118, col. 1683, 5 March 1903.
[9] Hansard, House of Lords, Vol. 125, col. 822, 16 July 1903.
[10] *Loc. cit.* col. 820-1.   [11] *Loc. cit.* col. 823.

Office view appears to have changed. In the previous year the Incest Bill of 1907 had been introduced with the full support of the Home Office, but after consideration by the House it was referred back for further statistical information to be collected. When it came back it was too late for legislation in the current Parliamentary session, and the Bill was reintroduced in 1908. Although once again serious doubts were expressed about the wisdom of legislating on the subject, this time in the House of Commons by Mr Rawlinson, the Hon. Member for Cambridge University.[12] He objected to the matter being dealt with 'at a late period on a Friday afternoon at the instigation of a private member' and thought that a sufficient case for the Bill had not been made out. He echoed the Earl of Halsbury's earlier doubts about the wisdom of giving such matters the prominence which prosecution would involve, with all the attendant publicity. He feared the danger of blackmail of every kind, and the risk of false accusations. On the question of alleged increase in incestuous behaviour, he asserted that such behaviour 'was far less known now than it was twenty or thirty years ago in parts of England'. There was no suggestion that this offence was on the increase. Prosecutions for this offence were practically unknown in Scotland. They should deal with the matter more by education that by extending the criminal law.

Mr Rawlinson's plea was supported by Mr Staveley Hill, but opposed by the Member for Bath, Mr Maclean, who argued that this crime was rife in certain parts of the country, 'and there was a case for the Bill on sociological grounds'. The cases which did occur were of the most grave kind.[13]

Mr Herbert Samuel, the Under-Secretary at the Home Office, supported the principle of the Bill, saying that 'the Home Office had long been aware, from the reports they had received from the police and other sources, that it was exceedingly necessary to add to the law provisions of the character proposed by this Bill'.[14] He mentioned that in Scotland the law was by no means a dead letter, there were every year a small number of convictions – about six a year. The offence might entail disastrous consequences. Though no one could say with any degree of certainty whether it was increasing or decreasing,

[12] Hansard, House of Commons, Vol. 191, col. 278, 26 June 1908.
[13] *Loc. cit.* col. 283.   [14] Col. 284

it was by no means rare. Society had a special interest that should lead to steps being taken to stop it.

Two other speakers expressed grave doubts about the wisdom of the measure, but the balance of opinion seems to have been in favour, and the attempt to stop the Bill was defeated. By five o'clock that Friday afternoon in June the debate was concluded.

In the House of Lords there was less difficulty. The Second Reading debate was opened by the Bishop of St Albans, who referred to the evidence of 'the great frequency of incest'. The Lord Chief Justice had sent a telegram supporting the Bill.[15] The Home Office spokesman (Earl Beauchamp) said that it was hoped the Bill would become law. The Home Office was convinced of the necessity for legislation 'to deal with this evil'.[16] Earl Russell had doubts as to whether turning this particular mischief into crime would necessarily reduce it. The Lord Chancellor (Lord Loreburn) thought it better to stigmatise this behaviour as a crime 'seeing that it produces not only moral depravity but also physical deterioration'.[17] The Bill became law after completing all its stages in both Houses.

The Present English Law

The present law about incest is contained in the Sexual Offences Act, 1956, which consolidated all the offences of a sexual kind in one measure, and repealed the Punishment of Incest Act, 1908. Section 10 provides that it is an offence for a man to have sexual intercourse with a woman whom he knows to be his granddaughter, daughter, sister, half-sister[18] or mother. This applies whether or not the relationship is traced through lawful wedlock. Section 11 provides that it is an offence for a woman of sixteen or over to permit a man whom she knows to be her grandfather, father, brother (half-brother)[18] or son to have sexual intercourse with her by her consent.

The penalty for completed offences is imprisonment not

---

[15] Hansard, House of Lords, Vol. 197, col. 1408, 2 December 1908.
[16] Col. 1409.   [17] Col. 1411.
[18] Sections 10(2) and 11(2) provide for the half-sister and half-brother to be included in the term brother or sister.

exceeding seven years, and in the case of an attempt imprisonment not exceeding two years.[19] However, if the incest is committed by a man with a girl under thirteen, and is so charged in the indictment, there may be imprisonment for life.[20] An attempt in such circumstances is punishable with imprisonment for not more than seven years.[20A]

Unless the prosecution is brought by or on behalf of the Director of Public Prosecutions, it is necessary to have the sanction of the Attorney-General.[21]

There are not many legal points which command attention in connection with prosecutions for incest. The most significant concern consent and the requirement of corroboration. As many acts of incest are permitted if not encouraged by the 'victim', consent is no defence to this crime. If the 'victim' gives evidence, then as this is the evidence of an accomplice, it will require corroboration. But the mere fact of submission by a female is not sufficient to constitute her an accomplice.[22] Independent evidence of a previous similar offence by the prisoner with the same person may be corroboration.[23] The purpose of the requirement of corroboration is to make it more difficult to make false allegations or to fabricate evidence.

The relationship of the parties to the incest must be proved. This may be done by oral evidence, or by tendering certificates of marriage or birth coupled with identification. Or there may be an admission by the prisoner.[24] A father who could prove he did not know it was his daughter with whom he was having sexual relations would have a defence.[25]

There must be proof of the commission of the offence. This may be inferred from all the circumstances of the case. Obviously direct evidence is rarely available. Evidence tending to show that a sexually passionate relationship existed between the parties beforehand is admissible.[26]

---

[19] Section 37 and Schedule II(15).
[20] Section 37 and Schedule II(14).
[20A] Indecency with Children Act, 1960, section 2.
[21] Section 37 and Schedule II.
[22] R. v. Dimes (1911) 7 Cr. App. R. 43.
[23] R. v. Hartley [1941] 1 K.B. 5; 28 Cr. App. R. 15.
[24] R. v. Jones (1933) 24 Cr. App. R. 55.
[25] R. v. Carmichael [1940] 1 K.B. 630; 27 Cr. App. R. 183.
[26] R. v. Ball [1911] A.C. 47, 6 Cr. App. R. 31, R. v. Bloodworth (1913) 9 Cr. App. R. 80.

On an indictment under section 10, Sexual Offences Act, 1956, the jury may find the accused guilty of the alternative offences under section 5 (intercourse with a girl under 13), under section 6 (intercourse with a girl between 13 and 16), or under section 7 (intercourse with a defective person).[27] On a trial for rape there is power to convict for incest.[28]

On conviction under section 10, an order may be made under section 38 divesting the convicted person of his authority as a parent over his child. Such orders are rarely made, presumably because today the protection afforded by the law relating to the care of children is regarded as sufficient.

Sentences for Incest

By no means all incest cases are followed by sentences of imprisonment but this is the fate of the majority of convicted offenders. When imprisonment is chosen, sentences of six or seven years have been upheld in modern times, and according to D. A. Thomas[29] shorter terms would seem to require the presence of mitigating factors. In practice few cases attract such long prison sentences. In a really bad case a sentence of fifteen years was imposed but was reduced on appeal to twelve years. D. A. Thomas says that the majority of appeal cases concern incest between father and daughter, the daughter being in her teens. Occasionally a younger child is involved.

Sometimes in incest there is an element of violence and the offence is tantamount to rape; often there is intimidation, and not infrequently there is mutual consent. Occasionally it is the 'victim' who has incited or encouraged the offence.

Thus viewed, incest becomes an offence of greatly varying moral turpitude, and the sentences will reflect the perception of the situation by the sentencing court. Either a conditional discharge, a suspended sentence or probation may be the appropriate penal measure in certain cases. The table on page 226 gives the disposal of convicted offenders in England and Wales in 1970.

[27] Section 37 and Schedule II(14).
[28] Section 37 and Schedule II(1)(a)(viii).
[29] D. A. Thomas, *The Principles of Sentencing*, 1970, p. 111.

226 *Incest*

ASSIZES AND QUARTER SESSIONS[30]

Persons convicted of incest (all ages)

Recognizance	1
Conditional Discharge	2
Mental Health Order & Restriction Order under section 65 Mental Health Act, 1959	2
Probation	16
Detention Centre	1
Suspended Sentence	12
Imprisonment	75
Total found guilty (including 5 females)	109

MAGISTRATES' COURTS

Persons found guilty of Incest[31]

Conditional Discharge	1
Probation	3
Fit Person Order	1
Approved School	1
Total found guilty	6*

* All these defendants were aged between 14 and 17 years. All defendants between 17 and 21 and all adult defendants were committed for trial.

Criminological Aspects of Incest

The non-public nature of the offence makes it exceedingly difficult to estimate the amount of incest which takes place or to describe its criminological characteristics with any accuracy. We do know however that between two and three hundred cases are reported and recorded each year as indictable offences known to the police in England and Wales. Because of the way these offences come to light, usually by the complaint of the 'victim' or a parent, there is very little doubt about the identity of the perpetrator of the crime. It follows that in any year a mere handful of the cases known are not cleared up. Of

[30] Home Office, Criminal Statistics (England and Wales), 1970, Table II(a) Cmnd. [31] Table I(a).

those 'cleared up' we have seen that there are something like one hundred or more convictions per annum (in 1970, 115). It is obvious then that at least as many cases are not followed by conviction or indeed by any legal proceedings at all. Clearly considerable discretion is exercised by the police and the prosecuting authorities in deciding whether to prefer charges. Of those charged in 1970 ten were acquitted at assizes or quarter sessions, and in three cases charges were withdrawn or dismissed at the magistrates' courts. Although proceedings were usually preceded by arrest rather than summons, half those committed for trial were granted bail.

The nature of incest varies so enormously that it is difficult to make any intelligent comment about the direction in which reform might proceed, short of abolishing the crime altogether. While there are some social scientists who see incest as one of the next candidates for removal from criminal law sanctions,[32] one is bound to say that at its gravest extremes this conduct may be exceedingly difficult and dangerous behaviour which sometimes has some of the elements of rape, or grievous bodily harm, not to mention its physical and psychological consequences. Even where physical violence is not used, there are frequently threats made to someone, a child or young person, who is necessarily in a very special position of physical, economic and emotional dependence on the parent. Sometimes there is sexual perversion, and the sexual relations may be homosexual rather than heterosexual in character. They may be prolonged over a considerable number of years, and with several children in the same family, either concurrently or consecutively.

One fact remains, and that is that after imprisonment it is a very difficult question whether the father should be allowed to re-establish himself in the home. Where there is already a divorce the question does not arise. Otherwise the interests of the children must be a paramount consideration. If the father goes home, the social services department may feel obliged to have the children removed from that home. If the children have already been taken into care, the father's reappearance in the home may delay if not altogether prevent their being allowed

---

[32] Norval Morris and Gordon Hawkins, *The Honest Politician's Guide to Crime Control*, 1970, p. 3 and pp. 18–19. Barbara Wootton, *Contemporary Britain*, p. 33.

home. The question of the father's residence in a hostel or lodgings may have to be considered unless there is another relative or friend with whom he can stay. In the end, we have the question of the father's future sexual behaviour to consider.

Is Incest a Predominantly Rural Crime?

It is sometimes suggested that incest occurs more frequently in rural areas, where it is prevalent among certain of the labouring population. There are signs in the debates of the 1903 Bill and the 1908 Act that this view was taken, and some hold it to be true today. An examination of the police figures in England and Wales for indictable offences known to them[33] does not bear out the suggestion that incest is a predominantly rural crime. There are just as many rural areas in the group of police districts reporting the lowest incidence of incest as in the group of police districts with a high incidence of incest. There are also a number of predominantly urban and metropolitan areas in each group. Nor is it possible to draw any conclusion about regional trends from an examination of these figures.

Incest in Scottish Law

The Incest Act, 1567, made incest criminal in Scotland. Dr Gordon considers this to have been merely declaratory of the common law.[34] Two differences may be noted between Scottish Law and that prevailing in England and Wales since 1908. Firstly, incest between bastard relations is not criminal in Scotland, but it is criminal in England and Wales.[35] Secondly, intercourse between uncle and niece is incestuous in Scotland but not in England and Wales.[36]

[33] Home Office Supplementary Statistics Relating to Crime and Criminal Proceedings, Table 4, Indictable Offences Known to the Police.
[34] G. H. Gordon, *The Criminal Law of Scotland*, 1967, p. 17.
[35] *Ibid.* p. 842.
[36] *H.M. Advocate v. Aikman and Martin*, 1917, J.C. 8. Gordon, p. 841.

Glossary of terms

Claustrophobia: fear of enclosed spaces.
Coitus: sexual intercourse.
Cunnilingus: stimulation of the female sexual organs with the mouth.
Defence mechanisms: unconscious psychological processes which have the aim of warding off unacceptable impulses and emotions and of suppressing them, so as to avoid guilt feelings and fear, and to soften conflicts. They are a concept of psychoanalysis (*q.v.*). The most important are repression (*q.v.*), projection (*q.v.*), sublimation (*q.v.*), rationalisation (*q.v.*) and reaction formation (*q.v.*).
Depression: disheartened emotional state accompanied by lowering of drive and initiative. If there is an external cause (e.g. a death) then one talks of reactive depression. When strongly marked and not accompanied by any observable external cause depression is a symptom of various psychoses (*q.v.*).
Encopresis: dirtying oneself (in children after the age of three).
Enuresis diurna: daytime wetting.
Enuresis nocturna: bed-wetting at night (in children after the age of three).
Fellatio: sexual excitement of the penis with the mouth.
Forensic Psychology: judicial psychology. The most important areas of work for forensic psychology are: examination of the state of mind and the responsibility of the accused; examination of the credibility of witnesses' statements; research into delinquent behavioural tendencies; research into the psychological effects of legal penalties and the possibility of social rehabilitation.
Frustration: failure of, or hindrance to, satisfaction of a need, a wish or an expectation, and the resulting emotional condition of disappointment, but also of excitement, exasperation and anger.
Hallucinations: deceptions of the senses; the subject becomes aware of (e.g. sees, hears, smells) something which does not exist in the world around him. Yet he is convinced of the reality of what he has perceived. Hallucinations are a symptom either of mental illness or narcotic poisoning.
Homosexuality: sexual attraction to persons of the same sex and sexual activity with such partners.
Hypersexuality: a very strong sexual desire, with heightened sexual activity.

Identification: the unconscious adoption of the modes of behaviour and attitudes of another person.

Impotence: a sexual disturbance in men. A lowering or loss of the capacity for erection. Impotent men can either not perform coitus at all, or only incompletely.

Indication: compelling grounds for the application of a particular cure or method of treatment.

Interruptio: termination of pregnancy.

IQ: intelligence quotient. A method of measuring intelligence as used in intelligence tests. The IQ points have the following meanings: over 120, very high intelligence; 110–119, high intelligence; 90–109, average intelligence; 80–89, limited intelligence; 70–79, very limited intelligence; under 70, weak-minded.

Libido: sexual drive, sexual desire.

Mania: mania belongs to the indigenous psychoses (*q.v.*). The different aspects of mania depend upon the phased course of the illness: periods of psychological 'normality' alternate with manic periods. The length of the individual periods differs from case to case. Some of the most important symptoms of mania are: unprompted and exaggerated cheerfulness, vanity, lack of restraint, heightening of sexuality and aggression, nervous excitement.

Manic-depressive insanity: this belongs to the endogenous psychoses (*q.v.*). This illness is characterised by the phased appearance of manic (cf. mania) and depressive (cf. depression) conditions.

Masturbation: sexual satisfaction of self. The excitement of one's own sexual organs with the aim of achieving sexual excitement and sexual pleasure.

Menarch: time of first menstruation.

Narcissism: sexually abnormal behaviour. For the narcissist his own body is the most important sexual object. Sexual excitement is achieved or heightened by the observation of his own body or mirror-image. For sexual satisfaction (mostly achieved by masturbation, but also through coitus) this observation of his own body is a vital or at least decisive ingredient. In a broader sense narcissism means any kind of 'being in love with oneself', exaggerated vanity, or unnecessarily high opinion of self.

Neurosis: psychologically abnormal way of behaving and perceiving (psychological illness), caused by unresolved conflicts. In contrast to psychoses (*q.v.*), neuroses are extensively influenced by external factors (childhood experiences).

Oedipal connection: abnormally strong and active affection for the parent of the opposite sex.

Oedipus complex: a stage in child–parent relationships (between the age of three and five) postulated by psychoanalysis (*q.v.*). According to the latter the child develops a very strong love for the parent of the opposite sex; the parent of the same sex is seen as an undesirable 'competitor', the child regards him/her with jealousy, hatred and – because of the threat of punishment – fear. This fear and the frustration of the 'incestuous' wishes by the parent of the opposite sex cause the child to suppress his oedipal wishes. At the same time the child identifies himself with the parent of the same sex and thus adopts the latter's behavioural tendencies, expectations and evaluations (commands and prohibitions). In girls the oedipus complex is often referred to as the Electra complex.

Ontogenesis: the development of the individual being from conception to the sexually mature adult.

Paedophilia: sexual attraction to children of the same or the opposite sex, and sexual activity with children.

Pavor nocturnus: 'night fear', being startled or shouting out in one's sleep. *Pavor nocturnus* is mostly present in children and can be a symptom of psychological disturbance.

Phobia: a morbid fear of certain objects or situations, without there being any real danger.

Phylogenesis: the collective history of life.

Projection: a defence mechanism (*q.v.*). One's own unconscious unacceptable drives and emotions are read into another person, ascribed to them, and in them criticised, devalued, despised and attacked.

Psychoanalysis: a theory of psychological illnesses (predominantly neuroses) founded by Sigmund Freud – and the technique of psychotherapy based upon it. The central points of psychoanalysis are theories of the psychodynamics of conflicts, and of the meaning of unconscious drives of the emotions.

Psychosis: mental illness. A distinction is made between exogenous psychoses caused by physical changes (e.g. brain damage following injuries or inflammatory fever, *inter alia*) and endogenous psychoses which are regarded as conditioned and not the results of acute physical changes. The most important endogenous psychoses are schizophrenia (*q.v.*), endogenous depression (*q.v.*), manic-depressive insanity (*q.v.*).

Psychosomatics: science of the effects of psychological processes on the occurrence and course of physical illnesses.

Psychotherapy: the treatment of psychiatric illness by psychological methods. The term is a general one and embraces various methods of therapy, e.g. psychoanalysis, group therapy, behavioural therapy, non-directive therapy, counselling, ontogenous training, etc.

Rationalisation: a defence mechanism (*q.v.*). A reasoned justification is made for an action whose main motivation is an unacceptable urge.

Reaction formation: a defence mechanism (*q.v.*). An unacceptable impulse or unacceptable emotion is turned into its opposite in order to overcome feelings of guilt and fear.

Regression: return to earlier, less mature patterns of behaviour, as the result of frustration or conflict; regression is a defence mechanism (*q.v.*).

Repression: a defence mechanism (*q.v.*). The suppression of an unacceptable drive or unacceptable emotion. Although subconscious, the repressed urges do have an effect. According to psychoanalytical theories they are a decisive factor in the formation of neuroses (*q.v.*).

Schizophrenia: an insanity of split personality. Schizophrenia belongs to the endogenous psychoses (*q.v.*). A factor common to the many forms in which it appears is that the personality is changed irreversibly. The most important symptoms of schizophrenia are: disturbed mental processes (absent-mindedness; illogical thinking); mania (persecution in or delusions of grandeur); deceptions in perception (hallucinations); emotional changes (excitement, extreme depression); loss of contact.

Sexual characteristics: a comprehensive term for all the physical characteristics which differentiate male from female. Primary sexual characteristics are the actual sexual organs (sperm glands and accessory sexual organs). Secondary sexual characteristics are specifically male or female characteristics of physical build and organ formation (e.g. breasts, rounding of the hips in the woman and beard and bodily hair in the man).

Somnambulism: sleepwalking.

Sublimation: a defence mechanism (*q.v.*). Unacceptable drives are placed at the service of goals which are socially acceptable (thus for example sexual impulses can become love poems and aggressive impulses can be put towards the development of sporting abilities – like fencing or boxing).

Bibliography

ADORNO T. W. *Eingriffe. Neun Kritische Modelle*, Frankfurt on Main 1963 (*Edition suhrkamp* 10)
AICHHORN, A. *Verwahrloste Jugend*, Bern–Stuttgart, 1925–7
ALEXANDER, F. *Psychoanalysis and Psychotherapy*, New York, 1956
APFELBERG, B., C. SUGAR and A. Z. PFEFFER 'A Psychiatric Study of 250 Sex Offenders.' *American Journal of Psychiatry, 100* (1944)
BADER, K. S. *Die Veränderung der Sexualordnung und die Konstanz der Sitlichkeitsdelikte*, Zeitschrift für Sexualforschung, 3/4 (1950)
BADER, K. S. 'Sexualität und Rechtsordnung', in: *Bekampfung der Sitlichkeitsdelikte*, Wiesbaden, 1959
BALLY, G. *Einführung in die Psychoanalyse Sigmund Freuds*, Reinbek, 1961 (Rowohlts Deutsche Enzyklopädie 131/132)
BAUER, F., H. BÜRGER-PRINZ, H. GIESE and H. JÄGER *Sexualität und Verbrechen*, Frankfurt on Main–Hamburg, 1963
BEER, U. 'Jugendsexualität.' *Recht der Jugend 8, 230*, 1960
BENEDICT, R. *Urformen der Kultur*, Hamburg, 1955
Bilder-Lexicon (Illustrated Dictionary) of Cultural History, Sexology, Literature and Art. Pubd. by the Institute for Sexological Research in Vienna, Vienna–Leipzig, 1928
BIRNBAUM, K. *Kriminalpsychopathologie*, Berlin, 1921
BLAU, G. and E. MÜLLER-LÜCKMANN (eds.) *Gerichtliche Psychologie*, Neuwied, 1962
BLEULER, E. *Lehrbuch der Psychiatrie*, Berlin, 1918
BLOCH, I. *Neue Forschungen über den Marquis de Sade*, Berlin, 1904
BLOCH, I. *The Sexual Life of our Time in Relation to Modern Civilization*, London, 1916
BÖHM, H. and A. BÖHM, 'Die Jügendliche Mutter', in *Jahrbuch Jugendpsychiatrie*, Vol. I, Bern, 1956
BOLTE, K-M. 'Mobilität, Schichtung'. In *König* (1964)
BOWLBY, J. 'The Effects of Mother–Child Separation: A Follow-up Study.' *British Journal of Medical Psychology, 3/4 211*, 1956
BRIFFAULT, R. *The Mothers*, Vol. III, London, 1927
BROMBERG, W. *Crime and the Mind*, Philadelphia, 1948
CAPRIO, F. S. and D. R. BRENNER *Sexual Behaviour*, New York, 1964
CASSIN, E., J. BOTTERO and J. VERCOUTTER (ed.) *Fischer Weltgeschichte*, Vol. 3: *Die alt-orientalischen Reiche II (Das Ende des 2 Jahrtausends)*, Frankfurt on Main–Hamburg, 1966

CHRISTIANSEN, K. O., M. ELERS-NIELSEN, L. LE MAIRE and G. K. STEURUP 'Recidivism among Sexual Offenders.' In *Scandinavian Studies in Criminology*, Vol. 1, Oslo, 1965

COHEN, A. K. *The Study of Social Disorganisation and Deviant Behaviour*. In MERTON

CORY, D. W. and R. E. L. MASTERS *Violation of Taboo*, New York, 1963

DAHRENDORF, R. 'Industrielle Fertigkeiten und soziale Schichtung.' *Kölner Zeitschrift für Soziologie*, Vol. VIII, 540–68 (1956)

DARWIN, C. H. *The Origin of Man and Sexual Natural Selection*, Stuttgart, 1919

DEVEREUX, G. 'The Social and Cultural Implications of Incest among the Mohave Indians.' *Psa Quarterly*, 8, 10 (1939)

DURANT, W. *Our Oriental Heritage*, New York, 1954

DURKHEIM, E. 'La prohibition de l'inceste et ses origines.' *L'année Sociologique*, I. V. VIII, 1898–1904

DURKHEIM, E. *Les formes élémentaires de la vie religieuse. Le système totémique en Australie*, Paris, 1912

EBER, A. 'Die Blutschande'. *Kriminal*, Vol. II, 68 (1937)

EDWARDES, A. and R. E. L. MASTERS *The Cradle of Erotica*, New York, 1962

ELLIOTT, M. *Crime in Modern Society*, New York, 1952

ELLIS, H. *Studies in the Psychology of Sex (4 vols)*, New York, 1936

ERIKSON, E. H. *Childhood and Society*, New York, 1950

ERIKSON, E. H. *Wachstum und Krisen der gesunden Persönlichkeit*, Stuttgart, 1953

ERIKSON, E. H. 'The Problem of Identity'. *Psyche 1–3, 114–76*, 1956

ERIKSON, E. H. 'Drive and Environment in Childhood' *Frankfürter Beiträge zur Soziologie*, 43–64, Frankfurt on Main, 1957b

ERIKSON, E. H. 'Identity and the Life Cycle'. *Theory, 2.*, Frankfurt on Main, 1966

ERMAN, A. *Ägypten und ä Leben im Altertum*, Vols. 1–2, Tübingen, 1885

EXNER, F. 'Die Reichskriminalstatistik von 1934 und Entwicklung der Kriminalität seit der nationalen Revolution.' *Mschr. f. Kriminalbiologie und Strafrechtsreform* 7, 336–43, 1938

FENICHEL, O. *The Psychoanalytic Theory of Neurosis*, London, 1960

FINK, H. T. *Primitive Love and Love Stories*, New York, 1899

FINKE, H. and F. ZEUGNER 'Inzest. Inzestzahlen und Bemerkungen auf Grund von 60 untersuchten Fällen'. *Mschr. Kriminalpsychologie und Strafrechtsreform*, 25, 305 (1934)

FLÜGEL, J. C. *The Psychoanalytic Study of the Family*, London, 1935

FORD, C. S. and F. A. BEACH 'Formen der Sexualität. Das Sexualverhalten bei Mensch und Tier' (Reinbeck, 1968) (*Rowohlts Sexologie, 8006/8007*)

FOREL, A. *Die sexuelle Frage*, Munich, 1905
FORTUNE, R. 'Incest'. *Encyclopaedia of Social Sciences*, Vol. VIII, 620 f., New York, 1932
FRANK, L. *Bruder und Schwester*, Leipzig, 1929
FRANKEL 'In Niederschiften, Strafrechtsreform', Vol. 8, esp. sections 76–90, *Session*, Bonn, 1959
FRANKL, V. E., V. E. VON GEBSATTEL and J. H. SCHULTZ: *Handbuch der Neurosenlehre und Psychotherapie*, Munich–Berlin, 1959
FRAZER, SIR J. G. *Totemism and Exogamy*, 4 vols., London, 1910
FRAZER, SIR J. G. *The Golden Bough*, New York, 1940
FREUD, S. *Collected Works*, London
FREUD, S. *Über Psychoanalyse. Fünf Vorlesungen, On Psychoanalysis: Five Lectures*, Leipzig–Vienna, 1922
FREUD, S. *Totem und Taboo*, Frankfurt on Main–Hamburg, 1964
FRIEDELL, E. *Kulturgeschichte der Neuzeit*, Munich, 1965
FRIEDEMANN, A. *Neurosen des Jugendalters*, 1959a
FRIEDEMANN, A. 'Die Frage der Entschädigung der Opfer von Sittlichkeitsverbrechen'. *Schweizer Arch. f. Neurol, n. Psych.*, 83, 2, 354–5, 1959b
FRIEDEMANN, A. 'Spätschäden bei Kindern und Jugendlichen'. *Beiträge zur Sexualforschung*, Vol. 33, Stuttgart, 1965
FRISCH, M. *Homo Faber*, Frankfurt on Main, 1964
FROMBERGER, H. *Das Sitzenbleiberproblem. Untersuchungen über das Versagen von Kindern in der Volksschule*, Dortmund, 1955
FROSH, J. and W. BROMBERG 'The Sex Offender; A Psychiatric Study.' *American Journal of Orthopsychiatry*, IX, 761–76 (1939)
GEBHARD, P. H., J. H. GAGNON, W. B. POMEROY and C. V. CHRISTENSEN *Sex Offenders*, London, 1965
GEBSATTEL, V. E. VON 'Daseinsanalytische und anthropologische Auslegung der sexuellen Verirrungen'. In *Prolegomena einer medizinischen Anthropologie*, Berlin–Göttingen–Heidelberg, 1954
'Gegenüberstellung des Entwurfs eines Strafgesetzbuches (E. 1962) und der Stellungnahm des Bundesrates.' Drucksache IV/650
GEHLEN, A. and H. SCHELSKY (eds.) *Soziologie*, Düsseldorf–Cologne, 1955
GEISLER, E. 'Das sexuell missbrauchte Kind'. *Bhft. z. Pr. d. Kinderpsychol. und Kinderpsych.*, 3 (1959)
GERCHOW, J. 'Über die Ursachen sexueller Fehlhaltungen und Straftaten bei ehemaligen Kriegsgefangenen.' *Deutsche Zeitschrift für Medizin*, 42, 452, (1953a)
GERCHOW, J. 'Zur Kriminologie von Heimkehrern.' *Mschr. Krim.* 36, 156 (1953b)
GERCHOW, J. 'Neue Ergebnisse über die Bedeutung soziologischer,

psychologischer und psychopathologischer Faktoren bei Inzesttätern der Nachkriegszeit.' *Mschr. f. Krim. u. Stratrechtsref.* 38, 168 (1955)

GERCHOW, J. 'Die Inzestsituation.' *Beiträge zur Sexualforschung*, 34, Vols. 39–50 (1965)

GIESE, H. (ed.) *Die Sexualität des Menschen*, Stuttgart, 1955

GIESE, H. *Psychopathologie der Sexualität*, Stuttgart, 1962a

GIESE, H. 'Zur Psychologie und Psychopathologie sexueller Fehlhaltungen'. In BLAU (1962b)

GIESE, H. *Das obszöne Buch*, Stuttgart, 1965a

GIESE, H. 'Zur Diagnose der Pädophilie'. *Beiträge zur Sexualforschung*, 34, Vol. 24–29 (1965b)

GIESE, H. Geleitwort (Preface). In SCHMIDT (1967)

GLUECK, B. C. JR. 'Final report, research project for the study and treatment of persons convicted of crimes involving sexual aberrations.' June 1952 to June 1955 (1956)

GORDON, P. *Sex and Religion*, New York, 1949

GREGOR, A. and E. VOIGTLANDER: *Die Verwahrlosung*, Berlin, 1918

GRIMAL, P. (ed.) 'Fischer Weltgeschichte', Vol. 6: *Der Hellenismus und der Aufstieg Roms*, Frankfurt on Main–Hamburg, 1965

GRIMBLE, A. 'From Birth to Death in the Gilbert Islands.' *Journal of the Royal Anthrop. Inst. of Gt. Britain and Ireland*, 51, 26 (1921)

GRIMM, J. and W. GRIMM: *Deutsches Wörterbuch*, Vol. 2, Leipzig, 1860

GROFFMANN, K. J. 'Die psychischen Auswirkungen von Sittlichkeitsverbrechen bei jugendlichen Opfern'. In BLAU (1962)

GRUHLE, H. W. *Die Psychologie des Abnormen*, Munich, 1922

GUYON, R. *The Ethics of Sexual Acts*, New York, 1934

HADDENBROCK, S. 'Das psychiatrische Gutachten zur Beurteilung der Schuldfähigkeit von Triebtaten zur besonderer Berücksichtigung der Pädophilie.' In *Die Pädophilie und ihre strafrechtliche Problematik. Beiträge zur Sexualforschung*, Vol. 34, 56–68 (1965)

HANHART, E. 'Zur mendelistischen Auswertung einer 33 Jahre langen Erforschung von Isolaten.' Vol. *Novant' Anni Delle Leggi Mendeliane* (Rome, 1956)

HARNACK, G. VON *Nervöse Verhaltenstörungen beim Schulkind*, Stuttgart, 1958

HARNACK, G. VON *Kurzlehrgang für Kinderheilkunde*, Berlin–Heidelberg–NY. In prep.

HEINTZ, P. and R. KÖNIG (eds.) 'Soziologie der Jugend-Kriminalität.' *Kölner Zeitschrift für Soziol. und Soziolpsychol.* Special Vol. 2 (1957)

HELLMER, J. *Recht*, Frankfurt on Main–Hamburg, 1961 (Fischer – Lexicon 12)

HENTIG, H. VON *Die unbekannte Straftat*, Berlin–Göttingen–Heidelberg, 1964
HENTIG, H. VON and T. VIERNSTEIN *Untersuchungen über den Inzest*, Heidelberg, 1925
HERSKO, M., and others 'Incest: A Three-way Process.' *Corrective Psychiatry and Journal of Social Therapy*, 7, 22–31 (1961)
HERZOG, J. J. *Realenzyklopädie für protestantische Theologie und Kirche* (1897)
HILLER, K. 'Das Recht über sich selbst' In *Sexus*, Bern–Leipzig, 1926
HILTMANN, H. 'Psychologische Begutachtung der Glaubwürdigkeit jugendlicher Zeugen speziell bei Sittlichkeitsdelikten.' *Zeitschrift. Diagn. Psychologie und Persönlichkeitsforschung*, IV, I (1956)
HILTMANN, H. *Kompendium der psychodiagnostischen Tests*, Bern–Stuttgart, 1960
HOBHOUSE, L. *Morals in Evolution*, London, 1912
HOCHHEIMER, W. 'Das Sexualstrafrecht in psychologische–anthropologischer Sicht'. In BAUER (1963)
HOFFMANNSTHAL, H. VON *Ödipus und die Sphinx*, Berlin, 1906
HOFSTÄTTER, P. and D. WENDT *Quantitive Methoden*, Munich, 1966
HOLDER, H. 'Zum Problem der Blutschande'. *Schweiz arch. Neurol. Psychiat*, 64, 175 (1949)
HUTH, A. H. *The Marriage of near kind*, London, 1887
JÄGER, H. 'Strafgesetzgebung und Rechtsgüterschut bei Sittlichkeitsdelikten.' *Beiträge zur Sezualforschung*, Vol. 12 (1957)
JANOWITZ, M. 'Soziale Schichtung und Mobilität in Westdeutschland.' *Kölner Zeitschrift für Soziol. und Sozialpsychol.* 1 (1958)
JESCHEK, In Niederschriften, Strafrechtsreform, Vol. 8, Session, Bonn, 1959
JONES, E. *Life and Work of Sigmund Freud*, Vol. II, London, 1962
KAHN, E. 'On Incest and Freud's Oedipus Complex.' *Confinia Psychiatrica*, 8, 89 (1965)
KAUFMANN, J., A. L. PECK and C. K. TAGIURI 'The Family Constellation and Overt Incestuous Relations between Father and Daughter.' *American Journ. Orthopsychiat.*, 24, 266 (1954)
KAYSER, F. and ROLOFF: *Ägypten einst und jetzt* Freiburg-in-Breisgan, 1908
KEPP, R. 'Kongress der Deutschen Gesellschaft für Familienplanning Pro Familia' (from a report in *Die Welt* of 4.11.1967)
KIELHOLZ, P. *Diagnose und Therapie der Depressionen für den Praktiker*, Munich, 1965
KINBERG, O., G. INGHE and S. RIEMER: *Incestproblemet Sverige*, Stockholm, 1943

KINSEY, A. C., W. B. POMEROY and C. E. MARTIN *Sexual Behaviour in the Human Female*, London, 1953
KINSEY, A. C., W. B. POMEROY and C. E. MARTIN *Sexual Behaviour in the Human Male*, London, 1948
KLEIN-MAYERN *Nachrichten vom Zustande der Gegenden und Stadt Juvavia*, Salzburg, 1784
KOHLER and WENGER *Kultur der Gegenwart*, Berlin–Leipzig, 1914
KOHLHAAS In Lindemaier-Mohring: Reference work of B.G.H., Munich–Berlin, 1961
KOHLRAUSCH and LANGE *Strafgesetzbuch mit Erläuterungen und Nebengesetzen*, Berlin, 1961
KÖNIG, R. 'Soziologie der Familie.' In GEHLEN (1955)
KÖNIG, R. *Handbuch der empirischen Sozialforschung*, Stuttgart, 1962
KÖNIG, R. 'Sittlichkeitsdelikte und Probleme der Gestaltung des Sexuallebens in der Gegenwartsgesellschaft' In BAUER (1963)
KÖNIG, R. *Soziologie*, Frankfurt on Main–Hamburg, 1964 (Fischer - Lexicon 10)
KRAEPELIN, E. *Lehrbuch der Psychiatrie*, Leipzig, 1914
KRAFFT-EBING, R. VON *Psychopathia Sexualis* (9th ed.) Stuttgart, 1894
KRETSCHMER, E. *Körperbau und Charakter*, 21 and 22 eds, Berlin–Göttingen–Heidelberg, 1955
KRIGE, F. J. *The Social Systems of the Zulus*, New York, 1936
Kriminalstatistik des Deutschen Reiches (1918)
Kriminalstatistik für das Jahr 1961–5. Bearbeitet im Osterreichischer Statistischen Zentralamt, ed. Federal Ministry of Justice (Vienna, 1961–5)
KROEBER, A. L. *Anthropology*, New York, 1948
KÜNZEL, E. 'Jugendkriminalität und Verwahrlosung'. *Beiheft zur Praxis der Kinderpsychologie*, 7 (1965)
LACKNER, K. 'Strafe ohne vernünftigen Sinn.' *Die Welt*, No. 139, 18 June, 1966
DE LANCRE *Tableau de l'inconstance des mauvais anges et démons*, Paris, 1613
LANGE, W. *Entwicklung und Erscheinungsformen der pädophilen Sittlichkeitskriminalität in Hamburg seit 1945*. Unpub. juristic dissertation, Hamburg, 1956
LANGELUDDEKE, A. 'Die Wirkung der Entmannung auf Homosexuelle und Pädophile.' *Beitrage zur Sexualforschung*, 34, Vol. 91–5 (1965)
LAWRENCE, D. H. *Sons and Lovers*, Penguin edition, London, 1959
LEA, H. C. *A History of Sacerdotal Celibacy in the Christian Church*, 1907
LENZ, W. 'Grundlagen der genetischen Beratung.' Special imprint from F. LINNEWEH, *Erbliche Stoffwechselkrankheiten*, Munich–Berlin, 1962

LEONHARDT, R. W. *Wer wirft den ersten Stein?* Munich, 1969
LEVI-STRAUSS, C. *Les structures élémentaires de parenté*, Paris, 1949
LEVI-STRAUSS, C. 'Natur und Kultur.' In MÜHLMANN (1966)
LEVY-BRUHL, L. *Le surnaturel et la nature dans la mentalité primitive*, Paris, 1931
LIGHT, H. *Sexual Life in Ancient Greece*, New York, 1953
LINTON, R. *The Study of Man. An Introduction*, New York, 1936
LINTON, R. *Culture and Mental Disorders*, Springfield, Ill., 1956
LOWIE, R. H. *Primitive Society*, New York, 1920
LUBKER, F. *Reallexicon des Klassischen Altertums*, Leipzig–Berlin, 1914
LUNDBORG *Medizinisch-biologische Familienforschung innerhalb eines 2,232-köpfigen Bauerngeschlechts in Schweden*, Jena, 1913
LUSTIG, N., J. W. DRESSER and S. SPELLMAN 'Incest, a Family Group Survival Pattern.' *Archives of General Psychiatry*, 14, 37 (1966)
MACKENROTH, G. 'Bevölkerungslehre.' In GEHLEN (1955)
MALINOWSKI, B. 'Practical Anthropology', *Africa*, II I, 1929
MALINOWSKI, B. 'Geschlecht und Verdrängung in primitiven Gesellschaften', Reinbeck, 1962. (*Rowohlts Deutsche Enzykläpadie 193/140*)
MANGUS, A. R. 'Sex Crimes in California.' In KARL M. BOWMAN, 'California, Sexual Deviation Research. Sacramento: Assembly of the State of California 9–46' (1953)
MANN, T. *Wälsungenblut*, Munich, 1921
MARCUSE, M. 'Zur Kritik des Begriffes und der Tat der Blutschande.' *Sexual Probleme* 4, 4 (1908)
MARCUSE, M. 'Zur Psychologie der Blutschande.' *Archiv für Kriminal-Anthropologie und Kriminalistik*, 25, 268 (1913)
MARCUSE, M. 'Vom Inzest. Juristisch-psychiatrische Grenzfragen.' 10th vol. issues 3/4 (Halle 1915)
MASTERS, R. E. L. *Eros and Evil*, New York, 1962
MASTERS, R. E. L. *Patterns of Incest*, New York, 1963
MATTHES, I. 'Kinderjährige "Geschädigte" asl Zeugen in Sittlichkeitsprozessen.' *Schriftenreihe des Bundeskriminalamtes, Wiesbaden*, Wiesbaden, 1961
MAURACH, R. *Deutsches Strafrecht*, Hanover–Darmstadt, 1952
MAURACH, R. *Deutsches Strafrecht*, Karlsruhe, 1964
MAUROIS, A. *Quest for Proust*, Peregrine Books, 1964
MAYNTZ, R. 'Begriff und empirische Erfassung des sozialen Status in der heutigen Soziologie.' *Kölner Zeitschrift Soziol.* 10, 58 (1958a)
MAYNTZ, R. *Soziale Schichtung und sozialer Wandel einer Industriegemeinde. Eine soziologische Untersuchung der Stadt Euskirchen*, Stuttgart, 1958b

MEAD, M. *Geschlecht und Temperament in primitiven Gesellschaften*, Hamburg, 1959 (*Rowohlts Deutsche Enzyklopädie 96*)
MERTON, R. K., L. BROOM and C. S. COTTRELL *Sociology Today*, New York, 1959
MEYER, H. *Lehrbuch des deutschen Strafrechts*, Erlangen, 1888
MEZGER, E. and H. BLEI *Strafrecht*, II, Munich–Berlin, 1964; 1966
MICHELET, J. *La Sorcière*, The Hague, 1863
MIDDENDORFF, W. 'Die Sittlichkeitsdelikte in historischer internationaler Sicht.' In *Bekämpfung der Sittlichkeitsdelikte*, pp. 45–8, Federal Crime Bureau, Wiesbaden, 1959
MITSCHERLICH, A. *Auf dem Weg zur vaterlosen Gesellschaft*, Munich, 1963
MITTENECKER, E. *Planung und statistische Auswertung von Experimenten*, Vienna, 1960
MITTERMAIER, W. 'Verbrechen und Vergehen wider die Sittlichkeit.' In *Vergleichende Darstellung des deutschen und ausländischen Strafrechts*, IV Vol., Berlin, 1906
MOHR, J. 'The Pedophiliacs. Their Clinical, Social and Legal Implications.' *Canadian Psychiatric Assoc. Journal* 7, 255–60 (1962)
MOHR, J., R. E. TURNER and R. B. BALL 'Exhibitionism and Pedophilia; Results of a follow-up study of forensic out-patients.' Paper presented at the annual meeting of the American Psychiatric Assoc. Toronto, May 1962
MOMMSEN, T. *Römisches Strafrecht* (1899)
MORGAN, L. H. *Ancient Society*, New York, 1877
MORUS (RICHARD LEWINSOHN) *Eine Weltgeschichte der Sexualität*, Reinbeck, 1965
MUHLMANN, W. E. and E. W. MÜLLER (eds.) 'Kulturanthropologie Neue Wiss.' *Bibliothek*, Vol. 9, Kohr–Berlin, 1966
MÜLLER-LÜCKMANN, E. 'Uber die Glaubwürdigkeit kindlicher und jugendlicher Zeuginnen bei Sexualdelikten.' *Beiträge zur Sexualforschung*. 14th ed. (1963)
MÜLLER-LÜCKMANN, E. 'Über die Wahrhaftigkeit kindlicher und jugendlicher Zeugen in der Hauptverhandlung.' *Beiträge zur Sexualforschung* 33 Heft. 100–8, Stuttgart, 1965
MURDOCH, I. *A Severed Head*, London, 1961
MURDOCK, G. P. *Social Structure*, New York, 1949
MUSIL, R. *Der Mann ohne Eigenschaften*, Hamburg, 1967
Nationalsozialistisches Straffrecht. Drückschrift des Preuss. Justizministeriums, Berlin, 1933
NAU, E. 'Die seelischen Auswirkungen von der in der Kindheit erlebten Sittlichkeitsverbrechen.' *Dtsch. Zeitschrift f. die ges. gerichtl. Med.* 55, 172 (1964)

NAU, E. 'Die Persönlichkeit des jugendlichen Zeugen.' *Beiträge zur Sexualforschung,* 33rd ed. (1965)
NICOLSON, A. B. and C. HANLEY 'Indices of physiological maturity: deviation and interrelationships.' *Child Development.* 24, 3–38 (1953)
NIEWENHAUS, A. W. 'Die psychologische Bedeutung der Inzesterscheinung in Australien.' *Internat. Archiv. f. Ethnographie,* 30, 1–32 (1929)
NÜRNBERGER, H. 'Inzestprobleme der Nachkriegszeit.' *Dtsch. Zeitschrift f. die ges. gerichtl. Med.* 44, 259 (1955)
OGBURN, W. F. 'The Family and its Functions.' In *Recent Social Trends in the United States,* New York, 1933
PARSONS, T. *Essays in Sociological Theory,* New York, 1964
PARSONS, T. and R. F. BALES *Family. Socialization and Interaction Process,* New York–London, 1955
PFLANZ, M. *Sozialer Wandel und Krankheit,* Stuttgart, 1962
PLAUT, P. 'Untersuchungen über den Inzest.' *Psychiatrische en Neurologische Bladen* (1934)
PLAUT, P. *Der Sexualverbrecher und seine Persönlichkeit,* Stuttgart, 1960
PRIESTER, H. J. *Die Standardisierung der Hamburg–Wechsler–Intelligenztests für Kinder (HAWIK),* Bern–Stuttgart, 1958
RADCLIFFE-BROWN, A. R. 'The Social Organization of Australian Tribes.' Vol. 1: *Oceania* (1930)
RAGLAN, R. F. *Jocasta's Crime,* London, 1940
RANK, O. *Das Inzest-Motiv in Dichtung und Sage,* Leipzig–Vienna, 1912
RAPAPORT, D. *Die Struktur der psychoanalytischen Theorie,* Stuttgart, 1959
RASCH, W. 'Die Frage nach der strafrechtlichen Verantwortlichkeit.' In GIESE (1962)
RECKLESS, W. C. *Crime Problem,* New York, 1961
REINHARDT, J. N. *Sex Perversions and Sex Crimes,* Springfield, Ill. 1957
RENNERT, H. 'Psychiatrische Betrachtungen zum Inzest und seiner Verbreitung.' *Zeitschrift Psychiat. Neurol. u. Med. Psychol.* 6, 80 (1954)
RENNERT, H. 'Zur Problematik des Inzest.' *Dtsch. Zeitschrift f. die ges. gerichte. Med.* 48, 50 (1958)
REYNOLDS, E. L. and J. V. WINES 'Individual Differences in Physical Changes Associated with Adolescent Girls.' *Amer. J. Dis. Child.* 75, 329–50 (1948/9)
RGst.: Entscheidungen des Reichgerichts in Strafsachen (Berlin, Vol. 4 1971)
RIEMER, S. 'Die Blutschande als soziologisches Problem.' *Mschft. Kriminalbiol.* 27, 86 (1936)
RIESMAN, D., R. DENNEY and N. GLAZER *The Lonely Crowd,* Yale, 1950

RINEHART, J. W. 'Genesis of Overt Incest.' *Compr. Psychiat.* 2, 338 (1961)
ROHLEDER, H. *Monographen über die Zeugung beim Menschen* 2. Teil: 'Die Zeugung unter Blutsverwandten', Leipzig, 1912
ROSENFELD, E. H. 'Grundsätzliches zur Bestrafung des Inzestes.' *Mschr. Kriminalpsychol.* Special Supplement 1 (1926)
SARTRE, J.-P. *Huis clos*, Methuen, 1962
SARTRE, J.-P. *Words*, H. Hamilton, 1964
SAUER, K. 'Zur Bedeutung des Inzests.' *Münchener Med. Wschr.* 43, 2105–7 (1965)
SCHELSKY, H. 'Die sozialen Formen der sexuellen Beziehungen.' In GIESE (1955)
SCHELSKY, H. *Die skeptische Generation*, Düsseldorf–Köln, 1957
SCHELSKY, H. 'Soziologie der Sexualität, Reinbek, 1965 (*Rowohlts Deutsche Enzyklopädie* 2)
SCHILLER-TIETZ, N. *Folgen, Bedeutung und Wesen der Blutsverwandschaft im Tier- und Pflanzenleben*, Berlin, 1892
SCHMIDT, G. and V. SIGUSCH 'Zur Frage des Vorurteils gegenüber sexuell devianten Gruppen.' *Beiträge zur Sexualforschung*, 40 vol. (1967)
SCHNEIDER, K. *Klinische Psychopathologie*, Stuttgart, 1959
SCHÖNFELDER, T. 'Die Rolle des Mädchens bei Sexualdelikten.' *Beiträge zur Sexualforschung*, 42 vol. (1968)
SCHÖNKE, A. and H. SCHRÖDER *Strafgesetzbuch*, Munich–Berlin, 1965
SCHWAB, G. 'Zur Biologie des Inzests.' *Mschr. Kriminalbiol. u. Strafrechtsref.* 29, 257 (1938)
SCOTT, J. A. 'A Report on the Heights and Weights and other measurement of School Pupils in the County of London in 1959,' London, 1961
SHELLEY, P. B.: *The Cenci*. In *The Complete Works of Percy Bysshe Shelley*. Newly edited by Roger Ingpen and Walter E. Peck, 10th vol., London, 1965
SIDLER, N. *Zur Universalität des Inzesttabu*, Stuttgart, 1971
SIEVERTS, R. and W. HARDWIG 'Sittlichkeitsdelikte'. In GIESE (1955)
SIMMEL, G. *Untersuchungen über die Formen der Vergesellschaftung*, 1908
SIMSON, G. 'Schwedische Erforschungen.' *Die Welt*, No. 139, 18 June, 1966
SLOANE, P. and E. KARPINSKI 'Effects of Incest on the Participants.' *American Journal of Orthopsychiatry*, XII (1942)
SLOTKIN, J. S. 'On a Possible Lack of Incest Regulations in Old Iran.' In MASTERS (1963)
SMITH, W. R. *The Religion of the Semites*, London, 1889–1907
SONDEN, T. 'Die Inzestverbrechen in Schweden und ihre Ursachen.' *Acta Psychiat. et Neuroligica*, 11, 379 (1936)

Bibliography 243

SOPHOCLES *Tragedies*, Cambridge University Press, 1904
SPECHT, F. *Sozialpsychiatrische Gegenwartsprobleme der Jugendverwahrlosung*, Stuttgart, 1967
SPITZ, R. A. *Die ersten Objektbeziehungen*, Stuttgart, 1956/7
Statistik der Bundesrepublik Deutschland, Vol. 158, 23 (1954)
Statistische Jahrbücher für die Bundesrepublik Deutschland, Statistisches Bundesamt Wiesbaden (1952 ff.)
STELZNER, H. F. 'Der Inzest.' *Zeitschrift f. ges. Psychiatrie und Neurol.*, 93, 647 (1924)
STERN, C. *Principles of Human Genetics*, San Francisco—London, 1960
STEUER, W. *Reife, Umwelt und Leistung der Jugend*, Stuttgart, 1965
Strafgesetzbuch (Stgb). Munich (Goldmanns gelbe Taschenbücher 714)
STÜRÜP, G. K. *Law and Contemporary Problems*, Vol. 25, No. 2 (1960)
STÜRÜP, G. K. 'Die Behandlung der Sexual Kriminalität in Skandinavien.' In BAUER (1963)
SUMNER, W. G. *Folkways*, New York, 1960
SZABO, D. 'L'inceste en milieu urbain.' *L'Année Sociologique, Troisième Série*, 1957-8 (1958)
TAMM, K. P. 'Die Unzucht mit Abhängigen' (174 No. 1 StGB). Unpub. legal dissertation, Hamburg, 1965
TANNER, J. M. *Wachstum und Reifung des Menschen*, Stuttgart, 1962
TAYLOR, G. R. *Wandlungen der Sexualität*, Düsseldorf–Köln, 1957
TÖBBEN, H. *Über den Inzest* Leipzig–Vienna, 1925
TUMLIRZ, O. *Die Jugendverwahrlosung*, Graz–Vienna, 1952
TYLOR, E. B. 'Method of Investigating the Development of Institutions Applied to Laws of Marriage and Descent.' *Journal of the Royal Anthropological Institute of Great Britain and Ireland*, Vol. 18 (1889)
VERSCHUER, O. VON *Erbpathologie*, Dresden–Leipzig, 1934
VERSCHUER, O. VON *Genetik des Menschen*, Munich–Berlin, 1959
VOGEL, F. *Lehrbuch der allgemeinen Humangenetik*, Berlin–Göttingen–Heidelberg, 1961
Vorentwurf zu einen Deutschen Strafgesetzbuch (1909)
WAGNER, E. and U. PLANCK *Jugend auf dem Land. Ergebnisse eine wissenschaftlichen Erhebung über die Lebenslage der westdeutschen Landjugend*, Munich, 1957
WAGNER, K. 'Das Inzest – Verbrechen und seine Kriminalbiologische Bedeutung.' *Kriminalbiolog. Gegenwartsfragen* Vol. VII, 41–7, Stuttgart, 1953
WAGNER, K. 'Psychiatrische Betrachtungen zum Inzest und seiner Verbreitung.' *Psychiatric, Neurol. und Grenzgebiete* 6, 80 (1954)

WAHL, C. W. 'The Psychodynamics of Consummated Maternal Incest. A Report of Two Cases.' *Amer. Med. Ass. Arch. Gen. Psychiat.*, 3 (1960)
WALLIS, H. In 'Das sexuell gefährdete Kind.' *Beiträge zur Sexualforschung*, 33rd vol., Part 1 (1965)
WECHSLER, D. *Die Messung der Intelligenz Erwachsener*, Bern–Stuttgart, 1956
WEGENER, H. 'Zur Psychologie der Kinderaussage.' *Prax. Kindpsychol.* 2, 195 (1953)
WEINBERG, S. K. *Incest Behaviour*, New York, 1963
WELZEL, H. *Das deutsche Strafrecht*, Berlin, 1965
WESTERMARCK, E. A. *Geschichte der menschlichen Ehe*, Berlin, 1902
WESTERMARCK, E. A. *Ursprung und Entwicklung der Moralbegriffe*, Leipzig, 1909
WESTERMARCK, E. A. *Christianity and Morals*, London, 1939
WHITE, L. A. 'The Definition and Prohibition of Incest 1948.' In MASTERS (1963)
WILCKEN 'Ehe zwischen Blutsverwandten.' *Globus*, LIX (1891)
WILHELM 'Die Sittlichkeitsdelikte in dem Vorentwurf zu einem schweizerischen StBG vom April 1908 und in dem VE zu einem österreichischen StBG vom September 1909' *Sexualprobleme*, 6, 820 (1910)
WILHELM: 'Die volkspsychologischen Unterschiede in der französischen und deutschen Sittlichkeitsgesetzgebung und -rechtssprechung.' *Sexualprobleme*, VII, 657 (1911)
WILUTZKI, P. *Vorgeschichte des Rechtes*, Breslau, 1903
WINTER, K. 'Akzeleration – nicht nur ein Problem des Jugendalters?' *Dtsch. Ges. d. Wesen.* (1962)
WÜLFFEN, E. *Der Sexualverbrecher*, Berlin, 1921
WYSS, R. 'Unzucht mit Kindern.' In *Monographien aus dem Gesamtgebiete der Neurologie und Psychiatrie*, Vol. 21, Berlin–Heidelberg–New York, 1967
ZULLIGER, H. 'Hintergründige Triebfedern von Eigentumsdelikten,' In HEINTZ (1957)
ZULLIGER, H. *Umgang mit dem kindlichen Gewissen*, Stuttgart, 1960

Index

abnormal sexual behaviour, 92, 95, 101, 107, 109, 196–207, 217
abortion, 40, 77, 211, 212, 213, 214
Adorno, T. W., 40
age, of victims, 102–3; of offenders, 103–4; relation between biological maturity and, 105–7, 176–177; and sexual forms of contact, 107–9; duration of sexual relations and, 109–10; of wives, 120–1
aggressiveness, 126–8, 133, 139
Aichhorn, A., 160
alcohol, alcoholism, 94, 124, 127, 130, 133, 135, 136, 139, 140–1, 142, 145, 171, 172, 174, 175, 177, 179, 199–200, 201
Alexander, F., 57
Alexander VI, Pope (Rodrigo Borgia), 29–30
anal intercourse, 101, 189
anxiety dreams, 161, 163–4, 165
Apfelberg, B., 130
Arabia, 23
Archeptolis, 24
Aretino, Pietro, 29
Augustine, Saint, 25, 47
authority *see* 'family tyrant'
aversion (abhorrence), 45–6, 54, 57, 75

Bader, K. S., 68, 73, 85
Bales, R. F., 111
Bally, G., 53, 56
Balthasar Cossa, Pope, 27
Bauer, F., 68, 73, 81, 86
Beauchamp, Earl, 223
Beer, U., 148
Belgium, 67, 68
Benedict, Ruth, 38
biological maturity, 105–7, 175, 176, 217; *see also* puberty

Birnbaum, K., 94
Bleuler, E., 77
Bloch, I., 32, 33, 94
Böhm, H. and Böhm, A., 148
Bolte, K. M., 111
Boniface, Archbishop of Mainz, 25, 26
Borgia family, 29–30
Bowlby, J., 160
breast buds, development of, 105, 175, 176, 177
Brenner, D. R., 69, 92
Briffault, R., 39
Brinvilliers, Marquise de, 32
Britain, 25, 26, 31; law in, 67, 89, 219–28
Bromberg, W., 137, 140
Bürger-Prinz, H., 205
Burton, Robert, 42
Byron, Lord, 16

Caligula, 25
Calvinism, 30, 32, 65
Caprio, F. S., 69, 92
caring-protective attitude (of adult partner), 182, 184, 189
Cassin, E., 22
Cenci, Beatrice, 30
Choiseul, duc de, 32–3
Christiansen, K. O., 90, 91
Cimon of Athens, 24
Claudius, Emperor, 25
claustrophobia, 161, 162, 229
Cleopatra, 21, 78
Cocteau, Jean, 16
cohabitation, 70–1, 74, 75, 83
Cohen, A. K., 93
coitus *see* sexual contacts
Commodus, 22
compulsion (to talk about the incest), 162–3

confession, 182, 187, 195, 196, 210
Constantine, Emperor, 25
Corneille, Pierre, 16
Cornelius Nepos, 24
Criminal Procedures Act (Scotland, 1887), 31
criminal records (of incest offenders), 119–20, 121, 133
criminal statistics, 86–92; nature and degree of penalties, 90–1; frequency of reversion, 91; forms of incest, 92; in Britain, 226–7; *see also* law
cultural history, 11–42
cunnilingus, 189, 229

Dahrendorf, R., 112
Darwin, Charles, 50, 55
Davey, Lord, 221
death, fear of, 153, 161, 162
degeneration, 14, 42–4, 128; *see also* hereditary-biological safeguards
delineation of the offence, 70–1
Deming, J., 105, 106
Denmark, 67, 90, 91
depression, 153, 165, 166, 168, 229
Devereux, G., 39, 40
Diamond, A. S., 219
Diderot, Denis, 13, 33
Diogenes, 24
dissociality, symptoms of, 154–60
divorce, 120, 121
Donoughmore, Earl of, 221
Durant, W., 22
Durkheim, E., 40, 44, 57

Eber, A., 77, 103, 126, 128, 132
Edwardes, A., 36
Egypt, 21–2, 34, 36, 78
Elizabeth I, Queen, 31, 220
Elliott, M., 69
Ellis, H., 45
emotional illness *see* psychoses
emotional partnership and free relationship, 99, 205–7, 217
encopresis, 153, 229
enuresis, 152, 153, 229
epic and dramatic writing, 12–21

epilepsy, 135, 136, 165
Erikson, E. H., 57, 58, 146, 147
Erman, A., 21
etymological interpretation, 11–12
Euripides, 16, 17, 23–4
excrementophilia, 204
exhibitionists, 103, 130
Exner, F., 87
exogamy, 41, 43; primitive cultures' rules of, 37–9, 44; politico-economic role, 47–9; oedipus complex and, 54–7
extra-family social orientation (role), 61–3, 110, 147, 184, 193, 194–5, 200, 217; *see also* social isolation

false information, 182, 183, 186–7
family, compulsory exogamy and, 48–9; psycho-sexual organisation of, 58–64, legal protection, 75, 81–5; sociology, psychology and psychopathology of incest, 93–123, 217; stabilisation of adult personality by, 111; social stratum, 111–13; and income, 113–14; size and living conditions, 114–16, 174–6; education and occupations, 116–17, 123; marital status of incest offenders, 118; criminal records, 119–20, 121; wives, 120–121; sociological characteristics of victims, 122–3; after-effects of incest on, 208–10, 217, 227–8
'family tyrant', 139, 140, 182, 183–4
fantasies, construction of, 204
favourable opportunities, 175, 176, 182, 185
fear, 182, 186–7, 188, 189, 190, 191, 194
fellatio, 189, 199, 229
female incest victims, 146–69; puberty, 146–8; school performance and intelligence, 148–52; psycho-somatic symptoms, 152-4; and dissociality, 154–60; special neuroses and behavioural disturbances, 160–6; depression, 166; diagnostic classification of per-

sonality disturbances, 167; time and manifestation of symptoms, 168–9; effect of incest on, 210–16; *see also* family; incestuous relationships
Fenichel, O., 165
Ferenczi, S., 165
Fink, H. T., 94
Finke, H. and Zeugner, F., 78, 95, 103, 109, 112, 116, 119, 136, 210
Fleck and Lidz, 132
Flügel, J. C., 86, 94, 115
force, adult partner's use of, 182, 184
Ford, C. S. and Beach, F. A., 35, 37, 38, 46
Ford, John, 16, 20
Forel, A., 94, 117, 126
Fortune, R., 63
France, 25, 32–3, 67, 82, 86
Frank, L., 17
Frazer, Sir J. G., 39, 40, 46, 50
free relationship *see* emotional partnership
Freud, Sigmund, 13, 18, 40, 46, 50–58, 59, 147
Friedell, E., 29
Friedemann, A., 214
Frisch, H., 17
Frisch, M., 18–19, 20
Fromberger, H., 149
Frosh, J. and Bromberg, W., 130

Gebhard, P. H. and colleagues, 95, 99, 100, 101, 102, 103, 104, 108, 112, 114, 115, 116, 118, 119, 120, 125, 126, 128, 129, 130, 132, 137, 138, 140, 145, 174, 176, 185, 190, 198, 199
Gebsattel, V. E. von, 197
Geisler, E., 151, 190, 210, 214
Gerchow, J., 77–8, 81, 82, 95, 96, 103, 119, 125, 129, 132, 135, 137, 144, 145, 173, 176, 181, 205, 207, 208
Germany, early Christian Church in, 25, 26; law on incest, 31–2, 67, 69–73, 76; and criminal statistics, 87–9, 90–1

Giese, H., 184–5, 197–9, 202, 204, 205, 206
gifts, 182, 184, 189
Glueck, B. C. Jr, 91, 126, 130
Gordon, Dr G. H., 228
Gordon, P., 40
Gratianus, 12, 65
Greece, Greek mythology, 11–12, 13–14, 16, 17, 18, 20, 23–4
Gregor, A. and Voigtlander, E., 155
Gregory I, Pope, 25, 44
Gregory II, Pope, 25
Gregory III, Pope, 28
Grimal, P., 22
Grimble, A., 39
Grimm, J. & W., 11
Groffmann, K. J., 147, 208
Gruhle, H. W., 131
Guala, Cardinal, 27
guilt and shame, 17, 18, 19, 20, 178, 181, 182, 187, 188, 190, 194, 195; *see also* oedipus complex

Haddenbrock, S., 197
Halsbury, Earl of, 221, 222
Hanhart, E., 79
Harnack, G. von, 122
health *see* hereditary biological safeguards; physical illnesses
heart trouble, 153, 166
Hebrews, 21, 23
Hellmer, J., 81
Henry VIII, 31
Hentig, H. von, 86, 87, 94, 103, 116, 126, 130, 174
hereditary-biological safeguards, 74, 75–81, 83
heresy, 27, 28
Hermant, Abel, 14–15
Herodotus, 22
Herzog, J. J., 12
hetero-homosexual triads, 96, 202–205
Hill, Staverley, 222
Hiller, K., 73, 82, 208
Hiltmann, H., 98
history, 21–33
Hobhouse, L., 45

248 *Index*

Hochheimer, W., 72, 197
Hofmannsthal, Hugo von, 16, 18
Hofstätter, P. and Wendt, D., 98
Holder, H., 94, 117, 123, 149, 214
Holland, 67, 86
Homer, 12
homosexuality, 27, 28, 29, 101, 103, 120, 126, 128, 130, 197, 198, 199, 200, 202–5, 227, 229
homozygotisation, 78–80
Huth, A. H., 42
hypersexuality, 94, 128, 133, 171, 229
hypochondriac fears, 162, 165

Ibsen, Henrik, 17
illegitimate births, 18, 111, 121, 122, 136, 141, 157, 158, 159, 194, 195, 200, 211–14
Incas, 22–3, 78
Incest Act (Scotland, 1567), 228
Incest Bill (England, 1907), 222
incest taboo, 41–64, 84, 216; degeneration, 42–4; 'blood tie' and sexual neutralisation, 45–6; politico-economic interests, 47–9; Oedipus and patricide, 50–8; function of, 58–64, 110–11, 146
incestuous relationships, 169–96; predisposition, 170–4; factors instigating or favouring, 174–81; sustaining, 181–92; and bringing about end of, 192–6
Innocent III, Pope, 27
Inquisition, 27, 28
intelligence, 94, 125, 126, 172; of female incest victims, 148–52, 172
Italy, 25, 29–30, 67

Jäger, H., 44, 73, 74, 75, 76, 81, 82, 83, 84, 85, 86, 197, 206, 208
Janowitz, M., 112
jealousy, 141, 143, 171, 173, 177, 183, 184, 189, 192, 193; *see also* oedipus complex
John XII, Pope, 27
John XXII, Pope, 30

Julius Caesar, 16
Justinian, Emperor, 25

Kahn, E., 132, 137, 200
Kay, J., 94, 115
Kayser, F., 21
Kepp, R., 148
Kielholz, P., 166
Kinberg, O. G., 140
Kinsey, A. C. W., Kinsey Institute, 86, 100, 102, 114, 118, 126, 128, 129, 132, 144, 145, 174, 198
König, R., 34, 57, 87, 111, 118
Kraepelin, E., 77
Krafft-Ebing, R. von, 94
Kretschmer, E., 131
Krige, F. J., 39, 40
Kroeber, A. L., 34
Künzel, E., 160
Kurnai culture, 38–9

lack of knowledge (victim's), 182, 187, 188
Lackner, K., 85
Lange, W., 109
Langeluddeke, A., 91
laws (regulating incest), 65–92, 216; historical survey, 65–6; variability of 66–9; in Britain, 67, 89, 219–28; in West Germany, 69–73; classification of motives, 73–5; hereditary-biological motives, 75–81; protection of the family, 81–5, 137; protection of young people, 85–6; criminal statistics, 86–92
Lawrence, D. H., 20
Lea, H. C., 27
Lenz, W., 79–80
Leo III, Pope, 25, 26
Leonhardt, Rudolf Walter, 13, 19, 20
lesbianism *see* homosexuality
Lévi-Strauss, Claude, 34, 36, 41, 42, 43, 44, 46, 49, 58, 63
Lévy-Bruhl, L., 41–2
Light, H., 23–4
Linton, Ralph, 36, 57, 58
'literary' incest, 12–21

living conditions, 115–16, 174–6
Livy, 24
Lockwood, Colonel, 220–1
Lowie, R. H., 45
Lubker, F., 12
Lucian, 21
Lundborg, 76–7
Luther, Martin, 47
Luxemburg, 67

magic *see* superstitions
magic tricks (rituals), 182, 189
Malatesta, 30
Malinowski, B., 37, 43
Mangus, A. R., 126
Mann, Thomas, 17
Marcuse, M., 65, 76–7, 82, 87, 94, 112, 115, 209
married couples, 124–45; husband and family father, 124–34; wives and mothers, 134–6; family disorganisation before incest, 137–145; social and emotional relations, 138–43, 171, 173, 179–80, 181, 185; sexual relations, 143–5, 173, 177, 179, 182, 185
Masters, R. E. L., 25, 26, 27, 28, 30, 36, 37, 39, 68, 69, 86, 89, 92
masturbation, 36–7, 71, 101, 107, 108, 109, 199, 200, 201, 202, 203, 204, 230
Matthes, I., 99, 108
Maugham, W. S., 17
Maurach, R., 65, 66, 70, 80, 81, 83
Maurois, André, 16
Mayntz, R., 111
Mead, Margaret, 47–8
Melville, Hermann, 16–17
menarch, 105, 106, 175, 177, 230
mental and emotional illnesses *see* psychoses
Messalina, 25
Metalious, G., 16
Meyer, H., 65
Mezger, E. and Blei, H., 66, 70, 80, 81, 83, 113
Michelet, Jules, 28

Middendorff, W., 66, 69, 73
Middle Ages, 25–9
Mirabeau, Honoré Gabriel Riqueti, comte de, 33
Mitscherlich, A., 28, 84
Mittenecker, E., 98
Mittermaier, W., 66, 73, 82, 208
Mohr, J. *et al.*, 102, 126
Mommsen, T., 12, 65
moral health *see* purity of the family
Moravia, Alberto, 17
Morgan, L. H., 35, 42–3
Morus (Richard Lewinsohn), 21, 23, 29
Müller-Lückmann, E., 98, 148, 186
Murdoch, Iris, 17
Murdock, G. P., 34
Musil, Robert von, 17
mysticism, *see* superstitions

Nau, E., 152
Navarre, Marguerite de, 16
Nero, Emperor, 25
neuroses, traumatic, 152, 162–5, 166, 167, 168, 230
Nicolson, A. B. and Hanley, C., 105
Niewenhaus, A. W., 38
North Africa, 36
Norway, 67–8
Nürnberger, H., 103, 112, 115, 132, 174

obesity, 153
object-relationship (of child), 59–60
oedipal connection, 171, 173, 187, 190, 191, 230
oedipus complex, 13, 14–15, 50–8, 231
Ogburn, W. F., 49
O'Neill, Eugene, 20
oral–genital contact, 101, 203, 204

paedophilia, 130, 197–200, 202, 208, 217, 231
Parsons, T., 58–9, 60, 61–4, 111
Pascal, Blaise, 66–7, 72–3, 84
passive sexual behaviour, 182, 186–9, 192; *see also* female incest victim

pavor nocturnus, 132, 153, 161, 231
penalties, nature and degree of, 190–191
'penis envy', 52
Persia, 21, 22
personality, 59–60, 61, 95, 111; normal and abnormal, 132–4; *see also* female incest victims; married couples; super-ego
Peru, 22–3, 34
Pflanz, M., 115
Philippe d'Orléans, Duke, 32
phylogenetic theory (of incest taboo), 50, 54
physical illnesses, 136, 139
Pippin, King of the Franks, 25
Plato, 24
Plaut, P., 68, 94, 96, 102, 103, 104, 112, 115, 117, 121, 126, 140, 149, 174, 210
Plutarch, 22
politico-economic theories, 47–9, 64
Pollock and Maitland, 219
Portugal, 67
potency, disturbances in, 129, 172
pre-genital psycho-sexuality, 59–60, 61, 63
pregnancy, 40, 43, 71, 77, 194, 195, 210–14, 217
primitive cultures, 33–41
Protestant Church, 65
Proust, Marcel, 15–16
Prussian Legal Code (1851), 66, 69
psycho-hygienic safeguards, 74–5, 82, 85
psychopathy, 131
psychoses, 131–2, 300–1, 231
psychosomatics, 152–4, 168, 231
puberty, 62, 63, 105–6, 146–8; *see also* biological maturity
Punishment of Incest Act (England, 1908), 221–3, 228
Puritanism, 30, 65
purity of the family, 68, 75, 83, 84–5

Radcliffe-Brown, A. R., 49
Rank, O., 12, 15, 16, 22, 23, 24, 30, 33, 35

Rapaport, D., 57
rape, rapists, 69, 102, 103, 104, 128 130, 174, 175, 179, 220
Rasch, W., 131
Rawlinson (M.P.), 222
recidivism, surveys on frequency of, 91
Reckless, W. C., 91
recurring dream, 162, 163–4
Reformation, 30–1, 33
regression, 60, 63, 232
Renaissance, 29–30
Rennert, H., 96, 125, 126
resistance to incest (passive and active), 192–6
Reynolds, E. L. and Wines, J. V., 106
Richelieu, Cardinal, 32
Riemer, S., 87, 94, 137, 174
Riesman, D. and colleagues, 111
Rinehart, J. W., 95 137, 140
Rohleder, H., 11, 22, 94, 117, 126
Roman Catholic Church, 25–9, 30, 31, 38, 65
Roman Empire, 24–5, 65
Romano, Giulio, 29
Rosenfeld, E. H., 77, 94
Ruskin, John, 78

Sade, Marquis de, 9, 17, 19, 20
Saller, K., 78, 79–80
Samuel, Herbert, 222
Sartre, Jean-Paul, 9, 14–15, 20
Schelsky, H., 34, 46, 47, 49, 57, 64, 111
Schiller, Friedrich, 20
Schiller-Tietz, N., 21, 22
schizophrenia, 132, 232
Schmidt, G. and Sigusch, V., 196, 201, 202
Schneider, K., 131
Schönfelder, T., 99, 152, 154, 190
Schönke, A. and Schröder, H., 80, 81
school performance, of fathers, 116–117; of girls, 149, 155, 156–7, 161, 162
Schwab, G., 77, 94, 103, 112, 113,

115, 117, 130, 132, 134, 135, 136, 137, 202, 210
Scott, J. A., 106
Scottish law, 31, 221, 222, 228
Seneca, 16
sex-free sphere (within family), 75, 83, 84-5
sexual contact, forms of, 99-110
sexual morality, 75, 82-5
sexual neutralisation, 45-6
Sexual Offences Act (England, 1956), 223-5
sexual perversions, 101, 172, 182, 184-5, 201-5, 227
sexual promiscuity, 135, 136, 141, 142, 179, 185, 214
sexual provocation, 175, 178, 182, 186, 187, 189-92
sexual relations, duration of, 108, 109-10; of married couple, 143-5
sexuality, 128-9
Shakespeare, William, 20
Shelley, Percy Bysshe, 15, 16, 19, 30
Sieverts, R. and Hardwig, W., 73, 77, 81
silence, adult partner's exhortations to, 182, 138-4; victim's motivation for, 182, 187, 189, 190
Simmel, G., 59
Simson, G., 85
sleeping, difficulties with, 153, 161
Sloane, P. and Karpinski, E., 214
Slotkin, J. S., 22
Smith, W. R., 50
social hygiene, 74, 81-2, 83
social isolation, 147, 153, 161, 162, 165, 173, 182, 184, 189, 191, 200
Socrates, 23-4
Solon, 23
somnambulism, 153, 161, 232
Sonden, T., 94, 102, 103, 117, 202
Sophocles, 16, 17, 18, 20
Specht, F., 111, 122, 155, 160
Spitz, R. A., 57, 59
Stelzner, H. F., 123, 149
Stendhal (Henri Beyle), 15, 19, 30
Stephen, Sir J. F., 220
Stern, C., 78, 79

Steuer, W., 105, 106
Strabo, 23
Stridon, Hieronymus of, 25
Sturm, 80, 81, 83
Stürüp, G. K., 90
suffocation, fear of, 153, 161, 162
suicide, suicidal tendencies, 18, 25, 39, 157, 160, 161, 162, 165, 166, 195, 201, 212, 213, 218
Sumner, W. G., 35, 39, 42
super-ego, 51, 53-4, 63; *see also* personality
superstitions, 39-41, 84
Sweden, 67-8, 76-7, 90, 102
Switzerland, 32, 67, 79, 130
Szabo, D., 137, 144, 192

Tacitus, 24
Tamm, K. P., 102, 109
Tanner, J. M., 105, 106, 176
Taylor, G. R., 26, 27, 29, 31
temptation-situations, 176, 177
Theodosius, Emperor, 25
Thidrek saga (Norse), 12
thigh-pressing contact, 71, 100, 101, 107, 189
Thomas, D. A., 225
Thomas Aquinas, 47
Többen, H., 11, 22-3, 24, 25, 31, 32, 65, 77, 94, 102, 103, 112, 115, 130, 137
totemism, totem-feast, 44, 50, 54-7
Toulouse-Lautrec, Henri, 78
triads (or trioles: 3-sided intercourse), 101, 202-5
Trobriand (New Guinea), 37
Tumlirz, O., 155
Turkey, 67
Tylor, E. B., 47

United States, laws on incest, 67, 68-9; and criminal statistics, 89

verbal threats and intimidations, 182, 183-4, 186-7, 189, 191, 195
Verschuer, O. von, 78, 79, 80
Viernstein, T., 103
Vogel, F., 78, 80

Voltaire, François Marie Arouet, 16, 32, 33
voyeurs, 103, 203, 204

Wagner, E. and Planck, U., 115
Wagner, K., 77, 94, 95, 103, 119, 140
Wahl, C. W., 132, 200
Wallis, H., 71, 210
Wegener, H., 109
Weinberg, S. K., 25, 31, 34, 37, 69, 87, 89, 92, 102, 103, 115, 116, 119, 123, 135, 140, 175, 176, 201, 205, 210, 215
Welzel, H., 66, 70, 82, 83

Westermarck, E. A., 26, 44, 45–6
White, L. A., 44, 48–9
Wilhelm, 82, 83
Williams, J. W. Hall, 219–28
Williams, Tennessee, 17, 20
Wilutzki, P., 23
Winter, K., 106
witchcraft, 28, 39
Wülffen, E., 77, 94, 117, 126
Wyss, R., 129, 130

young people, legal protection of, 68, 74–5, 85–6

Zulliger, H., 160